Linguistic Change and the Great Vowel Shift in English

PATRICIA M. WOLFE

Linguistic Change and the
Great Vowel Shift in English

UNIVERSITY OF CALIFORNIA PRESS
BERKELEY LOS ANGELES LONDON 1972

University of California Press
Berkeley and Los Angeles, California

University of California Press, Ltd.
London, England

Library of Congress Catalog Card Number: 71-630201
Designed by Douglas Nicholson
Printed in the United States of America

*To the ratepayers of Coventry,
who provided me with good schools and
supported me for three years at the
University of London.*

PREFACE

This book is a revised version of my doctoral dissertation, presented at UCLA in 1969 and written mostly while I was teaching at the University of California, Santa Barbara, 1968-69. I am grateful to a number of colleagues at both of these institutions for helping me to complete the work.

At Santa Barbara I would like to thank Jules Levin for drawing my attention to the vowel alternations in Old Prussian and to the work of Kellerman; C. Douglas Johnson for much stimulation and insightful criticism; and Arthur Schwartz for very helpful discussion of the whole and also (certainly not less important) for his constantly urging me to get on and finish the work. At UCLA I am indebted to all those who participated in Robert P. Stockwell's seminar in English historical phonology in the Spring Quarter of 1969, who by their questions and comments forced me to clarify both my ideas and my presentation of them, and to the members of my doctoral committee. The reader will notice that in this book I frequently have occasion to examine the work of Dr. Stockwell and, regretfully, to find that in general the data provides no justification for adopting his theory of the Vowel Shift. I would therefore like here to acknowledge an especially great debt to Dr. Stockwell for suggesting the topic to me, for encouraging the research even when it became clear that I was going to differ from him in my conclusions, and for insisting that I publish the work. Finally, I wish to thank William S-Y Wang for reading the completed work and making many helpful suggestions.

CONTENTS

INTRODUCTION

PURPOSE OF THE STUDY

The aims of this study are to review some of the theories which have
been held concerning one of the most striking phenomena in the history
of English, the Great Vowel Shift,[1] to reexamine much of the data
on which these theories have been based, and to attempt to evaluate
the different analyses proposed to determine which provides the best
description and explanation of the data. The following summary and
much simplified description of the Vowel Shift is taken from a standard
history of the language (Baugh, pp. 287-289):

In Chaucer's pronunciation [the long vowels] had still their so-called
'continental' value—i.e., *a* was pronounced like the *a* in *father* and
not as in *name*, *e* was pronounced either like the *e* in *there* or the *a* in
mate, but not like the *ee* in *meet*, and so with the other vowels. But
in the fifteenth century a great change is seen to be under way. All
the long vowels gradually came to be pronounced with a greater ele-
vation of the tongue and closing of the mouth, so that those that could
be raised (*a*, *ę*, *ẹ*, *ǫ*, *ọ*) were raised, and those that could not without
becoming consonantal (*i*, *u*) became diphthongs. The change may be
visualized in the following diagram:

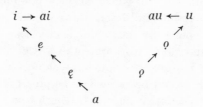

1

Baugh then gives a comparison of the supposed pronunciation of Chaucer and Shakespeare:

M.E.	Chaucer		Shakespeare
ī	[fi:f]	*five*	[fɑiv]
ẹ̄	[med:ə]	*meed*	[mi:d]
ę̄	[klɛ:nə]	*clean*	[kle:n] now [kli:n]
ā	[na:mə]	*name*	[ne:m]
ǭ	[gɔ:tə]	*goat*	[go:t]
ọ̄	[ro:tə]	*root*	[ru:t]
ū	[du:n]	*down*	[dɑun]

By this it is apparent that most of the long vowels had acquired at least by the sixteenth century (and probably earlier) approximately their present pronunciation. The most important development that has taken place since is further raising of M.E. ę̄ to ī. Whereas in Shakespeare *clean* was pronounced like our *lane*, it now rimes with *lean*. The change occurred at the end of the seventeenth century and had become general by the middle of the eighteenth.

METHODOLOGY

I use the symbols με as well as ME. με may be taken as a short way of saying "the normal development at the time under discussion of ME . . ." For instance, "ME ę̄ then merged with με ẹ̄" means "words which in ME had ę̄, at this time have the vowel which represents the normal contemporary development of ME ẹ̄."

Throughout this work, the forms cited partly follow the practice adopted in Chomsky and Halle (1968, chapter 6). That is, the forms given for early ModE are to be taken as representing the surface forms[2] described by the various orthoepists, grammarians, etc. The forms given for ME are, however, simply the traditional philological notation as given in the quotation from Baugh, namely ī, ẹ̄, ę̄, ā, ǭ, ọ̄, ū, *ai, ou, ę̄u, ẹ̄u, oi, ui.* There are two reasons for this choice. First, although these are probably to be interpreted as surface forms,[3] I do not wish to make any claim about their exact phonetic quality, since I do not think it possible to determine this with any accuracy for an earlier stage of the language for which we lack not only instrumental records but even impressionistic descriptions of the sounds. Second, although it would of course be desirable to give the ultimate underlying forms for ME, and thus incorporate the Vowel Shift into a complete grammar, much more work than has yet appeared on the phonology of OE and ME would be necessary before this could be done. These forms are the traditional surface categories as recorded in any standard historical grammar, and serve only to identify the entities I am discussing.

Chomsky and Halle (1968, p. 252) use different categorial labels. However, they also do not identify these as underlying or as intermediate forms, nor offer any justification for their adoption. They seem to be simply transliterations of the same surface categories I have used into the forms used throughout their work. The following table gives (perhaps redundantly) the correspondences between the traditional categories I use and those adopted by Chomsky and Halle:

Traditional	$\bar{\imath}$	$\bar{e}$	$\bar{\xi}$	$\bar{a}$	$\underset{.}{o}$	$\bar{\underset{.}{o}}$	$\bar{u}$
C. & H.	ī	ē	ǣ	ā	ɔ̄	ō	ū

Traditional	ai	$\bar{e}u$	$\bar{\xi}u$	au	ou	oi/ui
C. & H.	ǣy	ǣw	ēw	āw	ɔ̄w	ɔ̄y

The symbols for the short vowels are the same in this study as in Chomsky and Halle (or, indeed, in any other study).

I use both the slash notation, e.g. /ay/, and square brackets, e.g. [ai], to indicate sounds. These should not be taken as representing a phonemic level and an exact phonetic representation respectively. Rather, they stand for lesser and greater accuracy in indicating the quality of the sounds. For instance, Wallis (cf. Chapter III) has two distinct centralized vowels, and I discuss at some length the problem of identifying the quality of one of these, Wallis's *e feminine*, which may be [i], [ə], or [ɜ], in contrast with his *u obscurum*, which is probably [ʌ]. However, when an orthoepist records only one centralized vowel, I usually designate this as /ə/, since there seems no point in trying to establish the exact phonetic output. (At times, of course, the symbols are simply taken over from the source I am quoting.) It is possible that the symbols are not always rigorously differentiated in my usage, but I do not think any misunderstanding of my intended meaning will result from this.

QUESTIONS RELATING TO SOUND CHANGE

Many questions may be formulated with reference to linguistic change in general or to any specific change. The following are those which either have been most often treated with reference to the Great Vowel Shift, or which are considered of particular interest to present linguistic theory.

First, with reference to any particular change we may wish to establish when it first occurred. When there are not good contemporary

descriptions of the language, such changes can only be inferred from
the evidence of spelling, rhymes, etc. Much of the published work
on the Vowel Shift (e.g., Zachrisson (1913; 1927); Wyld (1927; 1936))
was aimed partly at establishing the chronology, and in particular
at showing that the changes must have begun to take place very much
earlier than had been believed at first.

Second, we may also ask in what part or parts of the country it
first began, and how and why it spread throughout all dialects. The
four-paper interchange between Sarrazin (1899; 1901) and Luick (1900;
1901) is largely devoted to questions of this kind, Sarrazin using the
very similar German vowel shift as a parallel to support his views
of the progression of the shift.

Third, if, as in the case of the Great Vowel Shift, the sound change
is a chain shift involving a whole class of sounds, we may ask if certain
sounds moved before others, and if so, which. Luick (1896) developed
a theory about the "primary impulse" of the Vowel Shift which was
later rejected by Western (1912) and with which Jespersen (1909)
also disagreed. Western was the first to adopt the view that it was
a simultaneous overall change, and that there was no evidence for a
"primary impulse," followed by Zachrisson (1913).

Fourth, one may try to establish with some accuracy what the
actual changes in phonetic output were, that is, what intermediate
chronological stages are attested for, e.g., ME ī on its way to the ModE
common (though not universal) value of /ay/. This was the basis
of Ellis's original pioneering works (1867-1889); he wished to determine
what pronunciation the spellings of such writers as Chaucer, Shakespeare,
Dryden, represented, and however faulty his methods and conclusions,
the intellectual curiosity and insight which initiated such a work,
and the sheer energy and perseverance which carried it through such
an immense survey, unsupported by any previous work or by any
tools such as an established phonetic alphabet (he invented his own—
Palaeotype—a very complicated and virtually unusable system, much
influenced by conventional spelling), must command the respect and
admiration of any subsequent worker in this field. Naturally, this
question has commanded the greatest amount of attention, in general
works (Zachrisson (1913); Dobson (1957a); Wyld (1923; 1927; 1936)),
in works devoted to a particular writer (Zachrisson (1927); Jespersen
(1909); Kökeritz (1953)), and also in works dealing with a particular
region (Orton (1933); Kökeritz (1932)). In addition, there have been
many critical editions of orthoepistical works (Danielsson (1955; 1963);
Dobson (1957b); Ekwall (1911); Holmberg (1956)) which have provided

the evidence from which one can find support for hypotheses about the actual stages in the development of any vowel participating in the Vowel Shift.

Fifth, one may ask why sound changes of this kind, that is, general changes which affect a certain sound (or class of sounds) regardless of its phonetic environment, should occur at all, and if there is any reason for them to go in some particular direction. (I exclude here sound changes resulting from contact with other languages or dialects, since this is merely another instance of the spread rather than of the initiation of a sound change.) Many theories have been advanced, both with regard to sound change in general and to the Vowel Shift in particular. Ellis, for instance, attributed the Great Vowel Shift to the confused conditions produced by the Wars of the Roses. Lotspeich to the extra effort involved in stressing vowels and to the Germanic tendency to stress the root syllable. Many others, including Luick, Martinet, and Mařik, have also produced explanations. None is convincing, and some are so unbelievable as to be ludicrous.

It has recently been claimed (Weinreich, Labov, and Herzog) that the initiation of a change is the basic question in linguistic change, since without understanding of the factors that activate a change we are unable to predict change, and prediction of linguistic change is a matter with which linguistic theory should be properly concerned. Labov (1965) criticizes the work of Halle for not providing any means of predicting sound change, claiming that all that is being offered is a description, and that (p. 93 n. 6) "In terms of a description . . . there is no greater probability of the change taking place in the observed direction, as in the reverse direction." But it should be observed that this paper offers no linguistic solution to the problem, and that much of Labov's other work (e.g., 1963; 1966) demonstrates merely that once a variant has acquired value, others who wish to identify with groups using this variant will adopt it also (without being conscious that they are doing so, though they may remark it in others)[4] and describes and quantifies in some detail the factors which motivate the adoption of such a change. In essence, he is formalizing the rules governing the use of different styles, whereas earlier linguists had tried to explain similar situations as coexistent phonemic systems (cf. Kučera (1958; 1961); Schmalstieg (1964); and the discussion in Wolfe (1968)), often without great success. Weinreich, Labov, and Herzog also deal with the diffusion of a change after it has originated, rather than providing the answer to what they regard as the basic question. Similarly, theories have been presented on the generalization of a change within a dialect (Kiparsky (1965; 1968b); Wang (1969)), but again the origin of the sound change is left unexplained. Postal (1968, pp. 283-285) considers this question and concludes (p. 283) ". . . it seems evident within the framework of sound change as grammar change that the 'causes' of sound change without language contact lie in the general tendency of human cultural products to undergo 'nonfunctional' stylistic change." It is interesting to note that a very similar opinion was expressed by Schuchardt in 1885 (p. M 15). Postal furthermore remarks (p. 284) that this is not at all incompatible with Labov's work, which relates to the spread of a change once it is initiated. However, Postal's theory seems to preclude the possibility of ever being able to predict the particular direction sound change is likely to take. Wang (1969, pp. 12-13 n. 9) rejects Postal's conclusion, and claims that there is laboratory evidence indicating that all sound change is phonetically conditioned (but does not cite any). It is certainly difficult to imagine the environmental conditions governing a change which occurred to all long vowels throughout the language. Further, Hoenigswald (1960, p. 79) notes that:

. . . even if all sound change could be made out to simplify articulation, this cannot claim to be a causal explanation, since the particular segments which are simplified, the particular direction in which they are simplified, and the particular time and dialect in which the segment, sometimes after millennia of undisturbed existence, is altered, all remain unpredicted . . . it is interesting to note that articulations lost by sound change are frequently reintroduced by another sound change within a short period of time.

A slightly different kind of observation was made by Sweet (1888, pp. 19-20, §§ 53, 55, 56) who suggested that long vowels raise and that short vowels tend to lower. Labov (n.d.; forthcoming) and Labov and Wald (1969) claim that there is now quite a lot of evidence to substantiate this with regard to correlated chain shifts.

Sixth, one may reasonably ask if there are any constraints on sound change, and, if so, what are they? In fact certain constraints have been assumed, often implicitly, in most work on language change (one of which is manifest in the description of the Vowel Shift taken from Baugh), often without any empirical evidence, and some are explicitly formulated, e.g. in Stockwell (1952). Recent developments in linguistic theory have caused a great deal of attention to be focused on this point, both in relation to linguistic change in general and to specific analyses which have been proposed for the English Vowel Shift.

SCOPE OF THE STUDY

There is an immense literature on various aspects of linguistic change and of the Great Vowel Shift in particular. No general survey of this literature will be presented, and much of the literature will be ignored completely, since recounting the history of linguistic theory or of theories of the Great Vowel Shift does not lie within the scope of this enquiry. Nor am I concerned with attempting to provide even cursory answers to all of the questions outlined above (even though they constitute only a selection of possible lines of enquiry). I am interested primarily in the fourth of these questions, that is, in attempting to establish the various stages in the Vowel Shift, and to decide which of the theories advanced is descriptively more adequate and explanatorily more satisfying. Further, I am confining my investigation mainly to long vowels in stressed syllables, that is, to the changes outlined in the summary quoted from Baugh. The development of the ME diphthongs and short vowels is included in less detail, and the treatment of some questions, e.g. the complicated problems of ME *oi/ui* words, is both cursory and sporadic. In general, vowels other than the traditional long vowels and questions other than the one cited are discussed only to the extent that they shed light on the main problem.

ORGANIZATION OF THE STUDY

Chapter I reviews different theories of the actual stages of the Great Vowel Shift. Chapter II reviews recent theories of grammars in general and of sound change in particular, insofar as they relate to the Vowel Shift. In Chapter III I reexamine the evidence of the early orthoepists and grammarians, and in Chapter IV the evidence of the writers of shorthand systems, of rhymes, and of occasional spellings. Chapter V presents and discusses miscellaneous data from other languages and from English dialects, both contemporary and earlier. In Chapter VI I present my conclusions on the questions considered.

CHAPTER I

The summary of the Great Vowel Shift quoted in the Introduction sufficiently if grossly indicates what is usually[1] assumed about the shift, namely, its beginning and its end. But there is great divergence of opinion as to the intervening stages. The purpose of this chapter is to review the major theories, indicating in some cases the bases for the differing hypotheses. Only controversial areas will be discussed; there is general agreement about the development of other vowels in the series.

THE DEVELOPMENT OF ME $\bar{\imath}$, $\bar{u}$

The major area of dispute is the development of ModE /ay/, /aw/, from ME $\bar{\imath}$, $\bar{u}$, respectively. In the following discussion, often the development of ME $\bar{\imath}$ only will be discussed, but this is to be taken as reflecting parallel views for ME $\bar{u}$.

The view most commonly held is shared by Luick (1900, p. 94; 1914-1940, pp. 559-581); Jespersen (1909, pp. 234-236); Horn (1908, pp. 56, 91); Ekwall (1914, pp. 49, 66); Zachrisson (1927, pp. 55, 60); and Chomsky and Halle (1968, pp. 249-289). This view holds that the normal development of ME $\bar{\imath}$ in Standard English was that $\bar{\imath} > $ /iy $>$ ey $>$əy $>$ ay/. That is, ME $\bar{\imath}$ diphthongized and the first element of the resulting diphthong first lowered, then centralized, and then lowered again. Because this particular hypothesis has been supported by so many scholars over so long a period, I refer to it henceforth as the traditional view.[2]

Orton suggests a development for Northern English in which centralization did not take place until lowering had been completed. He believes that:

The chief stages in the development of ME ī to the present sounds are almost automatically suggested by its correspondences in the living dialects. In fact, the following table, which illustrates a reconstruction of the course of sounds, is in the main a mere enumeration of some of the sounds now representing the vowel in the dialects under consideration.

$$
\text{ME } \bar{\imath} \ < [ii] \Big\langle \begin{array}{l} [ei] \\ [ei] \end{array} \Big\langle \begin{array}{l} [\varepsilon i] \\ [\ae i] \end{array} \Big\langle \begin{array}{l} [\varepsilon i] \\ [ai] \end{array} \Big\langle \begin{array}{l} [\ae i] \\ [ai] \end{array} \Big\langle \begin{array}{l} [ai] \\ [ai] \end{array} \Big\langle [ai] \ < [a]
$$

[slightly simplified—PMW]

He notes that this does not take into account one of the current recorded variants in the area, namely [əi], but suggests (without citing any evidence) that this may be an imitation of Standard English, or may have developed directly from [ei] or [εi] (pp. 201-202, § 352). These variants are also documented in Orton and Halliday.

This development is based on dialect studies in the North of England, and is suggested for that area only (as the reference to Standard English makes clear). However, Lehnert (pp. 98-99, § 111) seems to consider this a possibility for the standard dialect, suggesting īi > i̯i > e̯i > e̯i > ai (and cf. discussion of Wallis, Chapter III) as does Bliss. Sweet (p. 15, § 42) suggests (in his notation): [ɨ, [ᴛɾ,[ɾ, [ɾ,]ɪ,]ɪ, which is roughly ī > /iy > ey > εy > ɑy > ay/. Wyld (1936, p. 225) also suggests a line of development in which there is no intermediate centralization:

$$
i^{\scriptscriptstyle \mathrm{I}} \ < \ e^{\scriptscriptstyle \mathrm{I}} - \left[\begin{array}{ccc} & \text{Type A} & \\ \varepsilon^{\scriptscriptstyle \mathrm{I}} & < & \ae^{\scriptscriptstyle \mathrm{I}} \\ & \text{Type B} & \\ a^{\scriptscriptstyle \mathrm{I}} & & a^{\scriptscriptstyle \mathrm{I}} \end{array} \right\} \ < \ \alpha
$$

Ellis (Part V, pp. 826-827) appears to favor the development ī > /iy > ey > εy > ay/.[3] However, he is aware of the existence of dialects with /əy/, and is not at all sure how to fit them into his scheme. His discussion reads (p. 827):

But there is another set of these diphthongs, of which the first element
is (ə,ɜ) or even (æ). These are common . . . Whether they were derived through a progression similar to the former, or came from an
original (ə'ii) form of (ii) parallel to (éii), it is not easy to say.

That is, Ellis is unsure whether to incorporate these variations as
an offshoot of the main development, thus providing a secondary
line of development which agrees with the traditional one, or whether
to prepare an alternate development separate from the time ME ī
first diphthongized. Similarly, Kökeritz (1953) postulates two lines of
development, one in which ME ī diphthongized and then centralized
and lowered simultaneously to /əy/ (which is his primary line of
development), and an alternate one in which ME ī diphthongized and
then simply lowered to /ey/, without centralization. Kökeritz seems
quite sure of his ground, since he states categorically (1953, p. 216
n. 4):

The course of development from ME ī was certainly not that suggested
by Wyld (p. 223) [= Wyld (1936)] which pays no heed to the diphthonging tendencies in modern English. The first stage was not the
introduction of a slack [ɪ] after the [i:] but the introduction of a glide
[ɪ] before it, resulting in the rising diphthong [ɪi:]: with the gradual
lowering of this glide to [ə] and the change of the rising diphthong to
a falling diphthong, the whole development would be approximately
this: [i: > ɪi˙ > əi > əɪ > ʌɪ > ai].

This is for many reasons a very interesting statement. One wonders
where Kökeritz obtained the information about the initial stages of the
Vowel Shift which he describes with such certainty; he cites no evidence
for them. His only reference is to his study of the Suffolk dialect,
upon which he apparently bases his hypothesis. But when we turn
to this study we find only that ME ī must pass through the stage /əy/,
at which point it merged with ME oi—and, of course, it must end
up as /ay/ (Kökeritz (1932, p. 149)). But there is nothing in this study
to constrain stages earlier than /əy/. Further, it is not at all clear
what he means by "the diphthonging tendencies in modern English."
The most obvious reference would seem to be to the fact ModE generally has no pure long tense vowels but instead diphthongs consisting
of a vowel and off-glide. But this would not logically lead to the conclusion that ME ī necessarily acquired an on- rather than an off-glide.
Kökeritz nowhere defends this curious claim.

It is also interesting to see the way Kökeritz treats the evidence
he does cite. For instance, noting that Wallis and Wilkins both de-

scribe a diphthong with centralized first element, he adds that this (1953, p. 216) ". . . can also be deduced from Wodroephe's transcriptions *pyee, py-ee,* for Fr. *pays*; his *y* [one of the normal contemporary spellings for 'long *ī'*—PMW], which I interpret as [əi], is as near a substitute for Fr. [ɛi] as he could get at that time." But it is hardly a deduction from the evidence if one has to make an assumption as to the interpretation first; it seems not even to have occurred to Kökeritz that in fact Wodroephe's transcription may have been exact, that his *y* did represent /ey/, not /əy/, and that one could interpret the evidence literally rather than slanting it to fit preconceived ideas about the development of ME *ī*. Since the date of Wodroephe's work is 1623, and the earliest unequivocal evidence of /ə/ in stressed syllables is 1643 (cf. section on Hodges, Chapter III), it seems improbable that he meant /əy/. Kökeritz seems here to be perverting contemporary evidence because on the most obvious and literal interpretation it does not support his theory.[4]

Unlike Ellis, Kökeritz rejects the possibility of uniting the two lines of development, claiming (without giving reasons) that (1953, p. 216 n. 4) "Dialects . . . that have [ęi] for *ī* today could never have had the intervening stage [əi], but went from [ɪi˙] > [ei] > [ęi]." I believe the earliest formulation of a line of development for ME *ī* which postulated centralization before any lowering is that found in Stockwell (1952, p. 84) where it forms part of the justification for postulating /ɨ/ for one of the phonemes of ME. Stockwell here claims that this:

. . . was necessary in the ME frame of syllabic nuclei, since it is the key to understanding the development of certain ME complex nuclei (specifically the development of /ay/ from /iy/, which must have gone through the series /iy > ɨy > əy > ay/, and of /aw/ from /uw/, which must have been /uw > ɨw > əw > aw/; any different series postulated for these sequences will introduce crossing with other shifts within the system.

A footnote attributes the original postulation of these series to Trager and Smith, in unpublished material (p. 84 n. 26).

No further justification for this analysis is offered here, but later, in discussing the rule centralizing the first element of /iy/, /uw/, to /ɨ/, Stockwell notes that (p. 143):

There is no spelling evidence whatsoever for this change . . . The evidence comes from its later history. The reflex of EME /iy/ is NE /ay/. This cannot reasonably be presumed to represent a sudden change, during the 15th century great vowel shift, from /iy/ to /ay/. The full shift must have been this:

The assumption stated by [the centralization rule] is essentially that the shifts /iy/ > /ɨy/ and /uw/ > /ɨw/ were simply the first changes leading to the 15th century great vowel shift. The full shift of EME /uw/ to NE /aw/ then was this:

$$ɨw \leftarrow uw$$
$$\downarrow$$
$$əw$$
$$\downarrow$$
$$aw$$

Stockwell then quotes dialectal evidence to support his conclusion, instancing the occurrence of /əy/ for /ay/ in Philadelphian and of /əw/ for /aw/ in Virginia Tidewater dialects, and concludes that "the changes listed above, then, are simply a reasonable chronological guess in view of their later history" (1952, pp. 143-144).

A similar view has been presented by Dobson (1957a, p. 660). He claims that:

The usual theory . . . is that ME ī developed through the stages [ei], [ɛi], and [æi] to [ai]. This view is altogether impossible. If the development had been that suggested, ME ī would have crossed the path of ME ai developing to [æi] and [ɛi] . . .; most of the orthoepists who say that ME ī was ei still pronounced ME ai as a diphthong. Yet the two sounds are always kept distinct, as they are still. ME ī can never have been [ɛi].

Dobson then agrees with Stockwell in regarding the possibility of intersection with ME ai as an absolute argument against the possibility of lowering before centralization. This line of development is also accepted by McCawley and by Bailey.

It can be seen that the above hypotheses fall roughly into three groups: (1) those who believe centralization occurred after lowering was complete; (2) those who believe that centralization occurred before any lowering took place; and (3) those who believe that centralization occurred about in the middle of the Vowel Shift, after the first stage in the lowering had taken place but before the second. The relative chronology of centralization and lowering must then be investigated in detail to see what evidence can be found on these points.

THE DEVELOPMENT OF ME ẹ̄

There is also disagreement as to the development of ME ẹ̄. Wyld claims (1923, p. 50) that "during the sixteenth and seventeenth centuries, and part of the eighteenth, ME ẹ̄, ā, and ai were identical." If this were so, it is difficult to explain (as Wyld himself acknowledges) first why and how ME ẹ̄ and ę̄ are now identical, and second why ME ā and ai did not also raise to merge with ME ẹ̄ as [ī].

Wyld claims that the evidence of occasional spellings, of the orthoepists, and of rhymes all shows the identity of these three sounds, and adduces evidence from all three sources (p. 53). Both Kökeritz and Dobson accept Wyld's claims. Indeed, Kökeritz apparently takes this to be a self-evident fact, since he says (1953, p. 10):

Like him [Wyld] I believe, of course, that our present [i:] for ME ẹ̄ in *sea*, *speak*, is not the result of a phonetic change of [ε:] > [i:], via [ẹ:], at the end of the 17th century, but that it represents a parallel development within another dialect current in London that eventually ousted its rival [ẹ:], except in the five words *break*, *steak*, *great*, *yea*, and *drain*.

He claims further that acceptance of the development [ε:] > [ẹ:] > [i:] has (1953, p. 194):

. . . blinded the student to the linguistic realities. The law's inherent incompatibility with the very complicated history of ME ẹ̄ was either ignored as irrelevant or explained away with much ingenuity and not a little casuistry.

However, he makes no attempt to explain what these "linguistic realities" are or how and why the law is inherently incompatible with the history of ME ẹ̄. Kökeritz here seems to be relying on the persuasive power of his extremely strongly worded statements rather than on empirical data. He remarks that Wyld has (1953, p. 194)

convincingly repudiated the orthodox views. On the strength of incontrovertible orthographic and orthoepic evidence he suggested [that the StanE [ī] for ME ẹ̄ was] not in the nature of a sound-change . . . but merely the result of the abandonment of one type of pronunciation and the adoption of another.

Dobson (1957a, pp. 607-611) essentially agrees with this, although in an earlier work (1955) he maintained that in "the educated language at this time . . . ME ẹ̄ was maintained as a distinct sound, identified neither with ME ę̄ . . . nor with ME ā, until the very end of the seventeenth century."

Wyld further equates the dialect which merged ME $\bar{e}$, $\bar{a}$, with educated speech, as the following quotations (all from Wyld (1923)) illustrate:

... at the beginning of the eighteenth century it is tolerably certain that the majority of educated speakers pronounced *heat* as *hate*, *seat* as *sate*, and so on (p. 43).

While, so far as we can judge, the vast majority of educated speakers pronounced *heat* exactly like *hate* ... (p. 51)

... while for a long time the old pronunciation [i. e. με $\bar{a}$] of the B words [= ME $\bar{e}$] was the more usual in polite society ... (p. 51).

Kökeritz accepts this dialectal distinction (1953, p. 88), as do Weinreich, Labov, and Herzog (pp. 147-148).

However, as noted above, this supposed merger creates great difficulties in explaining modern Standard English. The difficulties entailed by this hypothesis, and evidence bearing on the two claims (that is, of the merger $\bar{e}/\bar{a}$ vs. $\bar{e}/\bar{e}$, and of the social limits of the dialectal distinction), will therefore be considered in some detail.

THE TRADITIONAL LONG VOWELS

Stockwell has also claimed (1952; 1961; 1964; 1969; forthcoming) that the Great Vowel Shift (and English historical phonology generally) is more easily explained if what are traditionally considered to be long tense vowels are instead interpreted as diphthongs. This suggestion has been accepted by some linguists and is assumed in, e.g., Nist (pp. 221-222) (without, however, any acknowledgment of Stockwell's work) and in Hockett (1958, pp. 375-379; 1959).[5] Reasons for Stockwell's interpretation of the Vowel Shift have been discussed above. He bases his general claims about the phonology of earlier stages of English mainly on the following arguments. First, he believes that such an analysis would have greater phonetic validity. In ModE generally there are no long tense vowels but only diphthongs, and it is reasonable to assume that this may be true of earlier stages of the language, since otherwise we have to postulate much greater diachronic changes (1952, p. 11, postulate XIII; 1961, p. 538 n. 9). He holds (1964, p. 665):

... that the laws of sound change are the simplest set of general rules, plus exceptions, which with earlier forms as input yield later forms as output; the most insightful analysis of the structure of the most investigable state of the language—contemporary speech—is evidence of a high order for the structure of earlier states.

The claim is, then, thatto postulate diphthongs instead of long vowels (even in the underlying forms) will be more accurate phonetically and will also lead to a simpler synchronic analysis and formulation of diachronic change. Stockwell also claims that some problems in English historical phonology can be handled only by this kind of analysis, and in particular that "ME and its reflexes cannot be correctly accounted for with only one type of 'tense' or 'long' vowel" (forthcoming). Evidence relevant to these questions will be presented and discussed in Chapters III, IV, and V.

CHAPTER II

In Chapter I I discussed some of the controversies over the chronological development of the Vowel Shift. One of the most detailed
of recently published accounts is in Part III of Chomsky and Halle
(1968), and much of recent dispute has centered around the analysis
proposed there. The disagreement has two bases: (1) whether the
interpretation of the data, and the consequent postulation of certain
chronological stages, is correct; and (2) whether the explanation of
the process is valid. Scholarly positions on the first issue have already
been outlined in Chapter I. In this chapter I am concerned to give
a brief account of the theoretical background to the second question.

OUTLINE OF TRANSFORMATIONAL THEORY

The account in Chomsky and Halle (1968) is written within the framework of the transformational generative theory of grammar.[1] Within
this theory, as noted by Chomsky and Halle (1968, p. 3), the term
"grammar" is used:

... with systematic ambiguity. On the one hand, the term refers
to the explicit theory constructed by the linguist and proposed as
a description of the speaker's competence. On the other hand, we use
the term to refer to this competence itself ... The person who has
acquired a knowledge of a language has internalized a system of rules
that determines sound-meaning connections for indefinitely many sentences.

That does not imply that the speaker is conscious of the system of
rules, or could formulate it at will (cf. Chomsky (1965, p. 8)). Indeed,

the very great difficulty encountered in attempting to describe explicitly the constraints on, e.g., pronominalization in English, by
linguists who are yet able to use this process without difficulty, sufficiently illustrates this point. The claim, however, is that the competence, however unconscious, is there. When a linguist writes a
grammar, this "is simply intended to be a precise representation of
the internalized linguistic knowledge of the native" (Postal (1968,
p. 306)).

Obviously, individual grammars may vary slightly. However, Chomsky has frequently pointed out that in order to talk about the grammar
of a language at all we have to abstract away from the variation between speakers and that within a speaker's usage which is produced
by various "performance" factors—e.g. memory span, fatigue, etc.
—and set up as it were an idealized speaker in an idealized homoge-
neous community (cf. discussion in Chomsky (1965, pp. 3-4)). This
necessity has long been recognized, and was commented on by Ellis
(Part I, pp. 18-19) who, after recognizing that different generations
in particular vary one from the other, said that in practice we have
to choose a kind of mean (for which he selected "the general utterance
of the more thoughtful or more respected persons of mature age"):

. . . which, like the averages of a mathematician, not agreeing precisely with any, may for the purposes of science be assumed to represent
all, and be called the language of the district at the epoch assigned.
Concrete reality is always too complex for science to grasp, and hence
she has to content herself with certain abstractions, and leave practice
to apply the necessary corrections in individual cases. Thus, if we
descended into every minute shade of spoken sound, the variety would
be so interminable, each individual presenting some fresh peculiarities,
that all definite character would be lost.

Linguists from Ellis down to the present day are, however, still aware
that they are dealing with an abstraction set up for a particular purpose, and in any discussion of the rules for a grammar one finds frequent reference to dialect variation.

There have recently been some interesting studies suggesting that
some generalization about variation within the dialect of the community and within that of the individual can be captured by means of
rules using different kinds of variable constraints. It has been claimed
(Labov (1970, p. 43)) that:

. . . the patterning within this variation is by no means obscure: it
does not need the statistical analysis of hundreds of speakers' records
as linguists traditionally feared . . . On the contrary, we find that

the basic patterns of class stratification, for example, emerged from samples as small as 25 speakers.

A transformational grammar has usually been considered to have three components which define the semantic, syntactic, and phonological structures of a language. The syntactic component is conceived of as a device which will recursively enumerate in some form all and only the grammatical sentences of a language. It will assign an abstract "deep structure" which will indicate the relationship between different parts of the sentence, e.g., subject and predicate, and it is upon this representation that the semantic component operates. There has in recent years been much dispute within transformational theory about this formulation of the relationship between syntax and semantics, but this is irrelevant to the present study and may therefore be disregarded here. The phonological component operates upon the "surface structure" generated by the syntactic component.[2]

The lexical items which are the input to the phonological component are still abstractions far removed from the actual phonetic shape of utterances. The following very simple analogy may help to illustrate this point. In a sentence such as *I've finished* we understand the item *I've* /ayv/ to "stand for" the two items *I have* /ay hæv/. We could simply say that we have elided all but the final consonant of /hæv/. Certainly, however, the two variants would be felt to be in some essential way the same, and we could provide some kind of explanation of the relationship. Similarly, a generative phonology wishes to describe all the linguistically significant generalizations about the pronunciation of a language, for instance the relationship between the two lexical items *divine/divinity*. For this reason, although the two words differ phonetically they are assigned the same abstract root, what in a generative phonology is called the "underlying form," i.e., *divīn*. An ordered series of rules will then relate this to the two distinct surface representations. In *divinity*, the second vowel of the root will be shortened (laxed) because it is followed by the two syllables of the suffix (trisyllabic shortening): in *divine*, the vowel will remain long (tense) and will be subject to diphthongization and to Vowel Shift, which will change /ī/ to /ay/ (cf. Chomsky and Halle (1968, pp. 84-85) for the details of this derivation). It is then claimed that the vocabulary of a speaker is represented in the lexicon by abstract underlying forms, which are related to their phonetic realizations by a series of ordered rules.[3]

The sounds are represented not by orthographic symbols indicating indivisible sounds, but by bundles of distinctive features, e.g. [± voice], which indicate the different components of the sound.[4] Distinctive features are used because of the claim that all sounds in natural languages throughout the world are combinations of a finite number of differentiations which the human mechanism is capable of, and that by using these features a linguist can achieve greater generality in the formalization of rules. The system of distinctive features now in use is in fact only a refinement of insights as old as the study of language itself (and cf. discussions of the phonetic theories of Wilkins and Holder, Chapter III). For most of the phonological component these features are merely classificatory and have only binary values. That is, /p/ and /b/ are distinguished by the feature [± voice]. However, toward the end of the phonological component these features are translated into phonetic features with scalar values indicating, e.g., the degree of voicing. The concept of the phonetic matrix has not yet been developed in great detail (but cf. references in Chomsky (1967a); Chomsky and Halle (1968); Postal (1968); Ladefoged (1967); and King (1969)).

There has been considerable controversy about this theory of the phonology of a language in general, and about more specific subtopics such as the use of distinctive feature matrices to describe lexical entries and the abandonment of a phonemic level of representation. It is not my purpose here to justify the theory of generative phonology; I take it as the current standard theory, the paradigm, as it were, within which I shall interpret the evidence pertaining to the Vowel Shift. The theory attempts to provide insight into the generalizations implicit in a native speaker's use of his language, and these generalizations are not, so far as I have been able to determine, equally capturable in other theories. Chomsky and Halle (1965), Chomsky (1967b), and Postal (1968) discuss and substantiate some of the claims of generative phonology in detail. Chomsky and Halle (1968) is a detailed application of this theory to the description and explanation of the phonology of present-day American English, and Part III is an excursus attempting to explain in part how this system developed from earlier stages of English.

The development of generative phonology has led to the reformulation of many concepts about sound change. Within the theory of a phonological component, it is clear that there are basically two mechanisms by which the phonetic realization of a sentence can be changed: by some change in the system of phonological rules, or by some change in the underlying forms in the lexicon upon which the rules operate. The basic concept of rule addition, first discussed in Halle (1962*b*), has been enriched to include the generalization of a rule (cf. below), changes in rule ordering, and the restructuring of rules to form an optimal grammar by children learning the language (cf. Kiparsky (1965; 1968*a*; 1968*b*); Chomsky and Halle (1968); Postal (1968); Halle and Keyser (1967); and King (1969*a*) for discussion of these). One consequence has been that many assumptions which had long been accepted implicitly have now been questioned and, by many scholars, rejected.

GRADUAL VS. DISCRETE SOUND CHANGE

The assumption of the gradual nature of regular phonetic change has now largely been abandoned (though the rejection dates back to long before transformational grammar). In the description of the Great Vowel Shift quoted in the Introduction were the words "all the long vowels gradually came to be pronounced . . ." (Baugh, p. 287). Similarly, in Jespersen's account of the Shift we read (1909, p. 232): "So comprehensive a change cannot, of course, have been accomplished all at once. It must have been very gradual, taking place by insensible steps." Quotations illustrating this viewpoint could be listed at length (cf. Kiparsky (1965); Postal (1968); Wang (1969); and Weinreich, Labov, and Herzog (1968) for an outline of pretransformational positions on sound change). One of the motivations for this view is (Chomsky and Halle (1968, p. 250)):

. . . that speakers are by and large unaware of the changes that their language is undergoing. The reason for this, it has been claimed, is that changes affect only the phonetic actualization of particular sounds —and, moreover, in so slight a measure that the changes appear to be gradual. In other words, in this view, what we might call the" gradual" view of sound change, phonetic changes are restricted—with a few notable exceptions such as epenthesis, elision, and metathesis —to changes in the low-level phonetic rules that assign the precise numerical value to the different features in different contexts. Thus, vowels may be articulated somewhat further back than before, or consonants may be actualized in some environment with aspiration of degree 4 whereas earlier they were actualized in that environment with degree 2.

Since processes such as metathesis could not be regarded as gradual, many linguists (e.g. Bloomfield) did not consider them as regular sound change. But there are changes in the realization of individual segments which also cannot plausibly be fitted into a theory of gradual phonetic change. Halle and Keyser note that (p. 780):

. . . the simple change of [χ] → [f] that occurred in English *enough, tough, cough, dwarf,* etc., cannot plausibly be formulated in terms of a theory of gradual change. (Think what intermediate steps would have to be hypothesized !)

Halle and Keyser seem not to have noticed that a physical rather than a mentalistic solution has been proposed for this very change. Danielsson (1963, p. 225, § 227), discussing this, says that:

. . . the groups [oχ], [uχ], etc. had become [f], i.e. the successive pronunciation of [uχ] was replaced by one single sound, in which the labial articulation of [u] and the voiceless fricative articulation of [χ] were simultaneous, i.e. the voiceless labial fricative [f].

It is interesting to speculate how Danielsson would explain the reverse change of [f] → [χ] in Dutch, in such words as German *Kraft.* Such changes are not described in Hockett (1965), which is the most recent full-scale attempt to explain and justify the structuralist view of sound change. The question really resolves into whether we think sound change is a purely physical, physiological phenomenon, i.e., a gradual altering of articulatory habits, missing targets, etc., or essentially a mentalistic phenomenon. The question in general, and Hockett's position in particular, is most clearly and forcefully discussed in Postal (1968), in which discussion Postal says that (p. 299) ". . . the fact that documented sound changes reveal all of the types of processes which must be represented by rules in synchronic grammars is amongst the strongest evidence that sound change is rule change . . ."

One of the drawbacks to a theory of gradual sound change, as pointed out by Hoenigswald (1964, p. 207), is that although such a theory has "surface plausibility" there is little data to substantiate it. Earlier, in a discussion of "Alleged Gradual Character of Phonetic Alteration," he had remarked on (1960, pp. 72-73):

. . . the view that sound change is a gradual matter: in this view, sound change proceeds in small "imperceptible" steps so long as no contrasts are imperilled or other structural changes are called for. When these things do happen, gradual sub-phonemic alterations "become" phonemic. In the almost total absence of large-scale questionnaire supported observations which would have to be extended or repeated over generations of speakers in a community, such a picture can be only guesswork. Among its weaknesses is the fact that, in spite of an appearance to the contrary, it fails to explain the phonemic reinterpretation of the lexicon which makes a change proper out of the alteration and which is by nature sudden.

That is, even if a consonant came to be articulated with degree of aspiration 4 instead of 2, at some point this has to be interpreted as the addition of a rule which changes [–aspirate] to [+aspirate]. The type of large-scale work mentioned is now being done (cf. Labov (1963; 1966)), and this may lead to further insights. It seems possible that evidence will be found that some sound changes proceed first by alteration of the scalar values of the phonetic values. For although the existence of such common changes as epenthesis demonstrates that not all sound change is gradual, it does not seem to me to be a logical conclusion from this that therefore **no** sound change can be gradual[5] in the sense that it cannot originate in alteration of the scalar values of the phonetic features. Since the theory provides for these features, there seems to me to be no principled non—ad hoc way of saying they may not be subject to alteration.

Further, since the rules converting the binary features to scalar values are presumably part of a speaker's competence, then changes here would still be within the definition of sound change as "changes in the phonological component of a grammar" (King (1969*b*, p. 6)) and would not necessarily entail acceptance of the belief that sound change originates in changes in performance. In fact, some of the variations discovered by Labov have been assumed by King (1969*b*, p. 15) to be "produced by late phonetic rules in the grammar, so late that we may make free use of non-binary rules in stating them." All this, however, leaves untouched the question of how, when a certain value has increased say from 2 to 4, it is suddenly reinterpreted as + rather than as –. Since so little work has been done on the systematic phonetic matrix and its relationship to binary features, there seems little to add.

The rejection of the gradual nature of sound change is (as indicated above) not a recent theoretical change cotemporaneous with the development of transformational theory. It has apparently existed at least as long as interest in the Great Vowel Shift, since we find it in the earliest work on that subject, namely in Part I of Ellis's study, when he discusses the nature of sound change. Ellis claims that (p. 18):

We may apparently distinguish three laws according to which the sounds of a language change.

First, the *chronological law*. Changes in spoken sound take place in time, not by insensible degrees, but *per saltum*, from generation to generation.

Second, the *individual law*. A series of spoken sounds acquired during childhood and youth remains fixed in the individual the rest of his life.

Third, the *geographical law*. A series of spoken sounds adopted as the expression of thought by persons living in one locality, when wholly or partly adopted by another community, are also changed, not by insensible degrees, but *per saltum*, in passing from individual to individual.

Ellis thus believes that all change is discrete but that an adult can add rules to his grammar only when they are borrowed from another speaker. The quotation from Jespersen (cf. above) shows how little Ellis's ideas were regarded. In the original version of *A History of English Sounds* (published by Trübner for the English Dialect Society in 1874), Sweet accepted Ellis's position, stating (p. 18) that ". . . the changes in early languages are not gradual, but *per saltum*. . . . Many philologists have assumed that in such changes as that of a back into a front consonant (Sanskrit *k* into *ch*) the tongue was shifted forwards by imperceptible gradations. Such assumptions are quite unnecessary, besides being devoid of proof." However, in the 1888 version he had changed his mind, claiming that in the original version "The most serious of my defects was my rejection of the principle of gradual sound-change in favour of change *per saltum*" (p. vii).

Later Sommerfelt (1923) noted that ". . . tous les changements phonétiques sont des sauts d'une articulation à une autre" (p. 138). This he demonstrates by showing that the two variants coexist side by side, even within the speech of one individual, as two distinct entities. He gives several instances, including (p. 139):

. . . le changement d'une *ā* anterior et long en *ǣ* long (du type anglais dans *cat*) que se rencontre dans le parler irlandais de Torr [Donegal]. . . Les deux phonèmes s'emploient côte à côte. Le même individu se sert un moment de *ā*, l'instant d'après de *ǣ* . . .

He differs from Ellis in rejecting the idea that language change originates with new generations, but notes that successive generations seem to use the new variant more often, until it replaces the old entirely.

However, it has been observed that sound change can be viewed as gradual in some ways. One is what Wang (1969) calls lexical diffusion. He discusses this in some detail, since he believes that residue may be caused at least partly by the chronological overlap of two sound changes applying to the same segment. He believes that sound changes do not apply instantaneously to all words containing the relevant segment, but that they apply first to one or two and then gradually spread to all (1968, p. 699 n. 8):

A change starts as a minor rule, which may be optional for those mor-phemes with dual pronunciations, making exceptions of the portion of the lexicon it covers; as it diffuses across the bulk of the lexicon it becomes a major rule, making exceptions of the portion of the lexi-con it has not yet reached.

Another way in which a sound change can occur so as to appear gradual is by generalization of a rule. This seems to have been first discussed by Schuchardt, who suggested that a sound change might originally be motivated by phonetic factors, and then become gen-eralized. He instances devoicing of final consonants, saying that although this common change is often considered "as a purely phonetic law . . . as such it can be valid only before voiceless initials and the generalization is due to conceptual identity" (p. M 12). We have here, then, an early statement on both rule generalization and the mentalistic character of such a change. Interestingly, Schuchardt also considered the question of lexical diffusion, asking whether, when a rule gener-alized to cover larger segments or all of the relevant class, it did so "in bulk" or spread from word to word (p. M 11). Kiparsky (1965; 1968b) discusses rule generalization at some length, postulating that one means of linguistic change is by rule simplification, one partic-ular form of which, simplification of the structural analysis, or envi-ronment, is the mechanism by which what is traditionally called extension by analogy is brought about. Kiparksy uses as an ex-ample the rule (still operative in ModE) which laxes underlying tense vowels either before two or more consonants, as in *keep/kept*, or in the third syllable from the end of a word, as in *vain/vanity*. The rules are (Kiparsky (1968b, p. 180)):

$$5' \qquad V \rightarrow [\text{-long}] \text{ /———CC}$$
$$5'' \qquad V \rightarrow [\text{-long}] \text{ /———C} \ldots V \ldots V$$

and Kiparsky points out that these collapse into a single rule:

$$5 \qquad V \rightarrow [\text{-long}] \text{ /———C} \begin{cases} C \\ \ldots V \ldots V \end{cases}$$

This is a simplified version of an OE rule, which laxed underlying tense vowels before three or more consonants or in the third syllable from the end of a word provided that two consonants followed the vowel, as in:

6'   V → [-long] /——CCC
6"   V → [-long] /——CC . . . V . . . V

which collapses to:

$$6 \quad V \rightarrow [\text{-long}] \; /\text{——CC} \begin{cases} C \\ \ldots V \ldots V. \end{cases}$$

The only difference between (5) and (6) is that the ME rule requires one less consonant in the environment. This simplification of the structural analysis has generalized the rule so that it will apply in more cases.[6]

This had also been observed by Hoenigswald (1964, p. 208), as the process by which a sound change:

. . . first becomes regular for a specific conditioning, only to attract to itself more and more allophones of the disintegrating phoneme. The history of /w/ (digamma) in Greek is a good specimen. Viewed on a sweeping scale, across a vast gap in time, /w/ simply disappears completely—that is, unconditionally. But we know the language well enough to see that it first went out before consonants, then after consonants, then before some and finally all vowels word initially. We can also see that different dialects went through the stages of this sequence at different times.

Putting aside for the moment the last sentence of this description, we can see that Greek first added the rule:

w   →   ø /——C

and then added a second:

w   →   ø /C——.

But according to Bach's neighborhood convention[7] this is not the addition of another rule, but a simplification of the first one to:

w   →   ø /C.

That is, /w/ → ø in the neighborhood of a consonant. Finally, the rule simplifies to:

$$w \rightarrow ø.$$

That is, it applies in all environments.

A third way in which sound change may appear gradual is that the additional rule may be optional at first. Sommerfelt's observations indicate that speakers of the dialect cited have added a rule fronting /ā/ to /æ/, but that they do not always choose to apply this rule. Labov (1963; 1966) and Weinreich, Labov, and Herzog also illustrate this, and show that it is possible to isolate and to some extent quantify the factors, often completely nonlinguistic, which trigger the use of such an optional rule.

A fourth way in which a sound change may appear gradual is that the rule is not added by everyone at the same time, or used to the same extent. Sommerfelt noted that older speakers tended not to have the rule, and that its use increased inversely with age. This may be called social diffusion. Similarly, not all areas may add the rule simultaneously; Hoenigswald noted that the rules deleting /w/ in Greek were acquired by grammars of different regions at different periods. Labov has documented the diffusion of a sound change across the different generations and its variation between people of different racial backgrounds (1966), and regional diffusion of a sound change is amply documented in work on historical linguistics and dialect geography.

CONSTRAINTS ON SOUND CHANGE

One of the objections to the explanation of the Great Vowel Shift in Chomsky and Halle (1968) is to the formulation of the rules. For the dialect of John Hart they postulate that rules were added to diphthongize the high vowels, to lower the first element of the resulting diphthongs, to raise the original mid vowels, and to lax (shorten) the first elements of the diphthongs. The central rule is Vowel Shift (p. 256):

$$\begin{bmatrix} \alpha high \\ -low \end{bmatrix} \rightarrow [-\alpha high] \Big/ \begin{bmatrix} \underline{\quad} \\ +tense \\ +stress \end{bmatrix}$$

The theory is at present so rich that almost any change can be formulated in a rule. The need for constraining the theory has frequently been acknowledged, for instance in Chomsky (1967*b*, p. 126):

> A general theory of rule plausibility is clearly needed as a supplement to the theory of generative phonology . . . This matter leads us into an entirely new and relatively unexplored domain—namely, into consideration of the system of substantive (not formal) constraints on phonological rules, and into the interaction of substantive constraints with the processes described by phonological rules.

In particular Stockwell (forthcoming) and McCawley (1969) have objected to the use of α-switching or exchange rules.[8] The Vowel Shift Rule above is an example of such a rule. The variable α is to be interpreted as meaning both + and - simultaneously, and the rule is an abbreviation of two rules:

$$
\begin{bmatrix} -\text{high} \\ -\text{low} \end{bmatrix} \rightarrow [+\text{high}] \Bigg/ \begin{bmatrix} \underline{\quad\quad} \\ +\text{tense} \\ +\text{stress} \end{bmatrix} \qquad (a)
$$

$$
\begin{bmatrix} +\text{high} \\ -\text{low} \end{bmatrix} \rightarrow [-\text{high}] \Bigg/ \begin{bmatrix} \underline{\quad\quad} \\ +\text{tense} \\ +\text{stress} \end{bmatrix} \qquad (b)
$$

The two rules cannot be formulated as two separate processes, since the second will then simply reverse the first. The notation allows the rules to be formulated so that the two processes apply simultaneously. Examples of the operation of such a rule have been given by Kiparsky and Wang. Kiparsky (1965, I: 20-21) points out that:

In the dialects of Northern Corsica, the vowels of Vulgar Latin . . . developed further in the following way:

(23) i   e   ε   a   ɔ   o   u
      | ╳ | ╳ |
      i   e   ε   a   ɔ   o   u

That is, mid and open vowels have exchanged places with each other.

Further, Kiparsky notes that the distinction between mid and open vowels has not been lost. It is, of course, possible that some other feature was introduced before the change to produce a distinction (like the off-glide following ME ī, ū, in English), and that it later disappeared, leaving no trace of its presence. But this seems an implausible way of handling the change, since it is quite unsupported, by any evidence.

Similarly Wang (1967, pp. 102-103) has discussed cases in Chinese in which high tone has become low tone, and low tone has become high tone, while mid tone is unaffected. He also discusses the possibility that some other factor such as a contour tone was introduced, but against this points out first that there is no trace of this where the diachronic change occurred, and second that where this occurs in alternations in the synchronic grammar the switch is simply between high and low tones, with no other feature present.

One objection to this kind of rule has been that its introduction into a language would impair intelligibility, or that the participating sounds would merge. Stockwell (forthcoming) quotes an argument from McCawley, which is taken up in McCawley (1969), where he discusses (pp. 16-18):

. . . the question of whether the interchange of two segments or classes of segments is a possible historical change . . . Since changes normally spread by being adopted first as optional . . . the spread of an exchange would give rise to speakers who produced e.g. both [pol] and [pul] for older [pol] and both [pul] and [pol] for older [pul]. The speech of these two individuals would not differ markedly from the speech of a person who simply had free variation between [pol] and [pul]. Thus the spread of an exchange would produce a tendency towards the obliteration of the underlying distinction between the segments it affected.

Stockwell would not object to the change as formulated in Chomsky and Halle (1968), since there the environment in which the high vowels lower (before a homorganic off-glide) is distinct from that in which the mid vowels raise, and the two are therefore kept distinct. But there is no mention of this environment in the actual Vowel Shift rule; as formulated it is indistinguishable from any other exchange rule operating where the environment does not distinguish the exchanged segments. The objection is, then, not to such a rule per se, but to its incorporation in a grammar under such conditions that intelligibility would be impaired. Chomsky and Halle (1968, pp. 257-258) have argued that such a condition on grammars should be excluded, and that the suppositions on which it is based are implausible. In any case, the examples cited by Kiparsky and Wang seem to indicate that such changes have occurred in languages without loss or impairment of intelligibility or merger of the sounds.

Stockwell (1952, p. 192) postulated a series of constraints on sound change, of which the following are relevant here:

1. When a simple nucleus changes, that change consists in its reclassification under the next contiguous phonemic notch in any direction within a structural frame.

2. When a complex nucleus changes, that change consists in either one of two possible changes:

   A. Reclassification of the vowel of the complex nucleus under the next contiguous phonemic notch in any direction within a structural frame

   B. Reclassification of the semi-vowel of the complex nucleus under one of the other semi-vowels in the system.

No justification is given for these constraints, nor any explanation why a change in semivowel is not similarly restricted to replacement by a contiguous semivowel. Apparently /ay/ → /aw/ was allowed. However, Stockwell would now claim that precisely the same constraint holds for off-glides (personal communication).

Exchange rules seem to be more easily justified in synchronic grammars. Chomsky and Halle admit (1968, p. 259) that "it is conceivable that the constraints on rules that can be added to a grammar may be more severe than those on rules that can figure in a grammar." Kiparsky (1968a, p. 17) goes further:

. . . the claim that the set of possible sound changes is the same as the set of possible phonological rules is clearly untenable, given any presently formulated phonological theory . . . it seems more accurate to say that sound changes are a set of very simple rules, and that more complicated rules, which could not be added as such to grammars, may still come to exist in grammars through phonological restructuring.

To the Chomsky-Halle formulation of the Great Vowel Shift, then, one of two objections may be made: (1) it should not figure in a grammar at all; (2) it can figure in a synchronic grammar as a result of restructuring, but cannot be added as a rule; therefore, it does not explain the chronological sound change.

CHAPTER III

In this chapter the work of several orthoepists and grammarians is discussed with a view to attempting to ascertain what evidence their analyses of English contribute to our understanding of the Vowel Shift. As outlined earlier, I consider primarily the development of ME ī, ū, and ẹ, and also evidence bearing on the possible diphthongal character of the traditional long tense vowels. The development of the English consonant system, and other controversies involving vowels and diphthongs, such as the development of ME *oi* and *ui*, will largely be ignored, except where they bear on the Vowel Shift.

Because of the very specific nature of the information sought, certain works (such as Edmund Coote: *English Schoole-Master*, and A. Hume: *Of the Orthographie and Congruitie of the Britan Tongue*) which contributed no data of value in these areas have been ignored. Further, I have in general limited myself to English orthoepistical works; many of the French grammarians are not yet easily accessible, and those I consulted (and the accounts in Zachrisson's (1913) survey of a large number of such works) did not in general seem sufficiently enlightening to be indispensable.

The works are discussed in the chronological order of their publication (or writing, where not published till much later). In the case of some, one could from autobiographical data perhaps infer the date at which the phonology of the author had been established. In some cases, however, we know little or nothing of the author, and in none of them can we be sure that the author is describing his own particular usage rather than what he conceives to be the best Standard English of the time (as some, e.g. Coles, specifically claim to do). Because of this, there seemed no point in trying to establish the chronological order of the phonologies described when this could not even be attempted for some, and would possibly be inaccurate for any.

The principle throughout this chapter has been to believe the writer's description of his pronunciation as much as possible. There seems no point in trying to decide on the exact phonetic output. Since the writers had no established phonetic alphabet to use, or exact traditional terminology, it seems to me quite pointless in most cases to debate at length over whether any particular centralized vowel should be labeled [ʌ] or [ə]. On the other hand, if an orthoepist describes both diphthongs and long vowels, and shows that he does understand the difference between them, it seems wiser to follow his analysis of his sounds. Once we begin to disregard what the writer says because it seems inconsistent with our preconceived ideas, there is no principled way of drawing the line between what we accept and what we reject. I can see no reason for seeking the information given in these works if we are going to disregard it as unreliable whenever we happen to dislike the consequences our accepting it would seem to entail. If, having interpreted the description as literally as possible, we later wish to propose a different solution, we can then see to what extent we are relying on our theory of sound change, or of phonology in general, to support our argument, rather than on the data provided by contemporary sources. I feel very strongly that where a reasonable solution can be found which does not conflict with the orthoepists' and grammarians' own testimony, then that solution should be accepted, even though it may contradict or at least disturb some particular theory we may happen to have held dear.

The value of the orthoepistical evidence has been disparaged in favor of that provided by orthography, rhymes, and contemporary dialects by scholars from Weymouth to Stockwell, generally on the basis of the difficulty of interpreting the descriptions given, the (claimed) artificiality of the pronunciation thus described, and the discrepancies between writers. As regards the second point, we shall see to what extent the pronunciation described by the orthoepists differs from that indicated by other evidence. On the first and last points, Weymouth's remarks are very much to the point (p. 5): ". . . if, instead of studying only fragmentary quotations, and misleading explanations, and 'transliterations' which assume every point that is in dispute, we read the books themselves . . . almost every difficulty at once disappears." I wholeheartedly agree with this statement—yet, of course, anyone reading this work is again faced with quotations, explanations, and interpretations. I have, however, tried to make the quotations not too fragmentary, and to prevent both them and the explanations from being misleading. I have also tried to indicate exactly where a description is ambiguous, or where my interpretation departs from the orthoepists' analysis (the latter very seldom, in accordance with the interpretive principles outlined above).

JOHN HART: 1551, 1569, 1570

Hart wrote three works dealing with English pronunciation and orthography: *The Opening of the Unreasonable Writing of Our Inglish Toung* (1551), in manuscript; *An Orthographie* . . . , published in 1569, and *A Methode* . . . [*of Teaching Reading*], published in 1570. The *Orthographie* is essentially a revised version of Hart's manuscript, but there are some differences, the most notable being that the *Orthographie* has extensive passages of transcription in Hart's phonetic notation.

We can determine Hart's pronunciation from the occasional comparisons he makes with foreign sounds, from his transcriptions, and from the following articulatory description (Danielsson (1955, p. 190)):

First I finde that we vse fiue differing simple soundes or voyces, proceeding from the brest, without any maner of touching of the tongue to the palet or foreteeth, or of the lippes close ioyning togither: or eyther of the lippes to their counter teeth . . . the first, with wyde opening the mouth, as when a man yauneth: and is figured a. The second, with somewhat more closing the mouth, thrusting softlye the inner part of the tongue to the inner and vpper great teeth (or gummes for want of teeth) and is merked e. The thirde, by pressing the tongue in like maner, yet somewhat more foreward, and bringing the iawe somewhat more neare, and is written i. The fourth, by taking awaye of all the tongue, cleane from the teeth or gummes, as is sayde for the a, and turning the lippes rounde as a ring, and thrusting forth of a sounding breath, which roundnesse to signifie the shape of the letter, was made (of the first inuentor) in like sort, thus o. For the fift and last, by holding in lyke maner the tongue from touching the teeth or gummes (as is said of the a, and o) and bringing the lippes so neare togither as there may be left but space that the sounds may passe forth with the breath, so softly, that (by their ouer harde and close ioyning) they be not forced thorow the nose, *and* is noted thus u.

Hart makes no qualitative distinction between short and long vowels, and (in the absence of any evidence to the contrary) this is in general accepted by the scholars who have discussed his work, though Dobson (1957a, p. 73) seems to suggest that there were some qualitative differences which Hart failed to notice. However, we may assume that Hart had [a]/[ā] for ME, *a, ā*; [i]/[ī] for ME *i, ẹ̄*; and [u]/[ū] for ME *u, ọ̄*. Jespersen (1907, p. 11), Dobson (1957*a*, p. 73), and Halle and Keyser (p. 782) all point out that Hart clearly distinguishes front from back vowels. However, like some of the other orthoepists (e.g. Wilkins, Holder), Hart does not discuss tongue height in relation to back vowels, and there is therefore no evidence from which to determine whether he has [ō] or [ɔ] for ME *ọ̄*. Halle and Keyser (p. 774) reject Danielsson's value of [ɔ] in favor of [ō] on the grounds that there is no evidence either way, and selection of [ō] will result in a more symmetric vowel system. But since Danielsson (largely on the basis of comparisons with French and German sounds (1963, p. 115)) identifies Hart's *e*, ME *ẹ̄*, with [ɛ], in fact he has a symmetric system, but not the one in Halle and Keyser or in Chomsky and Halle (1968). The essential difference is whether or not vowel raising has applied to ME *ẹ̄, ọ̄*, or whether these vowels still have their ME value. There is no empirical way of deciding this, and it is in any case unimportant for the issues with which we are more particularly concerned.

In his manuscript, Hart appears to assume that in all diphthongs[1] the second element is long and the first short (Danielsson (1963, p. 132)). However, in the *Orthographie* (p. 199) he differentiates two kinds, the first "made of two short vowels" and the second "of one short and another long." He exemplifies the first with "ui uil reid bei ionder uel, huer de uat uas ualnēr tākn bei ðe iung hound" (*we will ride by yonder well where the Wat was well near taken by the young hound*), and the second by "iū uēr uāking in de foūrþ toūr, huen az de buē did poūr uāter upon de[2] huēt floūr" (*you were waking in the fourth tower, when as the boy did pour water upon the wheat flour*). Note that με *ū* is included in both lists, whereas με *ī* occurs only in the first. (Dobson notes (1957*a*, p. 70) that in his actual transcription Hart rarely uses *oū* for με *ū*.) But Hart gives us no help here in determining the quantity of the ME diphthongs. Danielsson gives *ēu* for με *ẹ̄u*, and *iu* for με *ẹ̄u*. However, Hart transcribes με *ẹ̄u* as *eu*, with no length mark, and Danielsson gives no justification for his analysis. For με *au, oi*, Danielsson gives *au, oi*, whereas Chomsky and Halle (1968) have /āw/, /ōy/, assuming "that only the reflexes of ME nonlow tense vowels were laxed before glides" (p. 262). They give no reason for making this assumption except that Hart's analysis of diphthongs shows some uncertainty as to which had tense and which lax vowels. But there is no evidence either in Hart's discussion or his transcriptions for assigning tense first elements to ME *ẹ̄u, au*, or *oi*.

But Hart does show uncertainty as to the proper transcription of με *ou*. At first he transcribes it either as *ou*, in which case it is identical with με *ū*, or as *ō*, indicating monophthongization. Finally, in the *Methode*, he transcribes it as *ōu* (which agrees with Gil and Butler). This is the only diphthong which he marks as having a tense first element (except for the idiosyncratic lexical item *oyster*). One possible interpretation of the data is that Hart has an optional rule monophthongizing ME *ou* (for which there is evidence in other orthoepists). Chomsky and Halle (1968), however, believe that ME *ou* was always diphthongal in Hart's speech, but that because his original theory did not allow for diphthongs of this kind he did not recognize them. Similarly, although Hart uniformly transcribes με *ai* as *ē*, that is, as being identical with ME *ẹ̄*, Chomsky and Halle assume that this also was diphthongal, and that again Hart had simply failed to hear the off-glide. This is also the view of Jespersen (1907), who believes that in fact ME *ai* never monophthongized at all. He offers two explanations for Hart's transcription (1907, p. 34):

. . . either Hart represented a dialect confounding the two sounds, a dialect which was nowhere else mentioned, and which died out rapidly without leaving any traces, or else his notation was deficient.

But in fact the same dialect is described by Gil (who criticizes Hart, not for faulty transcription, but for describing a nonstandard dialect), by Butler, and by Bellot. There is therefore supporting contemporary evidence for Hart's analysis. Further, Hart is extremely clear about his identification of ME *ẹ̄* and *ai*. In his manuscript (which Jespersen does not use very much, since the *Orthographie* is so similar), he considers the use of *ai, ay, ei, ey*, and *ea* to be completely on a par as being improper representations of his long *e*, "as in this sentence, I may not beare their heathen deceites, which to do wel we shuld write thus, I mee not beer ther[3] heethen deceets . . ." (Danielsson (1955, p. 163)). Both Danielsson and Dobson accept the monophthongization of ME *ai*. Chomsky and Halle note that if Hart's evidence is here interpreted literally (as I would prefer to do, since he seems quite clear), then their rules must be amended to monophthongize these, optionally for ME *ou* but obligatorily for ME *ai*, but they also point out quite rightly that "these modifications, however, do not shed any new light on the evolution of the English vowel system" (1968, p. 262). But although it may be reasonable to assume that ME *ai, ou*, usually transcribed *ē, ō*, respectively, if diphthongal had tense first elements, there seems no reason to extend this to the ME diphthongs *ẹ̄u, oi*, and *au*, as discussed above. In fact, since in each case Hart is aware that these are diphthongs, and transcribes them as such, but (except for *oyster*) never marks them as having a tense first element, we may presume that in his speech they were different in structure from ME *ai, ou*, and that most probably the first element was not tense. This would mean that the Chomsky-Halle laxing rule would have to be extended to apply generally except to ME *ou* (which is in any case different, since it is the only case of optional monophthongization in Hart's dialect).

Chomsky and Halle (1968), Jespersen (1907), and Danielsson (1955; 1963) all accept that in Hart's dialect με *ī, ū*, were /ey/, /ow/, respectively. Dobson, however, assumes that the first element of each must be a centralized vowel. As Chomsky and Halle point out (1968, p. 255), this interpretation stems from Dobson's belief about the nature of sound change and is quite external to the evidence in Hart, with which it is, indeed, in conflict. That is (as discussed in Chapter I), Dobson believed that if ME *ī* diphthongized and lowered without centralization of the first element, so that at some point the resulting diphthong "crossed the path of ME *ai* developing to [æi] and [ɛi]," then the two would inevitably merge. But merger will follow from intersection only if sound change is considered to be gradual and exchange rules are not allowed. Further, as was pointed out above, all authorities, including Dobson, are convinced that Hart did clearly distinguish between back and front vowels. "There is, therefore, little reason to doubt that in Hart's speech the reflexes of ME *ī* and *ū* differed not only in their glide but also in their vowel . . . " (Halle and Keyser, p. 782). Further, since for Hart the amount of rounding is the characteristic by which he differentiates between his back vowels, it is at least odd that, if με *ū* were indeed /əw/, he did not comment on the lack of rounding in this manifestation of *o*.

Hart shows some instances of ME *ẹ̄* raising to merge with με *ẹ̄* before *r*, e.g. *appīr*. We shall see that this is quite commonly shown by other orthoepists. Hart also shows shortening of /ū/ < ME *ǭ* to /u/, as in *book, took, good, would*, and a back-glide following *a, o*, before *lC* or *l#* , as in *fall, wall, call, hold, soul*, as opposed to, e.g., *hallow, ballad, solid, follow*, and the deletion of /l/ before labials and velars, as in *talk, calf, yolk, holm*.

I assign to Hart the following pattern, which differs in some respects from the findings of Danielsson, Jespersen, Dobson, and Chomsky and Halle, as discussed above:

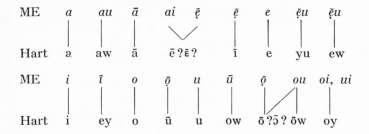

JACQUES BELLOT: 1580

Jacques Bellot's *The Englische Scholemaster* is the earliest surviving French-English grammar. It is particularly useful as evidence of the pronunciation of the vowels which participated in the Vowel Shift at a time very little later than Hart.[4]

Bellot treats of what he calls vowels, diphthongs, and triphthongs. It is, however, clear that by diphthong he means digraph, and similarly with triphthongs. He lists the English diphthongs as *Ai, Au, Ay, Ea, Ei, Eo, Ey, Oa, Oe, Oy, Ue, Ui, Uy, Ee*. He gives no examples or description of the pronunciation of *Oy*.

According to Bellot, *ai, ay, ea, ei, ey*, and *a* are all pronounced like the first *e* of *Estre*, "to be somewhat long and the mouth half open." The examples given are *pleased, affairs, either*, and *they*. Bellot notes that *a* is not pronounced in this manner when standing alone, or when it begins a word or syllable, or mostly when following a consonant (it is difficult to see what he meant by this last exception, since it would seem to exclude most of the occurrences of *a*; perhaps he means in word-final position), but he does not describe what the pronunciation is in any of these environments. He gives no examples of words with *a* to indicate any of its pronunciations. ME *ā* seems therefore to have generally fronted and raised to [ɛ̄]; however, since French does not have [æ], it is quite likely that he would also hear this as [ɛ̄]; it is therefore possible that ME *ā* had merely fronted to [æ]. We cannot come to any conclusion by comparing it with the exceptional pronunciation of *a* which Bellot mentions, since we have no way of knowing what that is; it could, for instance, be [æ], or he could be indicating an unstressed pronunciation [ə]. Bellot indicates that ME *ā, ai*, and *ę̄* are all identical; this is contrary to the evidence of any of the English orthoepists (cf. below) and perhaps lends support to an identification of ME *ā* with [æ] and ME *ę̄* with [ɛ̄]. This does not enable us to decide on a value for ME *ai*, which could have merged with either ME *ā* or ME *ę̄*, but which certainly seems to be monophthongal. French is said to have had the diphthongs /ai/ and /ei/, and there is therefore no reason why Bellot should not have recognized a diphthongal pronunciation. Alternatively one could assume (as Zachrisson does) that ME *ā* was [ɛ̄] and ME *ę̄* was [ē]. However, both these vowels existed in French, and there is therefore no reason why Bellot should have heard them as identical. We can explain his equating them (if they were different) only by assuming that one sound was identical with a vowel which did not occur in French, which he therefore could not identify, and to which he assigned the nearest French sound. This seems to point to ME *ā* having become [æ].

Ee, *y*, in word-final position (except when following *l*), and *e* when word- or syllable-final, are pronounced as "the I vowel of the Frenchmen." Some of the examples given are *hee*, *the*, *betweene*, *he*, *deedes*, *keper*, *me*, *se*, *we*. *Eo* is also said to be pronounced in this manner, but to occur only seldom; the sole example is of course *people*. Bellot states that when *e* is word- or syllable-final after *th* "it is sounded as the E masculyne of the frenchmen," as in *the*, *thether*; the same pronunciation is indicated for final *y* following *l*, as in *verily*, *partly*. Since he presumably distinguishes this from the sound of *e* in *Estre*, we may perhaps assume that the vowel of *Estre* is [ɛ̄] and that *e masculine* is [e]. But it would seem that the latter is only an allophonic variant of the sound he describes as the "I vowel of the Frenchmen," since it occurs so infrequently and only in specific environments. But whatever he means to indicate by this term, it seems fairly clear that ME *ę̄* has raised to [ī].

Oe is pronounced like *ou*, as in *doest*, *doeth*. *O* in word-final position is also pronounced like *ou*, as in *doing*, *to*, *do*. He notes some exceptions to this pronunciation of *oe*: *doe*, *loe*, *foes*, for which he gives the pronunciation of *o* long. *Oa* is said to be pronounced *o*, "keeping nevertheless the *a*, a little of his sound, which ought to be heard before *o*"; examples are *boast*, *coast*. It is possible that Bellot is accurately indicating the presence of an actual on-glide, but it may also be that he is influenced by the spellings (though one would not expect him to reverse the order of the vowels). ME *ǭ* and *ọ̄* seem then to be /ō/ and /ū/, respectively.

For both short *o* and short *u* he says that they are pronounced almost like French *o*. For *o* he gives as examples *Thomas* and *shorte*, which he says should be pronounced as if spelled *Tames* and *Chart*, and for *u* he gives *upon*, *up*, and *upsydowne*. *Au* is said to be pronounced as *u*, the only example given being *assuraunce*. We have no way of telling how the pronunciation of *o* and *u* differs from French *o*, or to what extent English *o* and *u* differ from each other.

Bellot then indicates that he hears the English vowel system of that period as consisting of *i, e, a, o, u*, and that each of these vowels could be either long or short. His general rule is that every vowel is long when followed by only one consonant, but short before two consonants. His examples are *fale (fail), mile, fell, fill, full.*

Bellot documents the existence of two diphthongs in addition to the simple vowels. *I* vowel plus *y*, and the digraphs *ui* and *uy*, are, he says, pronounced "as the Frenchmen doe sound Ey." His examples are *to guyde, to build, by, my*, and *Christ*, which is pronounced as if spelled *Chreist*. He notes that this last is an exception to his shortening rule, since *I* vowel is usually pronounced long only before one consonant, and short before two, as in *untill*, in which word *i* is, he says, pronounced as in French.[5] *Ou* is like the French *au*, *thou* and *thousand* being pronounced as if spelled *thau* and *thausand*. For both of these diphthongs, the question we are particularly interested in is the quality of the first element. Variant forms cited by Pope (§ 529) (from Meigret, 1554 and 1550), showing the development [ai] > [ei] > [ē], and illustrating that monophthongization tended to occur later in word-final position, and that in the sixteenth century both the diphthongal and monophthongal pronunciations are still current, are *j'ey, jé, jc sey*, and *ie sé*. This would seem to suggest that Bellot was indicating a front mid vowel for the first element. We cannot tell whether he really meant that the vowel was [ɛ] rather than [e]; since he was defining the pronunciation by equating it with a current French sound, he had to pick the nearest equivalent, and it would seem (from Pope's description) that the diphthong was always [ɛi], not [ei]. It does not seem very likely that at that period the English vowel had lowered to [ɛi]; it is relevant that Bellot did not equate the first element with either the vowel of *Estre* or with the *e masculine*.[6] With regard to *ou* (= ME *ū*) pronounced as French *au*, we find (Pope, p. 199, §§ 534-535) that during the sixteenth century the first element of the diphthong became rounded and that then monophthongization took place. We therefore assume that at this period Bellot intended to indicate a pronunciation something like /ow/. The only other pronunciations possible are /aw/, for which this seems rather early, or /ō/, which seems highly improbable.

We see then that, like Hart, Bellot's description of English would seem to indicate that με *ī*, *ū*, were /ey/, /ow/, respectively. Unlike Hart, it may be that Bellot recognized the existence of a centralized vowel, since it is possible that this is the sound he meant to indicate by *e masculine*. This is not the usual meaning of *e masculine*, but given the examples Bellot cites it is a possible one. However, it is strange that he did not then call the sound *e feminine*. But even if we decide that he did mean to indicate a centralized vowel, it is still true that he did not equate this sound with the first element of either diphthong. We must therefore conclude that to his ear the sixteenth-century developments of ME *ī*, *ū*, did not have centralized vowels as their first element, and that if we wish to claim that they did, then we are basing our analysis not on his description but on our own beliefs. There is also no evidence of diphthongization of the other long tense vowels, but there is evidence of monophthongization of ME *ai*.

We have no evidence here of the pronunciation of ME *ẹu*, *ęu*. Zachrisson (1913, p. 144) assumes that Bellot indicates a pronunciation *iu* [ju], but this is based on his misunderstanding of Bellot, who says merely that the letter "V, is pronounced in the alphabeth Yu as though it were of two syllables." This obviously refers only to the name of the letter, since he goes on to add that ". . . in any other place, it is pronounced almost lyke the frenchmen doe sound their O," and his examples are *upon*, *up*, and *upsydowne*. He tells us also that "ue, is pronounced u long," for which the examples are *rue* and *my due*. Unfortunately this very vague description does not enable us to identify the sound at all.

From the identification of *buck/book* as homonyms we may deduce that shortening had occurred in /ū/ < ME *ǭ*, but that /u/ had not yet lowered and unrounded to /ə/.

From Bellot's evidence we can formulate the following incomplete vowel system:

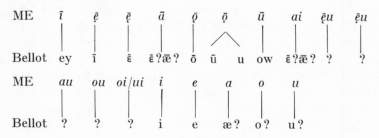

ME	ī	ẹ̄	ę̄	ā	ǭ	ǭ	ū	ai	ẹu	ęu
Bellot	ey	ī	ɛ̄	ɛ̄?ǣ?	ō	ū	u	ow	ɛ̄?ǣ?	?	?

ME	au	ou	oi/ui	i	e	a	o	u
Bellot	?	?	?	i	e	æ?	o?	u?

WILLIAM BULLOKAR: 1580

Bullokar wrote several works, all of which are described by Dobson (1957a, pp. 94-96), and used by Zachrisson (1927). The discussion here is based only on Bullokar (1580), Dobson, and Zachrisson.

Bullokar is interested in amending the orthography so that it will be easier for foreigners and for children to learn to read English, and in doing so with as little interference to the existing orthography as possible. He does not want to devise a new phonetic alphabet, nor is he interested in analyzing and describing the distinct sounds of English. He intends to ensure that any letter or digraph has only one possible pronunciation, but since he wishes to be able to differentiate homophones (p. 22) he does not attempt to limit any one sound to only one orthographic representation.

Both Zachrisson (1927, pp. 14-21) and Dobson (1957a, pp. 99-100) point out that there are several flaws in Bullokar's system of representation. First, despite all the diacritics used Bullokar is unable to distinguish all the ways in which a letter or digraph may be pronounced. Second, even when his system would enable him to represent the pronunciation he often does not do so because he wishes to distinguish homophones or to follow the conventional spelling. Third, he deliberately uses the same spelling for derived and inflected forms as for roots and stems, which means that they are often not equivalent to the phonetic output but more nearly represent a kind of underlying form.

Bullokar claims (p. 22) that there are in English eight distinct vowels, $a, e, e', i, o, \infty, v, v$. He goes on to say that a, e, i, y (these last two being the same, although Bullokar has as yet not explained this), and o may be marked with a superimposed accent or doubled, to show that they are long, e.g. $aa, á, e', \infty, v, u$ (again these two are the same), and $æ$[7] diphthong (which, he explains later, is a "pair" with e, i.e., is the same as ee or $é$) are always long. From this it seems that v is always short.

Bullokar then gives a definition of a diphthong, saying that "... when two vowels of diuers sounds com together in one sillable, they make a diphthong, that is to say, they are both touched short in sound together; but the sound of them is longer than the sound of a single vowel." He later (p. 24) modifies this, saying that when a diphthong consists of a vowel plus w, then the vowel is "perfectly sounded," but the w is only "lightly touched," except in $e'w$ ($=$ ME $\bar{e}u$) "where both are like sounded." He says nothing here of diphthongs not composed of a vowel plus w, and it is clear that he really means digraph, since he does not recognize the diphthongal quality of $\mu\varepsilon$ $\bar{i}$, and since he claims that some vowels and diphthongs are "of one sound," i.e., the same, and gives the following table of these equivalences (p. 23):

ai ay	aɣ aʉ aw	ei ey	eɣ eʉ ew	ó oa	oi oy	ow	oɣ oʉ ọw ꝏw v ʉ ọ ꝏ ꝏ
ꝏi ꝏy	e'a e'ae e'	e'ɣ e'ʉ v u e'w	al' aɣl	aṁ aɣm	ań aɣn	oń oɣn	uy seldom used

He then (pp. 23-24) gives examples of the eight distinct vowel sounds
and of the seven diphthongs, and later (pp. 30-35) indicates which orthographic symbols are "pairs," i.e., indicate the same sound. Combining these, and drawing on Bullokar's transcriptions for other examples, we find that Bullokar perceived the following sounds as distinct:

ME	Bullokar's symbols	Examples
a	a	lak (*lack*)
ā	aa á	bál (*bale*) Baal
e	e	hel
ę̄	é æ ae	laek (*leak*)
ę̣	e' e'ae e'a	he'l (*heel*)
i	i y	pillory, lyk (*lick*)
ī	í ý iy yi	pýl (*pile*)
o	o	lok (*lock*)
ǭ	ꝏ ó oa	nót (*note*)
ǭ	ꝏ	lꝏk (*look*)
u	ɣ ʉ ọ ꝏ ꝏ	lụk (*luck*)
ū	oɣ oʉ ọw ꝏw	họw (*how*)
ę̄u	e'v e'u e'w v u	ne'w (*new*) luk (*Luke*)
ę̣u	eɣ eʉ ew	heʉ (*hew*)
ai	ai ay	may; paier (*pair*)
ei	ei ey	they
au	aʉ aɣ aw	caʉz (*cause*)
ou	ow[8]	bowl (*basin*)
oi, ui	oi oy ꝏi ꝏy uy	boy (*boy*), bꝏy (*buoy*)

On the basis of Bullokar's descriptions and transcriptions, and using
other contemporary evidence, Zachrisson (1927, pp. 143-144) assigns
the following approximate phonetic values to Bullokar's symbols:

a	man	[æ] rather than [a]
á	nám	[ɛ:] rather than [æ:]
á	barn	[æ:]?
ay	day	[ɛ:i], possibly with a half long [ɛ·]
ae	mael	[e:]
e	men	[e]
e'	be'	[i:]
ý	wrýt	[ei] rather than [ij]

i	sit	[i]
ʉ	lʉk	[o] rather than [u]
ǫw	hǫws	[ou] rather than [uw]
oo	do	[u:]
aʉ	aʉtor	[au]?
o	not	[ə] with slight rounding
ó	gót	[go:t]
ow	blow	[o:u]
e'w, u	ne'w, due	[ⁱiu] or [iˈu]
ew	few	[e:u]
oi	joy	[əi]
ooi	booil	[ui] rather than [u:]
uy	ịuic' ịuyst	[əi]
ú	natúr	[o], [ə]
ó	thórn	[ɔ:]?

He notes also that Bullokar sometimes confuses ME ǭ and *ou* before *r* or *l*C, and that these may have been the same (Zachrisson (1927, p. 77)).

Bullokar also spells *roam* "rowm" and *sold* "sowld," and the herb *balm* as "baulm" (not using aʉ, which is his usual symbol for ME *au*, though of course this is probably just an oversight); these spellings suggest that Bullokar also knew that generally a glide was inserted following /a/, /o/, before *l*♯ or *l*C, but that he records this only when it is reflected in his ordinary spelling. Since he says that *a* is a "perfect letter" with only one sound, we must assume that it had not rounded either before or after *w*.

It seems that for Bullokar με ẹ̄ is distinct from με ę̄ and με ā̤, and that με *ai* is distinct from both με ā and με ę̄, that Bullokar knew of three pronunciations for ME *oi*, *ui* words, although one of these, "uy," was very uncommon, and that he differentiates ME *ai*, *ei* (though this may simply be based on the spelling; Zachrisson (1927, p. 38) notes that Bullokar sometimes confuses them in his transcriptions). We can, however, tell very little about the quality of the sounds. ME *o* is paired with ME ǭ, not with ME *au*, showing that it probably had not yet lowered. Bullokar says that με ẹ̄ was sounded "more sharpe [than με ę̄, e] between the old sound of the name of :e: and the name of :i:." However, this doesn't really help us very much, though it may indicate that Bullokar noticed a similarity between the sounds of με ẹ̄ and *i*.

Bullokar does not provide us with any very valuable evidence on the relative priority of lowering and centralization, since his descriptions of με ī̤, ṳ̄, are so vague. He considers με *i*, ī, to be the same sounds, differing only in quantity (p. 5), and says that με *u* is the same as the sound of "the diphthong ou," but short (p. 7). He gives no examples here. For με *i*, *ī*, he may simply be misled by the spelling, but this cannot be the case with με *u*, *ū*; "diphthong ou" may mean με *ū*, or he may mean *ou* before *r* pronounced like ME *ō*, as in, e.g., *court, mourn,* in which case, as Zachrisson (1927, pp. 61-62) notes, this might indicate that ME *ǭ*, *ū*, and *u* were qualitatively identical. But Zachrisson thinks it likely that Bullokar used *ou* for *court, mourn,* simply because that was the traditional spelling, not because he pronounced them with με *ū*. Since he presumably did not know that με *ū*, to him *ou*, was spelled *u* in OE, we must assume that his pairing here is made on the basis of some similarity of sound. There are four possibilities.

First, we might assume that in Bullokar (as is the case in Northern and Scottish dialects) ME *ū* had not diphthongized and shifted. Second, we might assume that με *ī*, *ū*, were /iy/, /uw/, respectively in Bullokar's dialect, contrasting with /ī/, /ū/, from ME *ę̄*, *ǭ*. This is also unlikely, and, further, if this were so με *i*, *e*, would pair just as well with με *ę̄*, *ǭ*, yet Bullokar does not suggest this. Third, it is possible that με *ū* was /ow/, that in Bullokar's dialect με *u* was /o/ (Zachrisson (1927, pp. 56-58, 144)), and that Bullokar noted the similarity between με *u* and the first element of με *ū*. If με *ī* were /ey/ and με *i* had lowered to /e/ (as was very common), this might also explain the pairing of με *ī*, *i*. But Bullokar does not suggest that ME *i*, *e*, were the same or similar in sound, or ME *u*, *o*. A fourth possibility (not suggested by Zachrisson) is that for Bullokar **all** με *u* were /ə/, and με *ū* was /əw/; again we would have a partial similarity, but against this explanation we must take into account that the earliest unequivocal description of ME *u* lowering and unrounding to /ə/ is in Hodges, over sixty years later, and that Bullokar would be unique in having no instances left of /u/. Further, this would not explain the pairing of με *i*, *ī*, since we have no reason to assume that με *i* was /ə/; equally, of course, there is nothing in Bullokar to make us suppose that με *i*, *ī*, were paired on the same basis as με *u* and "the diphthong ou."

All I conclude from this is that Bullokar affords us no help in determining the development of ME *ī*, *ū*. Further, since it is not at all clear that he understood the difference between diphthongs and monophthongs, there is nothing in his description that would help us to decide whether the traditional long vowels were in fact diphthongal.

RICHARD MULCASTER: 1582

Richard Mulcaster was born about 1530-31, and *The First Part of the Elementarie* was published in 1582, at which time he was the first headmaster of the Merchant Taylors' School. In his work, his aims are avowedly pedagogical; he is concerned with establishing a spelling standard, not with analyzing English sounds or with providing any kind of universal alphabet, or yet even with improving English spelling; he is concerned only that people should spell in the same way, and not that the particular spelling they choose be any kind of phonetic representation of the sounds. Because of this he provides no articulatory description or phonetic transcriptions.

It is extremely difficult to interpret Mulcaster's evidence. First, the terms he uses are very confusing; e.g. his use of *long* and *short* vs. *sharp* and *flat* (p. 122):

The vowells generallie sound either long as, *compāring, reuēnged, endīting, enclōsure, presūming*: or short as *ransaking, reuelling, penitent, omnipotent, fortunat*: either sharp, as *máte, méte, rípe, hópe, dúke*, or flat as *màt, rìp mèt, hòp, dùk.*

In this passage *sharp* and *flat* seem to mean *long* and *short*, but we must then decide what meaning to assign to Mulcaster's *long* and *short*. It seems possible that he was referring to the vowels of stressed and unstressed syllables, but there is no way of deciding. Similarly, when discussing the effect a word-final silent *e* has on the preceding vowel, he says that (p. 124):

. . . máde, stéme, éche, kínd, strípe, óre, cúre, tóste sound sharp with the qualifying E in their end: whereas, màd, stèm, èch, frind, strip, or, cur, tost contrast of tossed sound flat without the same E. And therefor the same loud and sharp sound in the word, calleth still for the qualifying e, in the end, as the flat and short nedeth it not.

Here *flat* and *short* seem to be equated, but *loud* is the term conjoined with *sharp* and opposed to *short*. We find later (p. 125): "E when it endeth the last sillab, with one or mo consonants cumming after it, either soundeth flat and full, and maketh a sillab, as in *rest, wretch, discent* . . ." and also: ". . . E, ending anie former syllab. soundeth of it self brode, and longish, as, *reprehend, delegate* . . ." Two more terms are introduced in his discussion of I, where we find:

If it [=I] end the last syllab, with one or mo consonants after it, it is shrill when the qualifying e followeth, and if it be shrill, the qualifying e must follow, as, *repine, unwise, minde, kinde, fiste.* If it be flat and quik, the qualifying e must not follow, as, *examin, behind, mist, fist.*

We have then the terms *long, short, flat, sharp, loud, shrill, broad, full*, and *quick*, for none of which Mulcaster provides any definition. It is possible that some are alternate terms with the same meaning, and Dobson (1957*a*, p. 123) believes that *sharp* and *flat* are used both for *long* and *short* and for *stressed* and *unstressed*. Hart originally uses sharp for stressed, and flat for unstressed, but later he too uses sharp for a mark to indicate short vowels also, even when unstressed. It seems impossible to determine the exact meaning or the terms used here. Mulcaster attempts no descriptions of the articulation of the vowel sounds, nor does he even indicate how many distinct sounds there are. His only comparisons with the sounds of a foreign language are references to Latin, as when he says that (p. 123) ". . . in *the*, the article, *ye* the pronown, and in Latin words, or of a Latin form, when these be used English like, as, *certiorare, quandare*, where e soundeth full and brode after the originall Latin."

Although Mulcaster distinguishes a sharp and a flat pronunciation of *i*, he gives us no further information and therefore we cannot even infer from his description that ME *ī* has diphthongized. Similarly, though *e* has two distinct pronunciations, we are given no help in identifying what they are; Mulcaster does not, for instance, note any similarity between short *i* and long *e*. ME *ę̄* is treated as the "diphthong" *ea*, as in *meat* (p. 131), *sea, yea, plea, weal, seal* (p. 153), but again we are given no indication of its sound. Mulcaster is a little more helpful in his treatment of *a*. He describes it as "sounding like a diphthong" before *l♯* or *lC* (pp. 134-135, 142), and says also that in *calm, balm, talk, walk, chalk, calf, salves*, and *alb* the *l* is pronounced like *w*, e.g. *cawm, baum*, etc. Further, he notes "Whene a, before the, n, soundeth like a diphthong, tho, u, be not to be writen"[9] (p. 143). His examples are *mane, cane, brane* [sic], *galance, france, change*. We have then some indication of diphthongal pronunciations of ME *ā* (and, in *brain*, that ME *ai* and *ā* were for him not distinct) but we have again been given no help with regard to the usual development of ME *a* and *ā*.

We are told that, like *a*, *o* is pronounced as a diphthong before *l♯* or *lC* (pp. 134-135, 149). Apart from this one item of information, Mulcaster is even less helpful with *o* and *u* than with the other vowels. He tells us that "V, & o, be so great cosens even in cosinage, as the one entermedleth with the others sound verie much" (p. 150). Dobson (1957*a*, pp. 123-124) notes that it is impossible to tell from Mulcaster's description whether he means to indicate *ū* or *u* in his discussion of words spelled with *o*. Similarly, in his discussion of *v*, we cannot from his descriptions differentiate /ew/, /iw/, /u/, and /ū/.

Mulcaster lists twelve diphthongs with examples: *ai decaie*; *ea meat*; *oo good*; *ou about*; *au audience*; *ei sleight*; *oi anoint*; *ow allow*; *aw withdraw*; *ew vertew*; *oy enioy*; *uy buy*; *iuyce*. It is clear that he means *u/w* to be alternate spellings for the same off-glide, *w* to be used in word-final position and *u* elsewhere, and similarly for the *i/y* variation (except for *iuyce*). Therefore it is obvious that all he really means here is that these are the only twelve digraphs for which he sees any need, and there is no implication that they are to be pronounced as diphthongs. It is, for instance, highly improbable that *ea* in *meat* was really diphthongal (unless, of course, all tense vowels were diphthongs consisting of a vowel plus off-glide). His discussion of the letters *a* and *o* shows that he often recognized a diphthongal pronunciation which is not indicated by the orthography and is not included in his list of "diphthongs."

It seems that for Mulcaster the spelling *ou* often represented a monophthong [ū], since he is unable to distinguish between ME *ǭ*, *ū*, and [ū] < ME *ǭ* before [χ]. In his discussion of the "diphthong" *oo*, he says that *food, stood, hoof, roof, look, took, book, hook, school, tool, groom, blook* (?), *hoop*, and *coop* could be spelled as easily with *ou* if it were not the custom to use *oo*. Dobson (1957*a*, p. 126) suggests that Mulcaster, who was of Northern origin, did not himself distinguish ME *ū* and *ǭ*, but had /ū/ for both.

Mulcaster seems to have known two pronunciations of ME *ai* (p. 132): "Ai, is the mans diphthong, & soundeth full: ei, the womans, and soundeth finish in the same both sense, and vse, *a woman is deintie, and feinteth soon, the man fainteth not bycause he is nothing daintie.*" However, it is possible that in his own speech ME *ai* was monophthongized and merged with ME *ā*, since in his discussion of *ai* he observes that, e.g., *mail, quail, sail, rail, gain, pain, remain, fair, pair, air, wait, strait,* and *aim* could just as easily be spelled *aCe* as *aiC* (though this may mean that the development of ME *ā* was diphthongal).

Generally speaking then, we find Mulcaster's evidence of little help in deciding anything about the stages in the Vowel Shift. His most helpful piece of evidence is on the alternate pronunciations of ME *ai*, but in view of the fact that he seems to have had no very clear idea of the nature of a diphthong as opposed to a digraph, not much weight can be attached to this.[10]

ROBERT ROBINSON: 1617

Robert Robinson was one of a number of phoneticians who were more concerned with providing an international phonetic alphabet than with reforming English spelling. Accordingly, in *The Art of Pronuntiation* Robinson transcribed a Latin poem, suggesting that he was not particularly concerned with the exact pronunciation of contemporary English. However, such details as an almost invariable transcription of orthographic *cl*, *gl*, with dental rather than velar stops, i.e., as *tl*, *dl*, show that he was careful to record what he perceived as the true phonetic facts. Robinson invented ten symbols with which to characterize vowel sounds; in addition, he used five digraphs to represent diphthongs, although of these only three fit his definition of diphthong. Since his symbols are difficult and expensive to reproduce, Dobson transliterated all Robinson's transcriptions, and this transliteration is used here.

In addition to his transcription of the Latin poem, Robinson made some attempt at an articulatory description of the vowels, and also provided a diagram. It is noteworthy that he observed that long and short vowels differed in quality as well as quantity, and that he described tongue positions for all vowels identified; however, he made no mention of lip-rounding. Unlike the other orthoepists, in his explanation of the theory Robinson gives no examples of English words having these sounds, nor compares them with sounds in other languages; in his original work we can identify the sounds only by examining the Latin transcription. In addition to this one work, however, there also exist two manuscripts containing transcriptions of English poems (which are included in Dobson (1957*b*)).

Robinson's diagram of the vowel sounds

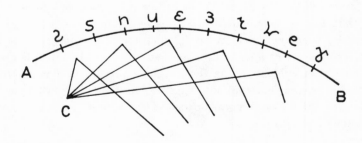

AB = the roof of the mouth. C = the root of the tongue.

The lines are the various positions of the tongue, and the angle shows where it bends, that is, where it nearly touches the roof of the mouth.

Robinson's first short vowel can be equated with ME *u*, and his first long vowel with ME *ǭ*, followed by ME *o*, *au*, *a*, *ā*, *e*, *ę̄*, *i*, *ę̄*. Note that for Robinson με *au* is a monophthongal long vowel, midway between με *o* and *a*, and therefore probably approximating to [ɔ̄], but this may only be the result of his having omitted με *ǭ* from his scheme; and, of course, he says that the short vowel is higher than its long equivalent.

Robinson has three diphthongs ending with front-glides, με *ī*, transcribed *eī*, με *ai*, transcribed *aī*, and με *oi/ui*, transcribed *oī*. The explanation for his transcribing the glide with *ī* may be found in his definition of a diphthong (p. 14): ". . . diphthongs . . . are caused by a continuance of the breath from any of the former [vowels], untill it finish it motion in the place of the last long vowel, and not otherwise." Robinson does not say that diphthongs ended with the last long vowel, but "in the place of the last long vowel," and presumably the only way he could indicate a place of articulation was to use the symbol for the vowel which was sounded there, in this case *ī*. Similarly, he uses the symbol for *ę̄* for the unstressed final syllable of, e.g., *dishes*, where it is highly improbable he used a long vowel, and the most likely explanation is that he was trying to indicate the place of articulation (cf. Dobson (1947)).

Robinson does not recognize combinations of vowel and back-glide (for which he uses the symbol for *w*) as a diphthong. He has four such combinations: *ow*, the symbol for με *ū*, *ew* for *ę̄u*, *iw* for με *ę̄u*, and *uw* for με *ǭ*. The first three are what we might expect, but *uw* for με *ǭ* is somewhat disconcerting. Dobson says (1947, pp. 40-41):

> It is inconceivable that it [ME *ǭ*] had reached the present diphthongal state so early; the use of the digraph must be an expedient to which Robinson was forced by his failure to include the vowel in the system of *The Art of Pronuntiation* and consequently to provide for it with a single letter.

But it is by no means obvious that Dobson's conclusion is correct. Robinson was a careful observer. If he had identified this as a long vowel, he could have inserted a new symbol before his symbol for *u*, and it is at least possible that his choosing not to do so is indicative of his actual pronunciation. In that case we have to believe that Robinson's diphthongization rule was asymmetrical, applying to ME *ī*, *ū*, and *ǭ*, or, alternatively, that in fact diphthongization was regular in Robinson, but that in his earlier work he was less skilled in perception and/or transcription and thus failed to record the diphthongal nature of what he then thought were long tense vowels. Later, when a new sound had to be accounted for, the gap was filled correctly, but Robinson did not switch to a completely new if more accurate system. This last view is completely speculative, since there is nothing in Robinson's transcriptions to support it; it is therefore directly opposed to the principle of accepting the orthoepist's evidence wherever possible.

Robinson apparently has optional monophthongization of ME *ai*, but, unlike Hart, Gil, or Butler, the monophthongal development is identified with μɛ *ā*. It seems probable, therefore, that ME *ā* had at least fronted to [ǣ], and may have raised to [ɛ̄]. ME *au* had monophthongized to [ɔ̄], except where traces of [χ] remain, in which case it is apparently still a diphthong, e.g., *pâwts* (Dobson (1957*b*, p. 57, line 3)). If we assume that this is [ɔ̄u], then it is the only example in Robinson of a diphthong with a tense first element. However, Jespersen (1909, § 3.63, pp. 99-100) describes the diphthong *ou* as having a lax nucleus before [χt] in ME, though it was *ōu* elsewhere. It is therefore possible that here also Robinson is using this particular symbol to denote the quality, i.e., [ɔ] rather than [o], and that in fact diphthong laxing is completely general in his dialect. ME *ou* has elsewhere monophthongized to [ō], thus merging with μɛ *ǭ*. Like, e.g., Gil and Mulcaster, Robinson shows *ow* for ME *o* before *ld*, as in *gowld, towld, bowld, kowld, fowld, owld*, and also before *l*# in *kontrowl, sowl* (but we also find *dōlful, sōldyer, kōlt*). In the same environment ME *a* has become [ɔ̄], as in *balk, call, fall, gall, talk, walk*.

Dobson (1947) claims that since Robinson differentiates ME *ār* and *ęr*, we would expect ME *ā* to be [ǣ] in his dialect, since had it raised to [ɛ̄], ME *ār* would have merged with ME *ęr*. But it is more likely that ME *ai* and *ā* would merge at [ɛ̄] than at [ǣ]. Dobson does not consider the possibility that ME *ā* had become [ɛ̄] in all positions except before *r*, just as ME *ę* raises to [ē] except before r—that is, that a following *r* prevents both ME *ā* and ME *ę* from raising.

Dobson (1957*a*) assumes without comment or discussion that in Robinson μɛ *ī* was /əy/ and μɛ *ū* /əw/, even though the symbols used for the first elements of these diphthongs, ɀ and n, do not seem to have this value elsewhere. In the introduction to his edition of Robinson (1957*b*), he states simply: ". . . Latin i, when made long, is identified with ME ī (transcribed eī = [əi]) . . ." But it seems clear that we have no evidence in Robinson for centralization of the first element of either μɛ *ī* or μɛ *ū*. It is true that Robinson has no symbol for a centralized vowel, nor does he even indicate in his description that he is aware of this possibility. It seems possible that his use of the symbol for ę in the unstressed plural morpheme is meant to indicate something of the quality of the sound, and since his diphthongs usually have lax first elements he might not wish to use ę here. On the other hand, we have already discussed the diphthong [ɔu], which is an exception to this, and which seems to suggest that he would have used the symbol for the tense vowel if useful here.

Although Robinson represents ME *ai* by both *ai* and *ā*, this almost certainly does not indicate that he was unable to differentiate these two sounds but rather, as suggested above, that he had an optional rule of monophthongization. If he had simply been unable to distinguish them, we would expect to find ME *ā* represented by *ai* at least occasionally, but this does not occur. Robinson's symbolization of ME *au* and *ou* also indicates that monophthongization of ME diphthongs was quite common in his dialect.

ROBINSON'S VOWEL SYSTEM

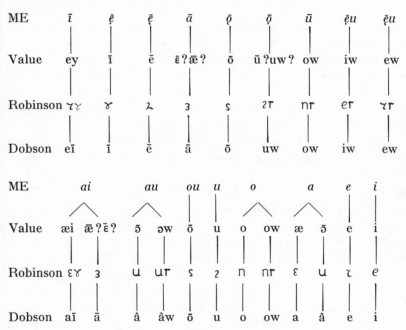

ALEXANDER GIL: 1619

Like Hart, Gil intended his *Logonomia Anglica* as a measure toward spelling reform; however, unlike Hart, Gil gives no articulatory description of the vowels, and so we can infer their pronunciation only from the distinctions he makes between them. Further, since he does invent distinct signs for vowels he wished to distinguish, we may assume that when the same symbol is used then the same sound is intended (but cf. discussion below on Gil's representation of unstressed vowels).

Let us first examine the description Gil gives of his pronunciation of με ī and ū. Both are diphthongal and we can make some inferences as to the nature of the first element. Gil differentiates με ū, in his dialect /ow/, from με ou, which was /ōw/; he symbolizes them as *ou* and *öu* respectively. Gil states that *o* and *ö* differ only in length and that this difference in length of the first element is all that distinguishes με ū from με ou; we must then accept that in Gil's dialect the first element of με ū was neither unrounded nor centralized.

Gil apparently has two sounds approximating to /ey/. To με ī he assigns the symbol *j*, stating that it is "almost the diphthong *ei*, but . . . a little thinner than if we were to spread it out into *e* . . ." Dobson (1957a, p. 150) says: ". . . we may take this to mean a diphthong of which the first element has the tongue raised to much the same height as *e*, but somewhat retracted to a middle position." Dobson wishes, in fact, to believe that Gil's *j* meant /əy/. But what evidence do we have that this is what Gil meant, i.e., that by "thinner" he meant "centralized"?

It is true that Gil used the symbol *e* for undifferentiated unstressed vowels. When discussing the value orthography has in showing the derivation of words, he notes (Dixon, pp. 109-110) that "in shortened syllables where either one of two sounds is heard without distinction, we shall decide that the origin of the word should be followed." His examples here are *scholar* and *divine*, which he prefers to spell *skolar* and *divjn*, though recognizing that *skoler* and *devjn* represent the phonetic quality more exactly. Similarly, he notes that an uneducated man, not knowing the etymology of the words, would write *oner* and *kunȝerer* rather than *onor* and *kunȝurer*. This, then, seems to establish the use of *e* for /ə/; *e* is also Gil's usual spelling for the vowel of the unstressed plural morpheme, as in *housez*. Dobson (1957a, pp. 148-149) is of the opinion that Gil's use of *a* for *o*, in the passage describing the dialect of the Mopseys,[11] also represents /ə/. Gil's claim is that *I pray you, give your scholars leave to play*, which should be pronounced *J prai you giv yur skolars*[12] *lev to plai*, is in this dialect pronounced *J pre ya gi yar skalerz liv ta plë*. However, Dobson seems to think that *skalerz* represents a genuine unrounding of /o/ to /a/, and there seems no reason to assume that within this same sentence Gil is indicating two completely different pronunciations with the one symbol *a*, particularly since, as noted above, he earlier uses *e* for unstressed vowels and, in fact, does so here in the second syllable of *skalerz*. If *a* in this example represented the unstressed vowel, then Gil could equally well have written *skalarz*. I therefore assume that Gil was here criticizing the kind of pronunciation we find satirized in Vanbrugh's *The Relapse* (1697), in which /o/ was generally unrounded to /a/, and was there meant to indicate an ultrafashionable pronunciation affected by fops.[13]

It seems then that *e* was the normal spelling for /ə/ in unstressed syllables. But *j* does not occur in unstressed syllables, and in other environments Gil uses *e* for a mid front vowel. We may then assume that he meant both *ei* and *j* to represent diphthongs with a mid front vowel as the first element. What meaning must we then attribute to "thinner"? "Thinness" is a term which has many meanings in Gil. With consonants it appears to mean voiceless, since he claims (Dixon, p. 128) that *v* is "thicker" than *f*. In his criticism of the Mopsey dialect (Dixon, p. 140), in which he speaks of that "greatly attenuated thinness of pronunciation which so shortens all sounds," he seems to be referring to monophthongization (*mëdz* vs. *maidz*), fronting and unrounding (*biccherz* vs. *bucherz*, *lën* vs. *laun*), and raising (*këmbrik* vs. *kämbrik*, *mït* vs. *mët*, *ʒintlimin* vs. *ʒentlwimen*, *këpn* or *kïpn* vs. *käpn*, and again *lën* vs. *laun*). In general, there seems to be a tendency toward raising and unrounding (and, of course, except in the *a/o* alternation discussed above, unrounding and fronting usually go together). Further, his description of [æ] *a*, and [æ̈] *ä* as "slender A" and of [ɔ] *â* as "thick A" suggests that to Gil unrounded vowels were "thinner." But there is nothing here to indicate that by "thin" he meant centralized. Cooper uses the term "slender," and Sundby (p. xxii) believes that this refers to tongue height, a "more slender" sound thus corresponding with "higher." An assumption that the first elements of the diphthongs differed only in height is then consistent with Gil's description.

Dobson suggests that in differentiating *ëi aye*; *ei eye*; and *J I*, Gil is not indicating differences in pronunciation at all but is, instead, allowing for the differentiation of homonyms as he says the orthography should do (Dixon, p. 110), and this is also Jespersen's opinion (1907*a*). However, Gil also distinguishes the ending of *barlei* (*barley*) from that of *puritj* (*purity*). Other examples of the *ei* spelling are: *ʒurnei* (*journey*); *valeiz* (*valleys*); *reineth~rainz* (*rains*); *ðeir~ðëirz* (*theirs*); *ðei~ðëi~ðeï~ðäi~ðai* (*they*); *ëiðer~eiðer* (*either*). Also, of course, we have his express

statement that *j* has a different sound from that which he would indicate by *ei*. We must believe then that for him *ei* and *j* represented
distinct sounds, and that both must be allowed for in the phonetic representation of his dialect. His representation of *rains, they, their*,
indicates that to him *ei* was slightly higher than *ai*, but not high enough
to be identified with the sound for which he used *j*. Dobson has suggested that Gil's dialect contained the front vowels [æ], [ɛ], and [ī],
but not [ē], and that this is shown by his criticism of the Mopseys'
dialectal pronunciation of *cambric*. Dobson thinks it unlikely that
the vowel would vary all the way from [æ] to [ī], and therefore assumes
that Gil's pronunciation was [kæmbrik] and that the Mopsey pronunciation varied between [kɛmbrik] and [kēmbrik]. However, since Gil's
dialect had no [ē], he associated the vowel of [kēmbrik] with the nearest
distinct vowel in his dialect, namely [ī]. If we accept Dobson's interpretation, this gives us a basis on which to interpret Gil's distinction
between *ei* and *j*. If *e* was, in Gil's dialect, normally [ɛ] and *ei* = [ɛi],
while *j* was [ei] but [e] did not otherwise occur in his dialect, then Gil
would want to distinguish *ei* = [ɛi] from *j* = [ei], but would not have
a vowel with which he could identify the first element of *j*. He therefore describes it simply as being not so wide as the first element of *ei*.
Against this interpretation, it should be observed that Labov's work
seems to show that so large a variation as /kæpn~kɛpn~kēpn~kīpn/
is possible. Further, accepting Dobson's interpretation of *kïpn* as
[kēpn] raises the question why, if *ï* = [ē], Gil did not use *ii* for [ei].
It seems faintly possible that the use of the symbol *j* was prompted
by his association of the sound with the high front vowel, since *ij*
was frequently used in earlier periods for /ī/.

A further theoretical difficulty is that if Gil does indeed differentiate
[ei] and [ɛi], then we must allow four different heights for the front
vowels in his dialect, [æ], [ɛ], [e], and [i], while for the back we need
only three, [ɔ], [o], and [u].

We can, of course, obviate this difficulty by deciding that *j* does
indeed represent a centralized vowel. As noted above, there seems
to be no justification for this in Gil's description, but it would in some
ways simplify our description. We can then say either that the high
and mid vowels switched, for both front and back vowels, and that
then the mid front vowel centralized, whereas /ow/ < ME *ū* remained
unchanged; or we can adopt Dobson's and Stockwell's theory and
assume that ME *ī* centralized before lowering, in which case in Gil's
dialect the high front vowel apparently behaved quite differently from
ME *ū*, and there is no possibility of generalizing the rule to cover both.

Of these possibilities I prefer to believe that *j* does not represent a centralized vowel, since this seems contrary to Gil's descriptions, and that by *ei* and *j* Gil was probably differentiating [ɛi] and [ei]. This interpretation has the advantage of not reading any a priori assumptions into Gil's analysis, and of not requiring different descriptions for the front and back vowels. But we are left with the problems of interpreting his description of the Mopsey dialect, and with allowing for four vowel heights. A solution to this last problem lies in the obvious phonetic fact that in ModE the phonetic realization of what Chomsky and Halle (1968) symbolize by *e* in the phonological rules is usually [e] when followed by a front-glide and [ɛ] elsewhere. It seems that the distinction is marginal in Gil's dialect, and, with the exception of a few idiosyncratic items, can be predicted, in that Gil has [ɛ], [ē], and [ei], and a few items which must in some way be marked as remaining [ɛ] and not becoming [e] in the systematic phonetic matrix even when followed by a front-glide. That is, when the binary features are replaced by features with scalar values (cf. Chapter II), then the first element of the diphthongs in items such as *barley, journey,* and the raised variants of *they, rains,* will have to be marked with some diacritic to ensure that they receive the same numerical index as a monophthongal /e/.[14]

However we interpret Gil's *j*, there is a problem when we turn to his criticism of Hart (Dixon, p. 108) for choosing to represent the Mopsey dialect. There he objects to the use of *ei* for *j*. Yet, by our interpretation, Gil would understand *ei* to mean [ɛi], which would have a **lower** first element than *j* = [ei], whereas normally the pronunciation he designates as typical of the Mopseys seems to have higher vowels. And he specifically states that his objection to Hart is based not on the grounds of a theory of orthography, but that "the dispute is a matter of sound only" (Dixon, p. 109), i.e., that Hart's symbols accurately indicated a pronunciation of which Gil disapproved. If Gil assumed that Hart's *ei* = [ɛi], whereas he himself had [ei] in these words, then the disapproval is understandable, but not the identification with Mopsey pronunciation.

Note that the inconsistency with regard to the interpretation of Gil's *ei* and his criticism of Hart is inherent in Gil's description and is not the product of this analysis. Gil gives us three facts: (*a*) Hart wrongly chooses to represent the Mopsey pronunciation *ei* where he should have chosen the standard, represented in Gil by *j*; (*b*) the Mopsey pronunciation is generally "thinner" than the standard; and (*c*)

the first element of *j* is "thinner" than that of *ei*. There is no way of
reconciling Gil's description of *j* as "thinner" than *ei*, and of *ei* as "thinner" than *j*.

It is interesting to note that in the North the reflexes of ME *ī*, *ū*,
seem to have already reached the stage of ModE, since Gil gives *faier*
as the Northern variant of *fjer* (*fire*), and *gaun* or *geaun* for standard
goun (*gown*). It seems that the Vowel Shift may have been more advanced in the North (though Gil regards this as a more archaic, "purer"
version of the English language).

As well as "thick I" (με *ī*), Gil discusses "slender I," which is, he
claims, short in *sin*, *win*, and *kin*, and long in *seen*, *ween*, and *keen*.
We can therefore assume that for Gil ME *i* had remained /i/, and that
ME *ę̄* had raised to /ī/. For *e* he gives only two variants, short as in
best, *net*, and long as in *neat* (adj.) and *beast*. ME *e* is then unchanged,
and με *ę̄* is the long equivalent; as discussed above, I agree with Dobson that it seems likely this was [ɛ̄] in Gil's dialect.

Gil differentiates two variants of "slender A," short as in *Hal* and
long as in *hale*. He mentions no distinction between them other than
that of length (though this does not necessarily mean that there was
none). We may assume that these had the values [æ] and [ǣ] respectively. Since Gil uses the symbol *a* for the first element in με *ai*,
we may assume that this also was [æ] and that laxing was here optional, since Gil has many alternates, apparently in free variation. Further, in a rather obscure passage he refers to the variants *sai*∼*säi* and
mai∼*mäi* as being "by nature common" (Dixon, p. 115). His meaning
here is not at all clear; however, it is clear that there is for him no
significant difference between these. Further support for the belief
that Gil would have chosen a different symbol for a different sound
is afforded by his symbolization of some developments of ME *a* as *â*.
This appears before *l♯* or *lC*, and represents [ɔ]. Gil uses this symbol
to represent the first element of ME *au* when not monophthongized,
and, indeed, Gil specifically contrasts the diphthongs and monophthongs
(Dixon, p. 136). Since, when discussing the three pronunciations of
orthographic *a*, he notes that "the *a* in the first two words [*Hal*, *hale*]
is briefer; in the third [*hall*] it is almost a diphthong," we may assume
that *â* is [ɔ] and *âu* is [ɔu].

Like the development of ME *ai*, ME *ę̄u* also seems to have been
subject to optional laxing, since we find both *ęu* and *eu*. But Gil does
not lax *öu* < ME *ou*, which contrasts with *ou* < ME *ū*.

Gil invents a symbol *v* and differentiates three variants, slender,
thick short, and thick long. His examples are: slender *yvth* (*youth*),

vs (*use*); thick and short *spun, us*; and thick and long *ooze, spoon*. From this it seems possible that slender and thick here differentiate the quality of two monophthongal pronunciations, since elsewhere Gil is careful to indicate diphthongal pronunciations, even when he uses a unitary symbol such as *j* for με *ī*. Further, he does not suggest that *v* is in any way similar to *eu* as in *beuty*. Also, in his criticisms of the Mopsey dialect "slender" often seems to indicate a monophthongal pronunciation, though in these cases it is always opposed to a diphthong. Dobson argues quite convincingly that *v* cannot be /yu/ or /yuw/, since Gil spells *youth* as *yvth*, which would then be *yyuth* if *v* were /yu/. Further, Gil criticizes Hart for representing *vz* as *iuz*, but it should be remembered that Gil also objected to Hart's *uī* (*we*) and to *uið* (*with*), in which case it may just be that his objection was to the use of the vowel sign for what he considered a consonant. If this is so, then that may be the cause of his objecting to Hart's *iuz*. Further, it should be noted that although *yvth* occurs five times we also find *yuth* once—though of course this may be an error; Gil is not always consistent in his usage. Dobson concludes that for Gil *v* really did represent [y], which is consistent with the comparison with slender and thick *v*. But bearing in mind his apparent identification of thinness and monophthongization, and also the absence of contemporary evidence for the retention of [y], it may be that *v* really signified /iw/. It seems impossible to identify the phonetic quality with any certainty.

Gil's long and short "thick" *v* seem to be /u/ and /ū/, that is, με *u* and *ǫ*, and in fact in the text he spells these with *u*, not *v*. Since these are said to differ in length only, there is no evidence for the lowering and unrounding of /u/ to /ə/.

Gil has only two sounds for *o*, short and long, illustrated by *pol* (*head*) and *kol* (*embrace*) for the short vowel, and *pöl* (*pole*) and *köl* (*coal*) for the long. I therefore assume that ME *o* remains /o/ and that ME *ǫ* has raised to /ō/.

Throughout his discussion, Gil distinguishes between long tense vowels and diphthongs consisting of a vowel plus off-glide. He claims a true diphthong in *aid, they, pray, play, maids, say, may*, and *way*. Gil obviously does not have the same theory of diphthongs as Hart, since he states (Dixon, p. 137) that in diphthongs:

. . . the preceding vowel time and again seems to sound more noticeably and clearly; for instance, in *ai* and *ei* it so fills the ears that it would be more proper for the *i* to be an addition than to be fastened to the side of the *a* and *e*.

He recognizes that there is a monophthongal pronunciation in use by some speakers of the language, citing the Mopseys' *plë* for *play* and *prë*[15] for *pray*, and criticizing Hart for representing this dialect with *pre, ue, ðe,* and *me*. It is obvious therefore that when he writes the symbol for a long tense vowel this is a claim as to the phonetic nature of the sound, not lack of ability to recognize a diphthong, and although he recognizes that some dialects do not differentiate the reflexes of ME *ẹ̄* and ME *ai*, he identifies με *ẹ̄* as a long tense vowel and με *ai* as a diphthong.

Similarly, he distinguishes what he calls "thick A" as in *tall* from the diphthong in *straw, law*. This is rather strange, since it seems probable that the same rule rounded the /a/ in /aw/ from ME *au* and in /aw/ from /a/ before *l♯* and *lC*. It seems possible that Gil deleted the off-glide except in word-final position, except that he claims a diphthong in *auger*. Since it seems unlikely that the two sources for /aw/ were really differentiated (cf. discussion in Chapter VI), it may be that *auger* is an error. Gil also detects an off-glide before *r* in *fjer* (*fire*), *hjer* (*hire*), *dier* (*deer*), *earl* (*earl*), though recognizing alternate pronunciations *ërl* and *erl* (Dixon, p. 136), and in his list of corrections (Dixon, p. 117) comments that an off-glide should always follow *o* before *ld*, as in *föuld, böuld*. Also, although he thought that the sound *â* in *hall* was "almost a diphthong," he makes no such claim about the similarity of *ä* and *ai*, which indicates that to him these sounds did not seem easily confusable. Since none of the other diphthongs had been monophthongized, it is possible that /aw/ was really still a diphthong, and that Gil could not hear the off-glide except in word-final position; but since in general he seems able to hear them, this position is difficult to justify.

GIL'S VOWEL SYSTEM

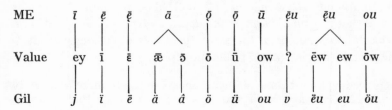

ME	*ī*	*ẹ̄*	*ę̄*	*ā*	*ǭ*	*ọ̄*	*ū*	*ẹu*	*ę̄u*	*ou*
Value	ey	ī	ē̄	ǣ	ɔ̄	ō	ū	ow	?	ēw	ew	ōw
Gil	*j*	*ï*	*ë*	*ä*	*á*	*ö*	*ü*	*ou*	*v*	*ëu*	*eu*	*öu*

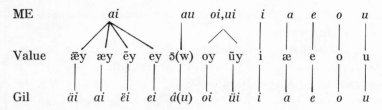

CHARLES BUTLER: 1633

Charles Butler's *English Grammar* was first published in 1633. However, he was at that time about seventy (having been born ca. 1560) and therefore we may assume that he is referring to the pronunciation of an earlier period—in fact, probably of the same period as Gil's, since the two are contemporaries. He was a schoolmaster, and his interest is in simplifying English spelling so that it will be easier for foreigners and children to learn to read and write English. He is, for instance, very anxious that [θ], [č], etc., should be spelled with one letter rather than with two. Butler is generally more concerned with giving instructions about the interpretation of the normal spellings than with providing a phonetic transcript or with giving any articulatory descriptions.

He uses only two innovations to represent distinct vowel sounds, *æ* and *∞*, as in *feed, meet, breed, goose, choose, soon.* He states that *æ* and *∞* have the same sound both long and short; and that short *æ* is the same as short *i*; he also identifies *æ* with the sound in French *qui*, *y*, and the last syllable of *honi*. We may then identify *æ* with ME *i* = /i/, and *ǣ* with ME *ę̄* = /ī/. Short *∞* is the same as short *u*, i.e., ME *u*, so that it seems that *ō̄* is /ū/, i.e., ME *ǭ*. Butler says that *good* and *blood* have the same sound, *∞* or *u* short, and mentions no other pronunciation for *u* short, so that it seems that although /ū/ < ME *ǭ* has shortened to /u/, it has not yet lowered and unrounded.

E and *o* are said to have the same sound long and short; I assume that by these he means με *e* and *ę̄*, *o* and *ǭ*. There is no evidence whether the long vowels have raised to [ē] and [ō] or not.

Butler claims that *i* differs greatly from *ī*, and gives minimal pairs such as *rid/ride, din/dine.* But he gives no indication of how *ī* is to be pronounced, so that we cannot tell from Butler that ME *ī* had diphthongized, although we know from the evidence of the other orthoepists and grammarians that it had. Since he does not indicate a diphthongal pronunciation, we have no way of drawing any conclusions about the quality of the first element.

Butler also states that *u* and *ū* differ greatly, but he goes on to identify the sound of "u long" with "*æ* and *i* short with *w*" (p. 9).[16] It is obvious from his examples that he is here talking about ME *ẹu*, as in *due, true, grew, knew*, which is for him /iw/; he stresses the importance of distinguishing this from ME *ęu*, which for him is /ew/. He claims that this is "manifestly different," and instances *dew, few, chew, strew, pewter*.

Butler says that orthographic *a* has two sounds, one short and one long, which are not the same, and gives *man/mane* as an example. However, he does not tell us what the difference is; we may hypothesize that *a* was [æ] and that *ā* was [ɛ̄], but this is pure surmise. He confirms Hart's and Mulcaster's claim that a back-glide is added following *a* before *l⧧* or *lC*, as in *palsy, also, alms, salve, calve*, and that the *l* is dropped before labials and velars and also before *s* and *t* (p. 18).

Butler notes (p. 12) that *o* is always long before *w* (by which he means ME *ou*), some of his examples being *bowl, known, though*. He also states (p. 25) that the "diphthong *ou* hath a distinct sound from *o* with the consonant *w*," as in "to bou a bow," *croun* vs. *known*. He does not state what the difference is, but since he has stressed that *o* is long before *w* (i.e., in µɛ *ou*), and says also (p. 27) that the "right sound of *ai, au, ei, oi, ou*, is the mixt sound of the 2 vowels, whereof they are made," instancing *cou* (*cow*), then we may assume that the difference is one of length, and that for Butler µɛ *ū* is /ow/, whereas µɛ *ou* is /ōw/.

We cannot tell either the length or the quality of the first element of ME *ai*, but we know that for Butler it was still a diphthong from the description given of how to pronounce this and other digraphs. He does not lack the ability to distinguish between a monophthongal and a diphthongal pronunciation, since he goes on to criticize the fact that "*ai*, in imitation of the French, is sometime corruptly sounded like *e*: as in *may, nay, pray, say, slay, fray, flay*." Like Gil, then, Butler knew of a monophthongal pronunciation, but disapproved of it. We assume that he was right in claiming that ME *au* was still a diphthong, especially since he equates it with a pronunciation of *a* followed by a glide before *lC*, but we have no way of knowing what the exact sound was; it is unlikely that it would have fronted at all before the back-glide (or that a back-glide would have developed in those cases which were not diphthongal in ME).

BUTLER'S VOWEL SYSTEM

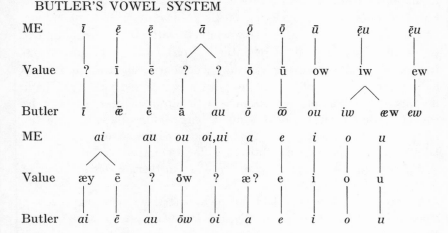

SIMON DAINES: 1640

The aim of Daines's *Orthoepia Anglicanae* is to teach "The Art of right speaking and pronouncing English." However, the author prevents himself from describing the pronunciation very clearly, in that, having admitted that many earlier writers had found it advisable to differentiate between the written letters of the alphabet and the sounds of the language, he then decides that this distinction is unnecessary, and proceeds to treat of the letters. One consequence of this is that having first given a reasonable definition of a diphthong, he continues with (p. 8): "Or briefly thus, A Diphthong is the contraction of two Vowels, which better suits our English Tongue, by reason we have some Dipthongs where one Vowell loseth its faculty in the pronunciation of the other." To Daines, then, any digraph is a diphthong. Fortunately, however, this does not lead him to conclude that a sound spelled with a single orthographic symbol cannot be diphthongal.

Generally Daines's approach is so very unphonetic, and his description often so vague, that he is of limited or even exiguous value; nevertheless, he is useful in confirming some other writers.

He tells us that με *ę̄* is sounded "almost after the manner of the Latin I," presumably /ī/, and that με *ę̄*, which "we write *ea*, as in *Bread, Sea*," is "what they call E," presumably /e/ and /ē/ (or Daines may have pronounced *bread* with a long vowel, though this is unlikely, in which case he is referring only to /ē/).

με *ī* "somewhat imitates the sound of the Latin Ei diphthong (though not altogether so full)." Since we do not know how Daines pronounced

Latin, all we can really tell from such a description is that he identified Latin *ei* with his pronunciation of με *ī*. However, to assume that he pronounced it /ey/ in no way conflicts with his evidence, and it is possible to understand his parenthetical reservation if his pronunciation of the Latin diphthong were /εy/; of course, his description may indicate that the diphthong began with a centralized vowel; we have no way of ascertaining his meaning with any exactness, but can be sure only that he heard it as a diphthong. Daines notes that in the North, they "abuse it [= με *ī*] with too broad a sound . . . like the Dipthong *Ai*, making no difference in pronunciation between *fire* and *faire*" (p. 6). This may indicate a Northern pronunciation of /εy/ for ME *ī*.

Apparently Daines still does not have a stressed centralized vowel, since *blood, wood, stood, wool, Edmond, Paighton*, are all said to have the pronunciation *u* short, which is evidently /u/. On the other hand, Daines notes that "*Er* is the same in pronunciation with *ir*, as it appears" and further that: ". . . *u* where *r* is doubled hath a flat or dull sound and short, where the pronunciation of the Syllable sticks chiefly in *r*, as in demurr'd." This may indicate /ə/, and, if so, is the earliest description in the English writers[17] of the development of a centralized vowel; it seems from this to have developed first before *r*.

ME *ai* is, he claims, still diphthongal (which is supported by his discussion of the Northern pronunciation of *fire* and *fair*) as in *faire*, though he notes that in *hair* and *say* it is monophthongized, and in *saist* and *said* shortened to *e*.

Dobson believes that Daines heard a diphthongal pronunciation of ME *au* in word-final position, but that it was monophthongized medially, except in *balm*, which appears to be an exception. I believe, however, that more probably Daines was misled by the spelling into thinking he heard a distinction where there was none. Since this directly contradicts his own testimony, I am reluctant to do this. However, the alternative is to believe that not only ME *au* and *ou* but also *ęu* and *ẹu* were diphthongal finally and monophthongal medially, since his note is as follows (p. 15):

These three [*aw, ew, ow*] differ in this from the Diphthongs *au, eu, ou*, partly in respect of their use, partly of their pronunciation. Their pronunciation, in that *aw* hath a more full and broad sound then *au*, which follows the Latin, from whence we tooke it.

Although he mentions only ME *au* in the second sentence, the first makes it improbable that *au* was the only diphthong he believed dif-

fered in pronunciation in this way. But we cannot believe that ME
ẹu, ẹu, had been monophthongized medially. (Daines's *ou* includes
both ME *ū* and *ou*, as his *eu* includes both *ẹu* and *ẹu*. He differentiates
the pronunciation of the latter, however, since he says that in *dew*,
few, *sewer*, and *ewe*, *ew* "retains the pronunciation of the Latin Dipthong
Eu. In all other words it has only the force of *U* single, as new, quasi
nu, &c.") Whatever our interpretation of Daines's note on *aw*, *ew*,
and *ow*, it seems that we must disbelieve part of his description.[18]
It should be noted that he does not identify the pronunciation of me-
dial *au* with his "full and broad" *a* developed after *w*, yet we expect
ME *au* to monophthongize to /ɔ/, before *a* after *w* becomes [ɔ] (cf.
Chapter VI).

Daines's description of ME *a*, *ā*, after *w* and before *r* is misleading.
It is clear that after *w* generally *a* has rounded to /ɔ/, for which he
uses the term "full and broad." However, *a* before *r* he describes
merely as "full" in *snarl*. But this is also the description he gives to
the vowel of *warn*, as opposed to *barn*, which has a "more acute" sound.
Dobson (1957a, pp. 332-333) believes that Daines is recording the
development of [ɑ]. This may be so, but his description is far from
clear. Since it does not bear on the issues with which we are more
concerned, we need not trouble about it further, except insofar as it
bears on the pronunciation of ME *au* medially.

Daines notes the distinction between με *ū* and *ou*, but gives us no
help in identifying the pronunciation of either. He does not identify
ME *ou* with με *ō*, so we may perhaps assume that they were still distinct, and, further, that ME *ou* had not monophthongized (which is
confirmed by his discussion of *ow* vs. *ou*; cf. above). Yet he claims
it has a "more quick and aspirate sound" than με *ū*, which seems a
strange description if it were distinct as /ōw/ vs. /ow/, as Gil and Butler
seem to indicate. It is always possible that ME *ou* had monophthongized, and that he was misled by the spelling into thinking it diphthongal,
though it is clear that he recognized some digraphs represented simple
sounds; for instance, he identifies the *ou* of *would*, *could*, *should*, with
"*oo* double" as in *soon*, *moon* (p. 12).

Generally, then, Daines says nothing which would lead us to
suppose our interpretation of other writers was incorrect, though
equally he is so vague that one could not base any interpretation
on his evidence alone. I include some indication of his vowel system,
though it is necessarily so incomplete and tentative as to be of little
value.

DAINES'S VOWEL SYSTEM

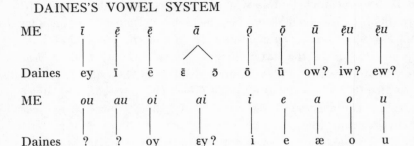

RICHARD HODGES: 1643, 1644

Hodges' works may be regarded as consisting of only two essentially distinct works: *A Special Help to Orthographie: or, the True Writing of English*, published in 1643 and later at several dates in slightly revised versions and under varying titles, and *The English Primrose*, published in 1644. The discussion here is based on *Most Plain Direction for True-Writing* (a version of *A Special Help . . .*) published in 1653, and on the British Museum copy of *The English Primrose*, which has bound up with it the page entitled "The New Horn book" and also an additional pamphlet, "Most plain and familiar examples (taken out of The English Primrose) . . ."

Hodges was a schoolmaster, and his concern, as his titles (and the additional matter on the title page of *The English Primrose*) show, was to make it easier for foreigners and schoolchildren to learn to write English. For this purpose he developed diacritics to be added to the normal letters to indicate when they were silent, voiced, long, etc., but this was intended only as a help to the teaching of reading and writing. He was not interested in developing a phonetic alphabet, and we have no analysis or description of the different sounds. We can therefore tell how many sounds he distinguished, and, from the copious examples and word lists, which words contained which sounds, but we are given little indication of the quality of the sounds.

Hodges (1644) says that English has nine vowels, five of which can be either long or short, one is always short, and three always long. His examples are (p. 7):

1.	a	pal	päle
2.	e	pel	peal
3.	æ	pil	peël
4.	awe	pol	pâul
5.	U-sher	pul	

6.	oo	pul	pool
		(wool)	
7.	eie		pîle
8.	owe		pôle
9.	yoo		pûle

From this we can tell that /u/ had probably unrounded to /ə/, but that many words, such as *pull*, could have either /u/ or /ə/. με *o* is given as the short equivalent of με *au*; we may assume then that the latter had monophthongized to /ɔ/, and that ME *o* had lowered to /ɔ/, and that there is no short equivalent of με *ọ̄*.

Hodges does not discuss the exact quality of the sounds, and he does not indicate any qualitative difference between με *a* and *ā*. Similarly, we do not know whether με *ẹ̄* is [ē] or [ɛ]. We note that he lists με *ī* and με *ẹ̄u* with the simple vowels, but his description is "The three vowels (as they are called) whose sounds are always long . . ." This may indicate that he realized their diphthongal quality, but this cannot be the case with his *owe*, με *ọ̄*, which is also listed here as having no short equivalent. In any case, though we may assume that in Hodges's speech με *ī* and με *ẹ̄u* were diphthongal, we cannot tell what the quality of the sounds was.

Hodges also lists five diphthongs (1644, p. 8):

1.	ai	day
2.	eu	dew
3.	oi	boy
4.	ọî	bọî-ling
5.	ou	bow-els

We see then that Hodges still differentiated ME *ẹ̄u* and *ẹ̄u*, that ME *ai* was still diphthongal and distinct from both με *ẹ̄* and με *ā*, and that he distinguished two pronunciations of the spelling *oi*. Dobson (1957a, pp. 173-175) notes that his distinction does not agree with the etymological distinction between ME *oi* and *ui*; however, it is important to see that he distinguished two word-classes here even though the spelling was the same, showing that he was not overly influenced by the spelling. Further, although he undoubtedly included two diphthongs in his list of simple vowels, he does not make the mistake of considering all digraphs to be diphthongs. He considered, e.g., the spelling *aw* to represent a monophthong, and so we may assume that the five diphthongs he claimed were in his speech, even though monophthongization of ME *ai* had already begun. There is some evidence that Hodges knew of monophthongal pronunciations of ME *ai*. In the pamphlet listing "Most plain and familiar examples . . ." he specifically contrasts *hail, pail, a-vail*, to which he assigns a diphthongal pronunciation, with *häir, päir*, and *a väil*, all of which have *ā*. Dobson suggests (1957*a*, p. 176) that *a vail = a vale*, and that the monophthongal pronunciation of *hair* and *pair* comes from ME variants with monophthongs. Since Hodges here is making a specific contrast with the diphthong, he clearly is drawing attention to a distinction which actually existed in his speech; but ME *ā* and *ai* are never listed as being exactly alike, although there are pairs giving them as words nearly alike, as *fare/fair, panes/pains, place/ plaice, rase/raise, vane/vein*. Curiously enough, however, though με *ę̄* and με *ai* are also often paired as being nearly alike, as in *maids/meads, plays/pleas, played/plead, say/sea*, they are once paired as being exactly alike, in *flea/flay*. Hodges seems to have had one idiosyncratic example of ME *ai* monophthongizing and raising to merge with με *ę̄*. These scattered examples would seem to suggest that although Hodges normally used a diphthongal pronunciation of ME *ai* (or perhaps merely that, as a schoolmaster, he regarded this as the better pronunciation), his speech had in fact been affected by the trend toward monophthongization.

One drawback to Hodges's lists of words nearly alike is that there is no indication of where the difference lies; therefore, even when με *ai, ā*, and *ę̄* are all distinguished one from the other, we have no idea what distinction he heard, nor, when they are merged, can we tell what sound they merged as. But these pairings seem to indicate that με *ę̄* was [ɛ̄], not [ē], in Hodges's speech.

Another interesting point is that although Hodges has added rules lowering and unrounding /u/ to /ə/, με *ū* is /ow/, not /əw/. We have, of course, no evidence as to his pronunciation of ME *ī*, but it would seem that the centralization of the first element of the diphthongs, developed from ME *ī, ū*, was subsequent to the lowering and centralization of ME *u*. (This would be confirmed by Holder, if he did have /ə/ < ME *u* (which is unlikely; cf. section on Holder), since he says that με *ī* is like *ai* or *ei*.)

Hodges's aligning *wool* with *pull* as an example of the short *ω* sound shows that shortening of /ū/ < ME *ǭ* had taken place. This is confirmed in *Most Plain Directions . . .* where he discusses (p. 46) ". . . the vowel *ω*, when it is short, as in *cook, hook, book*, and the like . . ."

Hodges's (1653) lists of words pronounced alike provide ample evidence of the monophthongization of ME *ou*, e.g. *roe/rose/row, thrown/throne, moan/mown*. We find confirmatory evidence for the monophthongization of ME *au* in his discussion of the pronunciation of *a*. He says that *all, gall, call, fall, hall, ball, wall, shall,* are pronounced as if they were written *aul*, etc. (pp. 43-44), and also that:

. . . you ought also to observe that the vowel *a* coming before *lt* or *ld*, in the end of a word, it must bee pronounc'd like *au*, as in *halt, salt,* . . . Whensoever the vowel *a* cometh before *lm, lf, lv,* or *lk*, it is to bee pronounct like *au*, and the *l* to be silent, as in these words, *qualm, qualms, half, halvs, balk, balks*; as if they were written thus, *quaum, quaumz, hauf, hauvz, bauk, bauks*: and so in all words of this kind.

As in other writers, we note in Hodges several examples of ME *ę̄* > /ī/ before *r*. He has the following identical pairs: *appear/a Peer, deer/dear, here/hear, shear/Buckinghamshire*. However, all except the last may depend on ME variants with *ę̄*. Since Hodges also has *bare/bear, pare/pair/pear*, we see the same differential development of ME *ę̄* before *r* that is illustrated in other grammarians. Lax /e/, /u/, and /i/ had all merged as /ə/ before *r* in Hodges, examples being *cur, her, sir* (1653, p. 73).

HODGES' VOWEL SYSTEM

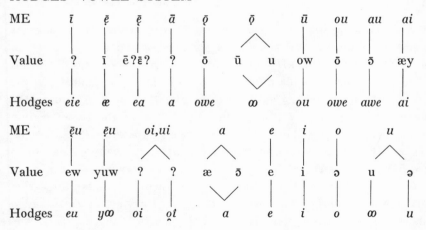

ME	ī	ę̄	ę̄	ā	ǭ	ǫ	ū	ou	au	ai
Value	?	ī	ē?ɛ̄?	?	ō	ū	u	ow	ō	ɔ̄	æy
Hodges	eie	æ	ea	a	owe	∞	ou	owe	awe	ai

ME	ę̄u	ę̄u	oi,ui	a	e	i	o	u
Value	ew	yuw	?	?	æ	ɔ̄	e	i	ɔ	u	ə
Hodges	eu	y∞	oi	o̧i̧	a	e	i	o	∞	u

JOHN WALLIS: 1653

Wallis's *Grammatica Linguae Anglicanae* was first published in 1653; his work was, however, reprinted many times into the next century. Since the only copy to which I had access was that of 1765 (which is a reprint of the final revised fifth edition of 1699 (Dobson (1957*a*, pp. 220-221)), all references are to that edition.[19]

Wallis describes the vowels of English twice, in *De Loquela*, a prefatory essay in which he also discusses the nature of speech and of the speech organs, and in the grammar proper. In *De Loquela* he explains his general classification (p. 5):

Ego illas omnes in tres omnino classes distinguandas esse judico; Gutturales, Palatinas, et Labiales; prout in Gutture, Palato, aut Labiis formantur.

[I therefore am of the opinion, that they ought to be distinguished into three classes; Gutturals, Palatines, and Labials; as they are formed by the throat, the palate, or the lips.]

The total of distinct vowel sounds in English is nine, three being formed in the throat, three in the palate, and three in the lips, depending on the degree of opening in the different places. Wallis described the guttural vowels first; these are, he claims (p. 6):

. . . in summo Gutture formantur, seu posteriori linguae palati parte, aëre moderate compresso.

[. . . formed in the top of the throat, or the lower part of the tongue and palate, with a moderate compression of the breath.]

With a large opening *o* or *a apertum* is formed, which, when short, is represented by *o*, but when long by *au* or *aw* and sometimes by *a*, as in *fall/folly, hall/haul/holly, call/collar, laws/loss, cause/cost.* Wallis claims that these sounds differ in quantity only, not quality. In the grammar proper, Wallis makes it plain that this sound is represented by *a* before *l♯* or *lC* (although he disapproves of the pronunciation *wauk, tauk,* for *walk, talk* (p. 55)), as in, e.g., *chalk, malt, half, balm, psalm,* which are, he says, pronounced *chauk, maut, hauf, bawm, psaum* (p. 51). This deletion of *l* apparently applies also following *o*, as in *folk.* Like Hodges and subsequent writers, then, and unlike the earlier orthoepists, Wallis couples με *o* with με *au*, leaving με *ǫ* without a short equivalent. For some reason this seems to bother Lehnert, who explains it as the result of Wallis's insistence on keeping his scheme symmetrical. However, even if his scheme forced με *ǫ* to be categorized as a labial vowel (cf. below), there seems no logical reason why Wallis could not include με *o* as the short equivalent if he wanted to, thus making it also a labial rather than a guttural. Further, if we accept Lehnert's interpretation of με *ǫ* as [ɔ], it is difficult to see what value to assign to με *au*—perhaps [ɒ̄]?

Wallis then says:

Eodem loci, sed apertura faucium Mediocri, formantur Gallorum *e* foemininum; sono nempe obscuro. Non aliter ipsius formatio differt a formatione praecedentis *a* aperti, quam quod magis contrahantur fauces, minus autem quam in formatione Vocalis sequentis.

Hunc sonum Angli vix uspiam agnoscunt: nisi cum vocalis *e* brevis immediate praecedat literam *r* (atque hoc quidem non tam quia debeat sic efferri, sed quid vix commode possit, aliter; licet enim, si citra molestiam fieri possit, etiam illic sono vivido, hoc est masculo, effere); ut, *vertue* virtus; *liberty* libertas, etc.

[In this place, but with a medium opening, is formed the French *e* feminine; an obscure sound. Nor does the formation of this sound differ from the formation of the preceding open *a* in any way except that the mouth is contracted more than in the former, but less than in the following vowel.

This sound the English recognize virtually nowhere except where the short vowel *e* immediately precedes the letter *r* (and this is sounded this way, not because it ought to be, but because it is not easy to pronounce it otherwise; for it is permissible, if it can be done without trouble, to pronounce *e* masculine there); as in *virtue*, *liberty*, etc.]

It will be best to consider this vowel along with Wallis's third guttural vowel, which he calls *o* or *u obscurum*, and which is again made in the same place, but with a yet smaller aperture of the mouth. According to Wallis, this is the sound the French use in the last syllable of *serviteur, sacrificateur*, and is found in English *burn, turn, dull, cut, come, done, country*, etc. (though Wallis disapproves of this pronunciation for words spelled with *o* or *ou*, such as *come, country*). In the grammar proper, he claims that this vowel (p. 67):

Differt a Gallorum *e* foeminino, non aliter quam quod ore minus aperto efferatur. Discrimen hoc animadvertent Angli dum pronunciant voces Latinas *iter, itur; ter ter, turtur; cerdo, surdo; ternus, Turnus; terris, turris; refertum, furtum*, etc.

[. . . differs from the French *e* feminine only in that it is pronounced with a less open mouth. The English may preceive this difference by pronouncing the Latin words *iter, itur*; . . . etc.]

In his *Defence of the Royal Society* (p. 18) Wallis refers to these two sounds, noting that even after much discussion Wilkins had still claimed that they did not differ. Wallis, however, perseveres in his opinion, and cites the same examples that are given here.

We may assume that his obscure *o* or *u* is [ʌ], and that *e feminine* is another, different, unrounded centralized vowel, [ə] or possibly [ɜ,] since he claims it exists only before *r*. It is apparently not at all common; Wallis seems able to find minimal pairs only in Latin, not English, except for ME *ī* and *oi/ui*. με *ī* is given as *e feminine* plus *y* (pp. 37, 68), whereas ME *oi/ui* is said to have two pronunciations, open *o* plus *y* or obscure *o* plus *y* (pp. 36, 69-70). Stockwell (forthcoming) would identify *e feminine* with [ɨ] and claim that this shows /ɨy/ in contrast with /əy/, and, further, that this supports his view that centralization preceded lowering. Lehnert, however, gives a very different interpretation. He believes that the identification of με *ī* with the French sound in *main*, *pain*, and with Greek ει indicates a pronunciation [ẹ], and also believes that the identification of the first element with *e feminine* supports a concept of lowering (even though he believes Wallis's *e feminine* to be [ə]). He assumes the line of development to be ịi > ịi > ẹi > ẹi > ai. This seems an improbable interpretation of Wallis's description. It should be remembered that we do not know how he pronounced Greek.

The distinction made by Wallis is almost identical with that found a century later in Tiffin (cf. Chapter IV). Tiffin also has a vowel which rarely occurs in English, and then only before *r*, but he claims that it is always long. Further, he does not assign this vowel to με *ī*, which is /ʌy/. It is possible that this vowel (Wallis's *e feminine*, Tiffin's vowel 9) is [ɨ], but it could equally well be [ə] or [ɜ], and its occurring only before *r* (except, in Wallis only, for με *ī*) makes the latter perhaps more likely. Wallis places it midway between [ə] and [ʌ], but it is not clear that one can accept this as a phonetic fact.[20] Since in words like *virtue*, *servant*, the vowel lowers to merge with με *a*, as evidenced by spellings as early as Chaucer and common as late as 18th-century literature, and still present in, e.g., *star* < ME *sterre*, and the *parson/ person* doublet, it may be that this unrounded centralized vowel is lower than [ə] or [ʌ]. At any rate, there do not seem to be any very convincing reasons for interpreting it as [ɨ], and the nature of the sound is sufficiently doubtful that it does not seem to provide unequivocal evidence for the priority of centralization over lowering. Chomsky and Halle (1968, pp. 267-268) assign it "the non-committal symbol ǝ," while Dobson (1957a, pp. 241-242) considers it to be [ə] in contrast with [ʌ], remarking rather misleadingly that Wallis distinguishes these sounds "even before *r*," whereas it would be truer to say that both Wallis and Tiffin contrast them **only** before *r* (except for με *ī*). Lehnert assumes Wallis's *e feminine* to be [ə], but says that it is impossible to determine the exact phonetic quality of *u*, *o*, *obscurum* (§§ 71, 73, 90, 103); he uses the symbol [ʌ] for it.

Wallis's next series is the Palatine vowels, which are formed in the palate (pp. 7-8):

. . . aëre scilicet inter palati et linguae medium moderate compresso: Dum nempe concavum palati, elevato linguae medio, minus redditur, quam in gutturalibus proferendis. Suntque hae in triplici gradu, prout concavum magis minusve contrahitur.

Quae quidam diversitas duobus modis fieri potest: vel fauces contrahendo, manente lingua in eodem situ; vel faucibus in eodem situ manentibus, linguae medium altius et interiores palati partes elevando: utrovis enim modo fiat, vel etiam si utroque, perinde est.

[. . . the air being moderately compressed between the middle of the palate and the tongue: that is when the hollow of the palate is made less by raising the middle of the tongue, than it is in pronouncing the gutturals. And these are of three sorts, depending on whether the hollow is larger or smaller.

And this difference may be made in two ways: either by contracting the mouth and leaving the tongue in the same place; or, leaving the mouth in the same position, by raising the middle of the tongue higher to the interior of the palate: but it comes to the same thing whichever way you do it.]

The first vowel in this series is *a exile*, or slender *a*, as in *bat/bate, pal/ pale, lamb/lame*. This corresponds to ME *a*, *ā*, and can be assumed to be [æ], [ǣ], since Wallis indicates no qualitative difference between the vowels. However, Lehnert believes that they were different, and assigns the values [æ], [ę̄] to them (§ 68).

"Ibidem item, sed Mediocri oris apertura, formantur Gallorum *e* masculinum" (p. 9). [In the same place but with a medium opening is formed the French *e* masculine.] This corresponds to ME *e*, *ę̄*, as in *tell/teal, set/seat, best/beast*. Wallis claims that, although the long *e* masculine is usually spelled *ea*, it is sometimes spelled *ei*, and in his discussion of diphthongs in the grammar instances *receive, seize, deceit* (p. 69). Dobson (1957a, p. 241) remarks that these particular examples could all have ME *ę̄*, and, of course, today they have /iy/, not /ey/.[21] This vowel is in Wallis's grammar presumably /e/, /ē/.[22]

The third Palatine vowel, formed in the same place but with the smallest aperture, is *i exile*, or slender *i*. Wallis notes that when short it is represented in English by *i*, but when long by *ee, ie*, or, sometimes, by *ea* (pp. 9-10). Some of his examples are *fit/feet, fill/feel/field, ill/eel, sin/seen*, and *near, dear, hear*. This then is με *i*, *ẹ̄*, the latter including some instances of ME *ę̄* raised to με *ẹ̄* before *r*, as we see in other orthoepists.

Vocales Labiales, in ipsis Labiis (in rotundum formam) collectis formantur; aëre ibidem moderate compresso. Suntque hae etiam in triplici gradu . . .

[The labial vowels are made in the lips, gathered into a round shape, the air there being moderately compressed. And there are three kinds of these . . .]

The labial vowel with the largest aperture is *o rotundum*, which is spelled *o* or *oa*, and in French *au*. Examples are *none, one*,[23] *hole, coal, boat, those*. Wallis notes that short *o* is usually open *o*, and that *o rotundum* is in English usually long. This is then μɛ *ǭ*, and from the discussion of the diphthongs it is clear that in many dialects ME *ou* has monophthongized to merge with it (cf. below). Lehnert (§§ 74, 122) claims that Wallis's *o rotundum* is [ɔ̄], since it is the monophthongized version of [ɔu]. He believes that Wallis placed this vowel among the labials merely to keep his scheme symmetrical (§ 150).

The labial vowel pronounced with a medium opening is *u pingue*, or fat *u*, usually spelled *oo*, some examples being *foot, shoot, full, fool, pull, pool, good, stood, wood, woo'd*, or with *ou*, as in *mourn, source, could*. Wallis says that *do, go*,[23] and *move* are better pronounced with *o rotundum* than with *u pingue*, from which it seems that they often were pronounced with *u pingue*. This vowel obviously includes μɛ *ǭ* and *u*, but it is not clear from Wallis's discussion and examples whether /ū/ < ME *ǭ* had shortened to /u/ in, e.g., *stood*.

The last vowel is the third labial vowel, pronounced with the smallest opening, *u exile* or slender *u*. In *De Loquela* Wallis is very clear that this is the same as French [ȳ], since he says (p. 12):

Hunc sonum extranei fere essenquentur, si diphthongum *iu* conentur pronunciare; nempe *i* exile literae *u* vel *w* praeponentes (ut in Hispanorum *ciudad*, civitas). Non tamen idem est omnino sonus, quamvis ad illum proxime accedit, est enim *iu* sonus compositus, at Anglorum et Gallorum *u* sonus simplex.

[Foreigners would learn to make this sound if they tried to pronounce the diphthong *iu*; that is, placing slender *i* before the letters *u* or *w* (as in the Spanish *ciudad*, city). However, this is not exactly the same sound, though it is close to it; because *iu* is a compounded sound, but English and French *u* is a simple sound.]

However, in the grammar Wallis describes it simply as "sono nempe quasi composito ex *i* et *w*" (p. 67) [a sound as it were composed out of *i* and *w*]. His examples include *lute, muse, cure, knew, brew, news* (pp. 11-12), but later in the grammar he gives *new* and *knew* as examples of the diphthong "*eu, ew, eau,* sonantur per *e* clarum et *w*" [sounded with *e* masculine and *w*] together with *neuter, few, beauty.* He notes that (p. 69):

Quidam tamen paulo acutius efferunt acsi scriberentur *niewter, fiew, bieuty,* vel *niwter, fiw, biwty*; praesertim in vocibus *new* novus, *knew* sciebam, *snew* ningebat. At prior pronunciato rectior est.

[But some pronounce them more sharply, as if they were written *niew-ter, fiew, bieuty,* or *niwter, fiw, biwty*; especially in the words *new, knew, snew* [= *snowed*]. But the first pronunciation is better.]

It is clear that Wallis differentiated ME *ę̄u, ę̄u,* and also that he knew a dialect in which ME *ę̄u* had raised to merge with με *ę̄u.* It is not so clear whether με *ę̄u* was [iu] or [ȳ]. Dobson believes that Wallis had [ȳ], while Chomsky and Halle give [iu]. It certainly seems that Wallis in one place claims to have [ȳ], but he is not consistent. Since there is very little contemporary support for [ȳ] this late, it may be that Wallis simply wanted a fully symmetrical vowel scheme, and, knowing the French pronunciation, included με *ę̄u* among the pure vowels. There seems no way of deciding from his inconsistent description. Lehnert (§§ 73, 140-146) believes that Wallis was describing an artificial, theoretical pronunciation, and really had [iu] or [ju].

I have already noted Wallis's descriptions of ME *ī, ę̄u, ę̄u,* and *oi/ui.* The last, however, needs further discussion. Wallis claims that both *ou* and *oi* have two pronunciations (p. 36):

. . . in *oi, ou,* vel *oy, ow,* praeponitur aliquando *o* apertum (ut in Anglorum *boy,* puer; *toys,* nugae; *soul,* anima; *bowl,* poculum); aliquando *o* obscurum (ut in Anglorum *boil,* coquo; *toil,* labor; *oil,* oleum; *boul,* globus; *owl,* bubo; &c. quandam non negem etiam horum nonnulla a quibusdam per *o* apertum pronunciare.

[. . . in *oi, ou,* or *oy, ow,* open *o* is sometimes set first (as in English *boy, toys, soul, bowl*); sometimes obscure *o* (as in English *boil, toil, oil, bowl*: &c. although I do not deny that some of these are pronounced by some with open *o.*]

In the grammar he says (pp. 69-70):

Oi, oy, efferentur per *o* apertum seu clarum sed correptum, et *y.* Ut in *noise* strepitus, *boys* pueri, *toys* nugae, *toyl* labor, *oil* oleum. Nonnulli tamen in quibusdem saltem vocabulis potius per *o* vel *u* obscurum efferent, ut *toil, oil,* vel *tuyl, uyl.*

[*Oi, oy*, are expressed by open or clear *o*, but short, plus *y*. As in *noise, boys, toys, toil, oil*. However some pronounce them with obscure *o* or *u*, as *toil, oil*, or *tuyl, uyl*.]

Chomsky and Halle (p. 268) assume that the normal development was /ɔy/, but that /ʌy/ was a variant, optional pronunciation, and that Dobson is wrong in trying to differentiate these on an etymological basis. I would certainly agree with this, since these sounds seem quite confused in the orthoepistical writings generally (as is understandable if we assume that the language had added rules lowering lax /u/ to /o/, and then unrounding /o/ to /ʌ/; cf. Chapter VI). But Chomsky and Halle are mistaken in the argument with which they try to support their case, namely, "the fact that the same alternation occurs in the reflexes of /ɔ̄w/ [= ME *ou*] where only a single historical source can be postulated." Chomsky and Halle have here misinterpreted Wallis. The misunderstanding may, however, be of Dobson, whom they quote, or may stem from the table of diphthongs in Lehnert (p. 70) which shows:

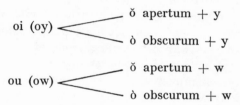

However, it is clear from the discussion that Lehnert is quite aware that Wallis was here referring to one orthographic digraph representing two disjoint word-classes; indeed, he points out (§ 155) that Wallis orthographically distinguishes *óu* < ME *ou* and *òu* < ME *ū*. Certainly the description cited above discusses two pronunciations of the digraph *ou/ow*, as Wallis does later in the grammar (p. 70):

Ou et *ow* duplicum sonum obtinent; alterum clariorem, alterum obscuriorem. In quibusdam vocabulis effertur sono clariori per *o* apertum, et *w*.

Ut in *soul* anima, *sould* vendebam, venditum, *snow* nix, *know* scio, *sow* sero, suo, *owe* debeo, *bowl* poculum, etc., quo etiam sono et *u* simplex nonnunquam effertur, nempe ante ld, ut in *gold* aurum, *scold* rixor, *hold* teneo, *cold* frigidus, *old* senex, antiquis, etc. et ante ll in *poll* caput, *roll* volvo, *toll* vectigal, etc. Sed et haec omnia ab aliis efferentur simpliciter per *o* rotundum, acsi scripta essent *sole, sold, sno*, etc.

In aliis vocabulis obscuriori sono efferentur; sono nempe composito ex *o* vel *u* obscuris, et *w*.

Ut in *house* domus, *mouse* mus, *lowse* pediculus, *boul* globus, *our* noster, *out* ex, *owl* bubo, *town* oppidum, *foul* immundus, *fowl* volucris, *bow* flectis, *bough* ramus, *sow* sus, etc.

Ou and *ow* have two sounds, one more clear, the other more obscure. In some words the sound is expressed more clearly by open *o* plus *w*.

As in *soul, sould, snow, know, sow, owe, bowl*, etc. with which sound the simple *o* is sometimes expressed, that is, before ld, as in *gold, scold, hold, cold, old*, and before ll in *poll, roll, toll*. But all these are by some pronounced simply with *o rotundum* as if they were written *sole, sold, sno*, etc.

In other words they are pronounced with a more obscure sound, that is, a sound composed of obscure *o* or *u* plus *w*.

As in *house, mouse, . . .* etc.]

It is quite clear that Wallis is referring to both ME *ū* and ME *ou*, and that they are distinct classes (with the exception of *bowl* (globus) and *owl*, which seem to be idiosyncratic), not merged, as Chomsky and Halle seem to think (cf. Wallis *in aliis vocabulis*). To consider them together is quite natural, since both are spelled *ou*, but Wallis does not confuse them. ME *ou* and *ou < o* before *l♯* or *lC* is either /ɔw/ or is monophthongized to /ō/, but is not realized as /ʌw/. It is obvious from the examples that /ʌw/ is a reflex only of ME *ū*, and that there is no merger at all. Wallis's description is exactly what we would expect, except that the first element of the diphthongal reflex of ME *ou* has not been raised and remains as /ɔ/. Dobson (1957*a*, p. 233 n. 1) suggests with regard to this that Wallis may have been misled by the desire to make the parallel with ME *oi/ui* more exact than it really was. Alternatively, since the diphthong evidently had a short element, the analysis may be the product of his vowel system, in which *o rotundum* is never short. But apart from this, his analysis is quite straightforward.

Wallis describes only a diphthongal pronunciation for ME *ai*, saying that (p. 69): "*Ai* vel *ay* sonum exprimit compositum ex *a* Anglico (hoc est, exile) correpto, et *y*" [*ai* and *ay* express a sound composed of short English (that is, slender) *a*, plus *y*]. His examples are *day* and *praise*.

In *De Loquela* (p. 36) he gives ME *au* as composed of slender *a* plus *w*, but in the grammar admits (p. 68):

Au vel *aw*, recte pronunciatum, sonum exhiberet compositum ex Anglorum *a* brevi, et *w*. Sed a plerisque nunc dierum effertur simpliciter ut Germanorum *a* pingue; sono nempe literae *a* dilatato, et sono literae *w* prorsus supresso.

[*Au* or *aw*, rightly pronounced, would give a sound composed of the English short *a* plus *w*. But by many nowadays it is sounded simply as the fat *a* of the Germans; that is, the broadened sound of the letter *a*, and the sound of the letter *w* completely suppressed.]

It seems then that με *au* was /ɔ/, but that Wallis thought /æw/ a preferable pronunciation; since Hart and Butler both give the diphthongal reflex, Wallis may be right in claiming that it was still used by some.

WALLIS'S VOWEL SYSTEM

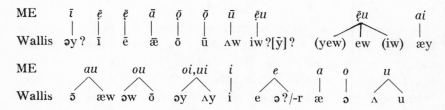

WALLIS'S VOWEL DIAGRAM

Apertura

	majori	media	minori
Gutturales	a⎱ o⎰ aperta	e foemininum	u⎱ o⎰ obscurum
Palatinae	a exile	e masculinum	ee⎱ i ⎰ exile
Labiales	o rotundum	oo⎱ u ⎰ pingue	u exile

JOHN WILKINS: 1668

John Wilkins's *Essay towards a Real Character and a Philosophical Language* was published for the Royal Society in 1668, at which time Wilkins was fifty-four. As the title indicates, Wilkins's real goal was to devise a language in which the symbols stood for concepts rather than words, so that it would be intelligible to people who did not have the same native language. However, as part of his discussion he devotes some time to the analysis of natural languages.

Wilkins tells us he has read the private papers of Holder and of Lodwick, and the published works of Smith, Bullokar, Gil, and Wallis (p. 357):

... the last of whom, amongst all that I have seen published, seems to me, with greatest Accurateness and subtlety to have considered the Philosophy of Articulate sounds.

It is with Wilkins's "Philosophy of Articulate sounds," and in particular with his description of contemporary English sounds, that we are here concerned.

Wilkins says that (p. 357):

The Essence of Letters doth consist in their *Power* or proper sound, which may be naturally fixed and stated, from the manner of forming them by the instruments of speech; and either is or should be the same in all Languages.

What variety there is of these, may appear from the Distribution of them into their several kinds, according to the following Table; wherein it is endeavoured and aimed at, to give a rational account of all the simple sounds that are, or can be framed by the mouths of men.

Wilkins then seems to be aiming at an exhaustive categorization of distinctive features on an articulatory basis. Despite his claim, however, his description of vowels is limited to those in his dialect of English, plus [y] which he knows from French.

He admits only five vowels, those "*Apert* and free" sounds which are "greater," and divides them into:

Labial; being framed by an emission of the breath through the lips contracted,
    Less (o)
    More, with the help of the tongue put into a concave posture long ways, the whistling or French (u)

Lingual; the breath being emitted, when the Tongue is put into a posture
    More concave and removed at some distance from the palate (α)
    Less concave or plain, and brought nearer the palate (a)
    Somewhat *convex* towards the palate (e)

Besides the vowels, Wilkins recognizes three glides, these being also "*Apert* and free," but "*Lesser*"; they may be either voiced or voiceless. Of the voiced sounds, he says (p. 360):

. . . they do somewhat approach to the nature of Consonants, and *mediae potestatis*; because when they are joyned with any Vowel to compose that which we call a Dipthong, they put on the nature of Consonants; and when they are not so joyned, but used singly, they retain the nature of *Vowels*.

His description of the three voiced glides is as follows:

Labial; by an emission of the breath through the Lips, more *contracted* (γ)
Lingual; when the breath is emitted between the middle of the Tongue in a more *Convex* posture, and the palate (i)
Guttural; by a free emission of the breath from the Throat (χ)

This analysis leads Wilkins to count glide and vowel combinations as diphthongs, as will be seen below. For this he is criticized by Dobson (1957a, p. 255), who says that ". . . he overlooks, in the interests of theoretical symmetry, the distinction in articulation of [w] and [ū], [j] and [ī], and [h] and [ʌ]." In his further discussion of the vowels (in which he includes the glides), Wilkins notes that they may be distinguished by either quality or quantity, since the same vowel may be either long or short. He omits from further discussion the "whistling *u*," on the grounds that its "laborious and difficult pronunciation" makes it of less general use. He therefore finds only seven different simple species of "Vowels, easily distinguishable, whose powers are commonly used." He gives the following table:

α	Short	Bot*tom*	Fol-*ly*	Fot	Mot	Pol	Rod
	Long	Bought	Fall	Fought		Paule	Rawd
a	Short	Batt	Val-*ley*	Fatt	Mat	Pal	Rad-*nor*
	Long	Bate	Vale	Fate	Mate	Pale	*T*Rade
e	Short	Bett	Fell	Fet	Met	Pell	Red
	Long	Beate	Veale	Feate	Meate	Peale	Reade
i	Short	Bitt	Fill	Fitt	Mit-*ten*	Pill	Rid
	Long	Beete	Feele	Feete	Meete	Peele	Reede
o	Short						
	Long	Bote	Foale	Vote	Mote	Pole	Rode

γ	Short		Full	Fut		Pul	
	Long	Boote	Foole	Foote	Moote	Poole	Roode
χ	Short	But	Ful	Futt	Mutt-*on*	Pull	Rudd-*er*
	Long			Aaaa			Amongst

Following this list, he again describes the articulation of the sounds, but does not change it in any interesting way. Note that, like Hart, (γ) and (o) are described only by means of lip-rounding, the position of the tongue being unspecified; (α), which seems to be [ə] from the examples, is described only as "the most Apert amongst the *Lingua palatal Vowels*" and by the position of the tongue. He notes that in English there is no short (o) and no long (γ).

We can equate Wilkins's (i), ME $\bar{e}$, with a high front unrounded vowel, ME $\bar{ę}$, Wilkins's (e), with a mid front unrounded vowel, and ME $\bar{a}$, Wilkins's (a), with a low front unrounded vowel. Dobson thinks Wilkins's description of (a) indicates pronunciations of [a] and [æ] where he would expect [æ] and [ɛ]. However, it does not seem possible to ascribe exact phonetic qualities to Wilkins's vowels; we know merely that he differentiated three heights of front vowels. (α) is used for ME *o* and *au*; as noted above, Wilkins makes no mention of lip-rounding. It seems improbable, however, that he used an unrounded vowel, and I therefore assume that his (α) was a low back rounded vowel approximating to [ɔ]. (o), ME $\bar{ǫ}$, is a mid back rounded vowel, which Wilkins claimed had no short variant in contemporary English (as we should expect, since ME *o* had lowered to [ɔ]). (γ) is the high back rounded vowel, representing ME *u* and $\bar{ǫ}$ (where ME *u* had not lowered and unrounded to [ə]). There is a slight problem here, however, in that the only three examples given for short (γ) are *full*, *foot*, and *pull*, which also appear in the list for (χ), which must be approximately [ə]. It seems that Wilkins knew of variant pronunciations of these words. It should also be noted that from Wilkins's list (p. 16) illustrating the various spellings of (χ), it is obvious that Wilkins had [ə] not only from ME *u* and from /u/ < /ū/ < ME $\bar{ǫ}$, but also from ME *i* before *r*, since he says there:

And as for the *Power* of the Vowel (ɥ)[24] this also is written five several waies; namely by the Letters

i	Sir, stir, firmament, &c
o	Hony, mony, come, some, love, &c
oo	Blood, flood
u	Turn, burn, burthen
ou	Country, couple.

In his discussion of diphthongs, Wilkins lists six: *ai boy, ai aye,*
χ*i bite,* α*γ awe, e*γ *ewe,* and χ*γ owl.* In his transcription, however,
he also gives *cri*γ*sifyiëd* and *cammi*γ*nian,* which indicates that he also
distinguishes /iw/ < ME *ẹ̄u.* ME *ou* is monophthongized to /ō/, and,
despite his listing α*γ awe,* from his table of vowels it would seem that
ME *au* is usually monophthongized as α = [ɔ]. It is possible that
Wilkins retained an off-glide in word-final position, but one word
seems insufficient data on which to base such a conclusion.

WILKINS'S VOWEL SYSTEM

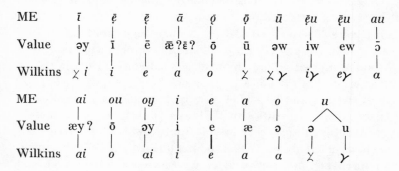

This system is almost identical with that of Wallis. Wilkins differs
only in lacking some of the variants mentioned by Wallis, and in not
indicating that /ew/ < ME *ẹ̄u* has a long first element (Wilkins does
not indicate length in his transcriptions). This similarity may be
due to the fact that both were of a similar age and social standing
and were known to each other. Alternatively, we know that Wilkins
was acquainted with Wallis's work and thought highly of it, particularly of Wallis's analysis of sounds, and that they had discussed the
differences between their analyses. Wilkins may therefore have been
influenced by Wallis's work. In this light, therefore, it is interesting
to note that, like Wallis, he makes no mention of monophthongal
pronunciations of ME *ai,* but that unlike Wallis he does not differentiate
the first elements of με *ī* and *ū.* If he were influenced by Wallis, then
he did not follow his system slavishly. However, the differences are
all simplifications, and it may be that Wilkins was interested more
in the phonological patterning than in the exact phonetic facts. His
using the glides (i) and (γ) for both vowels and consonants suggests
that this was in fact his main interest.

WILLIAM HOLDER: 1669

William Holder's *Elements of Speech* was published at almost the same time as Wilkins's *Essay*, that is, in 1669, only one year later, but we know that it (or, at any rate, writings on a similar subject) was in existence earlier, since Wilkins acknowledges having read it. However, the scope and purpose of Holder's work were very different from Wilkins's. Holder is interested only in the sounds of natural speech, and with a very practical end in mind (p. 15): ". . . to prepare a more easie and expedite way to instruct such as are *Deaf* and *Dumb*, and Dumb onely by consequence of their want of Hearing . . . to be able to pronounce all Letters, and Syllables, and Words . . ." He is primarily interested in English, but includes his description of English sounds in the framework of a theory of universal phonetics, laying down the hypothesis (p. 54): "That the number of Letters [= sounds] in Nature, is equal to the number of Articulations, severally applyed to every distinct matter of Sound." Because of his purpose he is particularly concerned to give as accurate a description as possible of the articulation of all sounds distinct in English; he is not, however, concerned with the problem of English spelling, and therefore does not provide any phonetic transcriptions of texts; we are provided merely with a very few words as illustrations.

Holder notes that theoretically a very large number of vowel sounds is possible, but concludes that in English there are only eight which are distinct, *a a e i o oo u γ*, "the sounds whereof, according to the vulgar pronunciation, are this

Long, or accented in the *Vowel*	*a*	*a*	*e*	*i*	*o*	*oo*	*u*	*γ*
	Fall	*Fate*	*Seal*	*Eel*	*Cole*	*Fool*	*Rule*	*Two*

| *Short*, or accented in the *Consonant* | *Folly* | *Fat* | *Sell* | *Ill* | *Full*." | | | |

He adds that "There is so much space between *a* and *e* that there may be a vowel inserted between them, and a fit character for it may be *æ* . . ." (p. 81).

Although he neither assigns symbols for the short vowels nor lines them up with their long counterparts, we may reasonably assign them to the first four and the sixth long vowels, and considering only these, might suggest the values [ɔ̆], [æ̆], [ĕ], [ĭ], [ŭ]. Dobson (1957a, p. 365) suggests [a] and [æ] for *a*, and [æ] and [ɛ] for Holder's hypothetical *æ*.

However, Holder suggests no qualitative difference between the long and short vowel. *O* as in *coal* has no corresponding short vowel; apparently ME *o* is now [ɔ] and corresponds with [ɔ̄] as in *fall*, while ME *ǭ* has raised to [ō]. We now come to some severe problems with Holder's analysis. He lists two more long vowels, *u* as in *rule* and *γ* as in *two*. Of these, Holder says (p. 88):

And in this, *γ* and *u* are peculiar, that they are framed by a double motion of the Organs, that of the Lip added to that of the Tong; and yet either of them is a single Letter, and not two, because the motions are at the same time, and not successive, as are *eu*, *pla*, &c. Yet for this reason they seem not to be absolutely so simple Vowels as the rest, because the voice passeth successively from the Throat to the Lips in *γ*, and from the Palat to the Lips in *u*, being there first moulded into the figures of *oo* and *i*, before it be fully articulated by the Lips.

Dobson interprets this to mean that *u* is [y] and that *γ* is [ū], and that they are opposed to the unrounded vowels *i* = [i] and *oo* = [ʌ], respectively. He believes that *oo* was included among the long vowels by mistake, and that *fool* was chosen as an example again by mistake, since *oo* often was used for the unrounded vowel, as in *blood*. Dobson bases his belief on Holder's analysis of *γ* and *u* as simple sounds and on his claim that the different articulatory motions are simultaneous, not successive; also Dobson bases his claim on the fact that, if *oo* ≠ [ʌ], then Holder apparently has no example of the lowering and unrounding of /u/ which is evidenced by his contemporaries. Jespersen (1907), however, equates *γ* with /uw/, and *u* with /iw/, since in places Holder's description seems to indicate that the sounds are successive, and since there is little contemporary evidence of [y]. He notes that Holder's only example of *γ* is *two*, and suggests that he may well have heard an off-glide in word-final position but not before a consonant (pp. 54-55). Further, as Jespersen notes, Holder claimed that this labial element could be added to every vowel, yet he had described *o* as being rounded already. Zachrisson (1927, pp. 84-85) also concludes that Holder is describing a diphthongal pronunciation. Another argument against *γ* = [ū] and *oo* = [ʌ] is that Holder describes the vowel which represents *γ* without the labial element as being "most open and backwards" (pp. 89-90), which seems an odd description of [ʌ]. Holder follows this description with a very important passage (quoted by neither Jespersen nor Dobson) (p. 90):

. . . there being reason to allow a Vowel of like sound in the Throat with *γ*, but distinct from it as not being *Labial*; which will be more familiar to our Eye if it be written *oo*; as in *Cut, Coot, Full, Fool, Tut, Toot*, in which the Lip does not concur; and this is that other.

The meaning of this passage is not completely clear; however, it seems to imply that all these words are examples of the nonlabial vowel. If this is so, it seems improbable that Holder meant [ʌ], since although [ʌ] alternated with [u] in the lax vowels (cf. Wilkins's examples) this variation is otherwise unattested. We should therefore have to believe either that Holder had a very idiosyncratic dialect in which [ū] > [ʌ], or else that he has again erroneously indicated [ʌ] to have both tense and lax forms and has this time given three erroneous examples, again omitting, e.g., *blood, flood*, which probably were lax unrounded mid vowels, in favor of words which survive only with tense high back rounded vowels. Either explanation seems curious. If we instead interpret this passage to indicate contrasting pairs of the labial and nonlabial vowels, and if we believe that *oo* = [ʌ], we must believe the first of each pair to be [ū] and the second to be [ʌ]. But this is even more incredible, since we are then reversing the values they have in modern English (and for Holder's contemporaries), except for *full*, which has not unrounded in ModE, but which is also attested with [ʌ] by the orthoepists. If a contrast is intended, then it is easier to believe that *cut, full, tut*, are examples of [ʌ], and *coot, fool, toot*, of [ū], rather than the other way round. Since the vowel contrasted with *oo* is symbolized by γ, this suggests that he intended this for the vowel in *cut, full, tut*. But this is difficult to reconcile with the instance of *two*, or with his describing γ as having the labial element, or with his originally including γ amongst the long vowels. It seems impossible to find any consistent interpretation of the whole of Holder's discussion. In any case, when he states that "Our vulgar (*i*) as in (*stile*) seems to be such a Diphthong . . . composed of *a.i.* or *e.i.* . . . ." (p. 95), we must assume that even if he had developed a centralized unrounded vowel, the first element of με ī either had not centralized, or if it had, he did not recognize this fact or identify the sound as in any way resembling [ʌ].

Generally, then, it seems to cause less problems to follow Jespersen's interpretation, noting, however, that it is extremely odd that Holder should not have had a centralized lax mid vowel, since this is well attested by other writers, and since he claims to be representing not a conservative but "the vulgar pronunciation" (p. 81).

However difficult of interpretation Holder's description of the back vowels is, this has no effect on our interpretation of his evidence concerning the Vowel Shift, since he offers none on most points. Although he identifies με *ī* as a diphthong, he is vague about the sound of the first element, and certainly does not indicate centralization; further, we have no examples of με *ū* with which to compare it. Holder does not go into any details concerning diphthongs, nor does he give any transcriptions, so we cannot tell the development of ME *ai, ou,* or *au.* It seems possible but not certain that με *ęu* was /ew/ in his dialect, and the development of ME *ęu* is similarly uncertain, depending on the interpretation of Holder's *u.* Holder assumes a monophthongal pronunciation of all long vowels—at least, there is no evidence of any off-glide except in the case of *γ* as in *two* and *u* as in *rule.* However, if he regards these as single sounds, then we cannot tell whether the other long vowels which he also heard as single sounds in fact had off-glides or not.

In general, we can conclude only that ME *ī* had diphthongized and the first element lowered, that ME *ẹ̄, ę̄, ǭ,* and *ǭ* had raised, that ME *ā* had fronted and perhaps raised, and that ME *ęu* and *ęu* were still distinct. We can therefore assign Holder only the following tentative and incomplete vowel pattern:

ME	*ī*	*ẹ̄*	*ę̄*	*ā*	*ǭ*	*ǭ*	*ū*	*ęu*	*ęu*
Value	?	ī	ē	?	ō	ū	?	iw?	ew?
Holder	*ai,ei*	*i*	*e*	*a*	*o*	*oo*	-	*u*	*eu?*

ME	*ai*	*oi,ui*	*ou*	*au*	*a*	*e*	*i*	*o*	*u*
Value	?	?	?	?	æ	e	i	ɔ	u
Holder	-	-	-	-	*a*	*e*	*i*	*a*	*oo*

ELISHA COLES: 1674

The Compleat English Schoolmaster by Elisha Coles consists largely of two tables of words, the first arranged phonetically and the second alphabetically. The second, with which we are not concerned, marks stress (unless it falls on the first syllable, in which case it is omitted) and shows the syllable division. Following the tables are three brief essays, two on orthography and one on the tables. In this latter Coles explains his purpose in writing the tables, saying that "Children are not to be troubled with Rules and Exceptions . . ." since ". . . Their Judgment is little or none at all" (p. 103). Since, however, "they are actively capable of imitation," he believes in giving them plenty of practice. It is for practice in spelling, and presumably in associating particular spellings with certain sounds, that the lists are intended. It should be noted that he claims to have followed "that pronunciation which I have for many years observ'd to be most in use among the generality of Scholars."

This essay is interesting in that in it Coles refers to Wallis's grammar, and alludes to the division of sounds into "Guttural, Palatine, and Labial" which Wallis had used. It is this analysis which Coles uses as a basis for ordering his first table, always placing the list with short vowels first, though he does not always agree with Wallis. He gives no description of the articulation of the sounds nor any comparison with other languages, so that his list has value only in establishing which vowels and diphthongs are distinct and in which words they occur.

Coles begins with με *au*, presumably [ɔ] approximately. This is also the value of ME *a* before *l*‡ or *lC*, as in *bald, ball, balk, halt, false,* of ME *ou* before [χt], and sporadically of ME *a* following *w* and/or before *r*, and of ME *o* before *r*. The short equivalent of this vowel is με *o*, which must therefore be [ə]. The next vowel is [ə] < ME *u* and from [u] < [ū] < ME ǫ (*blood, flood*), and from ME *ou* before [χ] (*tough*). The list gives ample evidence that ME *ur, ir,* had merged as [ər], but there is only one example of ME *er* (*her*). There is also only one example, *full,* of a word which has [u] in ModE; *pull,* which is often shown with [ə] in other writers, does not occur in Coles except with [u]. Like all the writers except Wallis, Coles has only one centralized vowel.

Coles follows these with three diphthongs. First he lists με ī. We can assume from its place in the tables that he meant this to be a diphthong, and that the first element was a "guttural," and therefore that this was approximately /əy/. No words spelled *oi* or *oy* are included in this list. However, the next list is of *oi* words; again Coles has one less distinction than Wallis, since he has only one diphthong here, presumably /əy/ but possibly /ʌy/, instead of making the differentiation usually attributed to the etymological distinction between ME *oi* and *ui*. The last diphthong in this class is με ū, which we may again assume to have had [ə] as its first element. *Plough* is included in this list.

Coles's next list, με ā, shows no merger with either ME ę̄ or ME *ai* (excepting *waste/waist*), except before *r*. Like Hodges, he has the triplet *pare/pair/pear,* and also gives *fare/fair, hare/hair, air/are/heir, bare/bear, stair/stare, there/their, ware/wear/were.* Included in this list are examples of ME *a* lengthened before *lf, lm, nt*, and of ME *au* > *ā* before *nt*; examples are *calf, half, alms, psalm, chant, haunt, vaunt*. In these last three Coles is different from, e.g., Butler, Hodges, who show the development here as [ɔ]. The following list, ME *a*, includes *waft, war, swan, wan, swash, wash, wattle, watch*, showing that in the dialect Coles is describing rounding of *a* following *w* had not taken place generally. Also included in this list are *dance, lance, haunch, branch*, which in other writers are often given with [ɔ]. It seems that Coles has far fewer occurrences of [ɔ] than have other writers.

The next list is με *ę̄*, which is completely distinct, showing no merger with ME *ai*, ME *ā* (except before *r*; cf. above), or ME *ę̄*, followed by ME *e*, including *er*, which seems not to have centralized. Next comes ME *ẹ̄*, followed by ME *i* and then by ME *ẹ̄* and *ę̄* before *r*. A reason for Coles's listing these (i.e., *ẹ̄r, ę̄r*) separately might be that a glide had developed before the *r*, causing a diphthong, and that Coles is therefore differentiating these from the pure tense vowels. Yet this is not done in the case of ME *ā* before *r*, examples of which occur in their alphabetical place between *āp* and *ās*. A comparison of Cooper's list of *ee lingual* before *r* (Sundby, p. 50) with Coles's list (p. 18) shows that Coles includes almost all Cooper's examples of *ea* words, although in Coles's dialect ME *ẹ̄* and *ę̄* are undoubtedly quite distinct.

Coles next lists words with ME *ai*, which apparently either was still a diphthong in his speech, or was considered by him to be more correctly pronounced as a diphthong, followed by ME *ǭ* and *ou* in one list, showing presumably that ME *ou* had monophthongized (on the evidence of the other orthoepists and grammarians), though from Coles alone all we can certainly tell is that the two sounds had merged. In this list are many examples of ME *ǭr* and *ọ̄r*, which have evidently not lowered to (or not remained as) [ɔ], even with a preceding *w*, as in *worn, sworn*. There is no short equivalent of this vowel.

Next Coles lists ME *ọ̄*, followed by ME *u*. *Rook, nook*, are listed with long vowels, though *book, brook*, have evidently shortened, as has *tooth*. Coles concludes with ME *ẹu* followed by ME *ę̄u*; he apparently still distinguishes these from each other.

Coles's evidence indicates that in the dialect he has chosen to represent ME *ai, ā, ę̄*, and *ẹ̄* are still all distinct one from the other, except that ME *ai, ā*, and some *ę̄* merge before *r*, as do *ẹ̄* and some *ę̄*. There are no cases of ME *ẹ̄* before *r* included in the normal ME *ẹ̄* list, nor is ME *ai* before *r* included in the *ai* list. ME *ẹu, ę̄u*, are still distinct, but ME *ou, ǭ*, seem to have merged. Coles shows only one /oy/ diphthong and one centralized vowel. ME *au* has monophthongized and rounded to [ɔ], and ME *o* has lowered to pair with με *au*, so that με *ǭ* has no short equivalent. Rounding of ME *a* after *w* or before *r* is evidenced only sporadically, but it occurs regularly before *l‡* or *lC*.

COLES'S VOWEL SYSTEM

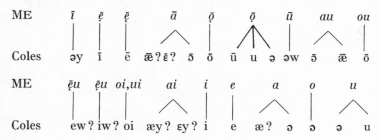

ME	*ī*	*ẹ̄*	*ę̄*	*ā*	*ǭ*	*ǭ*	*ū*	*au*	*ou*
Coles	əy	ī	ē	ǣ?ɛ̄?	ɔ̄	ō	ū	u ə əw	ɔ̄	ǣ	ō

ME	*ẹu*	*ęu*	*oi,ui*	*ai*	*i*	*e*	*a*	*o*	*u*
Coles	ew? iw?	oi	æy? ɛy?	i	e	æ?	ɔ	ɔ	ə	u

FRANCIS LODWICK: 1686

Francis Lodwick (or Lodowyck) is known mainly by three published works: *An Essay towards an Universal Alphabet*, which was published as an anonymous pamphlet and in the *Philosophical Transactions of the Royal Society* June 1686; *A Second Essay Concerning the Universal Primer*, which was added to his first essay in the Royal Society publication; and *A Common Writing*, published anonymously in 1747 but ascribed to Lodwick on the strength of a note on it signed "Jo. Aubrey" attributing it to Lodwick. The latter publication is concerned solely with a philosophical language suitable for international communication and is therefore of no relevance to the topic here. There are also certain unpublished notebooks of his in manuscript in the British Museum.

As the title of his Royal Society essay indicates, Lodwick wanted to devise a universal phonetic alphabet "which should contain an Enumeration of all such single Sounds or Letters as are used in any Language" (p. 126). Lodwick claims that there are in all fourteen vowels, for three of which he can find no English examples. His table is (p. 128):

1.	a	as	tall	8.	ui	—	muis Lowdutch
2.	a	—	tallow	9.	y	—	tile
3.	a	—	tale	10.	o	—	tone
4.	e	—	tell	11.	u	—	tunne
5.	e	—	teal	12.	u	—	*une French*
6.	i	—	till	13.	oo	—	tool
7.	u	—	*dure French*	14.	ou	—	tould

Following this table, he states: "These are the *Vowels*, each of which are long and short. Short as in the words, God, Man, Sin. Long as in Ball, Demand, Seen, &c." (p. 129). As stated, this is ambiguous, and could be interpreted to mean that all fourteen vowels have long and short variants. It is, however, taken by Dobson (1957*a*, p. 276) to mean that vowels 1, 2, and 6 can be either long or short, and this seems the more reasonable interpretation. Lodwick says (p. 133) that "a prick" should be added to distinguish the long vowels, but did not himself do so in his transcription of the Lord's Prayer.

There are obvious anomalies in his vowel system as described here. First, although *sin* is heard as the short equivalent of *seen*, *tell* is equated neither with *teal* nor with *tale*. Dobson (1957*a*, p. 277) attributes this to there being a greater difference between *e* and *ę̄* in English than in Dutch (in which the difference is more nearly that of [ɛ] and [ɛ̄]), so that Lodwick did not consider the short and long English vowels to be variants of one sound. Vowel 11 is used both for ME *u* and also for the unstressed vowel in *forgive*; it seems probable therefore that it represents /ə/, and that Lodwick has omitted to provide for /u/, which does not occur in the Lord's Prayer. The example given in the list for *ou* is *tould*; however, in the Lord's Prayer we also have *our* transcribed with vowel 14. It seems then that in Lodwick, as in Robinson, ME *ū* and ME *o* before *lC* had merged.

In his "Essay of An universall Perfect Alfabet" (Sloan MS 897) he gives the following table of simple vowels:

Stạ̄ll	Stę̱ạle	Stę̱ēle	Stǭle	Stǭǭle
Stānd	Stę̱m	Stı̱̄le	Stū̱nne	dū̱re french
Stạ̄ı̱ne			ū̱ne french	
	Lǭū̱d			

Underneath he comments:

These vowells are long or short

long	stạ̄ll	Sę̄ę̄ne	fǭǭle	demā̱nd
short	Gǭd	Sı̄n	fṳll	stạ̄nd	&c.

This list omits the *ui* given for "Lowdutch" in the Royal Society article, but fills in one of the omissions by indicating that the vowels of *fool* and *full* differ only in quantity.[25] Later, in his discussion "of Diphthongues and double letters," he says that ". . . oo, in the word fọọle is

no otherwise sounded than Single u, in the word full the former being
long, the Latter short . . ." This confirms that his distinct Vowel
11 is meant to be /ə/.

In other respects the lists agree. In his discussion of diphthongs
he claims that "ai, in the word plain is no otherwise sounded than
the Single a̲, in the word Same . . .," and in his vowel table the example *loud* makes it clear that his Vowel 14 is με ū, probably /ow/.
Further, με ę̄ is listed as different in quality from both με ę̣ and με ā.
However, if the spatial arrangement is meant to indicate any classification of the sounds (which Lodwick nowhere suggests), then he
apparently perceived με ę̄ as closer to με e than to με ę̣ or to με ā.
Similarly, /ə/ is grouped with με ǭ, presumably /ō/, rather than with
με ǫ̣, presumably /ū/.

But the really interesting point is that in both accounts με ī, ū,
are listed by Lodwick with the simple vowels. His reasoning is quite
clear. His third rule states (1686, p. 128):

That in every composition of single Sounds, the particular single Sounds
which make up that Composition, ought to be truly and clearly dis-
cerned in the Sound of the Composition, otherwise it cannot be truly
said to be a Composition, and composed of such single Sounds.

This agrees with the account of diphthongs in his notebook, but there
it is plain that his primary emphasis is to show that digraphs (including those for consonants, e.g., *th, sh, ck, sh, gh*) are often not diphthongal. He gives no examples of what he would consider true diphthongs. In his discussion of the so-called diphthongs in English *ea,
ou, oo, eo, ai*, he claims that these are in fact single sounds, since if
you utter the two vowel sounds indicated one after the other the result will not be the sound usually indicated by the digraph. His example is *teal*, and, assuming this to represent the normal development
of ME ę̄, i.e., [ē] or [ɛ], it seems clear enough. But it is difficult to believe that με ī and ū were monophthongs. Again Dobson (1957a, p. 277)
attributes this to Lodwick's Dutch origin, suggesting that he equated
με ī and ū with the Dutch diphthongs *ij* and *ou* respectively, and that
he was denying that these (which are "short" diphthongs and very
different from the Dutch "long" diphthongs) are diphthongal in nature. Be that as it may, it is clear that we cannot draw any conclusions about με ī and ū from Lodwick's evidence. His spelling *day,
daily,* and *against* with vowel 3 may indicate monophthongization,
but may again only be the product of his theory of diphthongs, as
may be his monophthongization of ME *au* and *ou*. He completely

ignores ME *oi*, *ēu*, and *ẹu*, none of which occurs in the Lord's Prayer. On the whole Lodwick gives us very little useful data. He documents the development of [ə] and of the continued existence of ME *ę̄* as a distinct entity, but he contributes nothing on the other issues with which we are particularly concerned, namely, the development of ME *ī* and *ū*, and the diphthongal or monophthongal nature of the traditional long tense vowels.

HEINRICH KELLERMAN: 1686

A second-generation Russian named Heinrich Kellerman spent the years 1661-1678 traveling and studying in various parts of Europe. For political reasons he later left Russia again, and in 1686, while still in exile, wrote back to Russia proposing he undertake to provide a definitive text of the Bible in Russian.[26] To support his claim that the different vernacular texts were inconsistent with each other, he provided transcriptions of parallel passages in eight languages: Hebrew, Greek, Dutch, German, English, Latin, Italian, and French. He gives each passage twice, the first being a direct transliteration from the native spelling into the Cyrillic alphabet and the second being an attempt at a phonetic transcript. When in England he stayed in Oxford, and we may perhaps assume that he is attempting to transcribe Standard English. He is, of course, handicapped by his alphabet, but does not seem to be greatly influenced by the original spelling. For instance, he transliterates both [θ] and [ð] with θ, but uses this symbol to transcribe only [θ]; for [ð] he uses the same symbol as for [d]. This shows that he could hear the difference in voicing, but that his alphabet did not allow him to make the three-way distinction between [d], [ð], and [θ]. He apparently considered the distinction between [ð] and [θ] as more important than that between [d] and [ð].

Some relevant examples are (Alekseev, pp. 144-148):[27] *this day*, θis dai, dis" dĕ; *thy name*, θv name, dei nĕm"; *our daily bread*, our dailv bread, aur dĕlĕi brĕd; *thine*, θine, dein; *three*, θree, θri; *and the earth*, ĕn de ĕrθ (note assimilation of the final [d] in *and* to the following [ð]); *be done*, bi dan"; *God*, gad; *power*, pauĕr; *amen*, ĕmĕn.

Note that ME *ę̄*, *ā*, *ai*, and *e* are all transcribed with *ĕ*; this is also used for unstressed *and* and for the unstressed second syllable of *heaven* (not given above) and *power*. Apparently he knew only the monophthongal reflex of ME *ai*. ME *ī* is transcribed *ei*. The Russian alphabet did not permit Kellerman to represent a mid central vowel. However, he could have used a high central vowel, but chose not to do so.

He uses this symbol only once, for the second syllable of *deliver*, which he transcribes /lɪv/. Another interesting point is that he does not use the same symbol for the first element of both με ī and ū; με ū is transcribed /aw/. *God* and *not*, both of which are transliterated with a rounded vowel, are transcribed as *gad* and *nat* respectively, and *done* as *dan*". There is ample evidence of the unrounding of /ɔ/ to /a/ elsewhere, and this may be another example of it. At this time we would expect both με ī and ū to have centralized first elements. It is possible that ME ū had reached a more advanced stage in the Vowel Shift, and was already /aw/, whereas ME ī was /ɔy/. However, it does not seem possible to determine this with any accuracy from Kellerman's transcripts.

His transcriptions of ME ę̄, ā, and *ai* support Wyld's claims of a merger between these, but are a little surprising in face of Kökeritz's statement (1953, p. 9) that in the East Midlands ME ę̄ and ẹ̄ had merged as /ī/. Since Kellerman apparently learned his English at Oxford, one would expect him to have this merger rather than the one he shows. But his transcriptions are very consistent. It is possible that με ę̄ was [ē] whereas με ā was [ɛ̄], and that he really had a three-way distinction between ME ę̄, ẹ̄, and ā which he did not know how to represent (as with [θ], [ð], and [d]). If this were so he would be in agreement with the English orthoepists and phoneticians such as Cooper. However, his actual transcriptions show no such distinction, and on the most straightforward and literal interpretation they lend support to the claim that ME ę̄, ā, and *ai* at this time were merged in educated English.

CHRISTOPHER COOPER: 1687

Christopher Cooper's *Grammatica Linguae Anglicanae* (edited by J. D. Jones in 1911) was published in 1685. Two years later *The English Teacher* appeared; it is a translation of Parts I and II and chapters 9 and 10 of Part III of the *Grammatica*, but omits the rest, which deals mainly with syntax and morphology. I have used *The English Teacher* here, and all examples are taken from there.

Cooper's purpose is "to teach the present way of writing," not, like Smith, Hart, Wade, Bullokar, Gil, and Butler, "wholly to reform" (preface, p. 5). He acknowledges that others have attempted to do the same thing, but claims that they failed because they ". . . have not rightly distinguished between Vowels and Dipthongs, or truly shown which are the proper or improper, neither does it appear that

they understood the Philosophy of Sounds, or the Nature of Char-
acters, or which were single, or which double . . ." In his Part I,
then, Cooper first discusses the mechanism of speech and then goes
on to describe the individual vowels, diphthongs, and consonants,
finishing with a critique of the English alphabet. Part II contains
(among other things) spelling lists of words spelled with a particular
vowel, together with instructions for the pronunciation. These lists
then illustrate and supplement the descriptions given in Part I.

Cooper claims that English has eight distinct vowel sounds. The
first he calls *a lingual*, and this is, he says, "formed by the middle
of the Tongue a little rais'd to the hollow of the Palate" (p. 4). It
is apparently short in *can, pass* (p. 4), and in, e.g., *cap, cat, gash, land,
pat* (p. 34), but long in *cast, past* (p. 4), and in *carp, gasp, lance, path*
(p. 34). Thus ME *a* seems to have become [æ] and to be subject to
lengthening before a continuant followed by a voiceless stop, before
two continuants, or before [θ].

The next vowel, *e lingual* (p. 5), ". . . is formed by the Tongue more
rais'd toward the end and extended than in *a* foregoing; whereby the
passage for the breath between the Tongue and the Pallate is made
narrower and the sound more acute." It is short in *sell, sent, tell,
tent,* and long in *sail, saint, tail,* and *taint* (p. 5). He also states that
u guttural (= /ə/; cf. below) is heard after long *e lingual,* except in
a few idiosyncratic words such as *cane, wane, age, strang(er), manger,
mangy,* and all words spelled with *ai.* He describes this in more detail
in Part II (p. 34) ". . . which *u* is nothing else but a continuation of
a naked murmur after *a* is formed; for by reason of the slenderness,
unless we more accurately attend, the tongue will not easily pass to
the next consonant without *u* coming between." However, his phonetic explanation based on the conditioning effect of the following
consonant is obviously not correct since (p. 35) he gives a list of minimal pairs, e.g. *main/mane, hail/hale,* in which supposedly the *ai*
spelling has the pure *e lingual* whereas the *a* words have *e lingual* plus
a centralizing off-glide. We may take it then that ME *ā* has raised to
/ē/ (more probably to [ɛ̄], for reasons that will appear later), and ME
ai has monophthongized and raised to /ē/ also; however, since ME *ai*
is not subject to Cooper's (possibly nonstandard) diphthongization
rule, which otherwise seems fairly general, it would seem that this
rule must apply at some stage before the two vowels merge. If the
rule is formulated to apply only to [æ] before consonants, and inserted
(in the formulation in Chomsky and Halle (1968, p. 280)) after Fronting
but before Monophthongization, it will apply to those words with ME *ā*;

it will not be affected by Monophthongization, since that is formulated to apply only to vowels followed by homorganic glides.

Cooper next discusses what he calls *i lingual*, which (p. 6) ". . . is formed by the Tongue nearer to the end, higher raised and more expanded, whereby the passage for the Breath is rendred narrower, and the sound more subtle, then in *ken* and *cane*; as in *win, priviledge*." Examples of *i lingual* long are *fe-male, wean, deceive, pea, plea, sea*, and word-final *y* as in *gravity* (p. 6). Other examples with the spelling *ea* are *bead, beat, cheap, east, great, wheat* (pp. 49-50). There has been considerable dispute about the nature of this vowel, which can perhaps best be considered in relation to the next, Cooper's *ee lingual*, which (p. 6):

. . . is formed by the end of the Tonge fixed to the lower Teeth, both expanded and raised to its highest degree, whereby the passage of the Air is most of all straightned, and the sound made the closest of all Vowels, and coming nearest to the nature of Consonants; as in *feet, feed*; and therefore there is the least difference between the shortning and lengthning thereof . . .

This clearly seems to be /ī/, and the difference in length noted by Cooper seems to be the usual variation caused by a following voiced vs. voiceless consonant, or no consonant at all (Cooper's later example of the difference (p. 7) being *ween/wee*). *I lingual* short seems to be [ɪ], but we are left with *i lingual* long. Sundby believes Cooper when he claims to distinguish this vowel from *ee lingual* long, and, wishing to explain its pairing with the vowel of *win*, assigns it the value [ī]; there is then the tense/lax distinction between *ween* and *wean*. Sundby takes this to indicate a gradual raising of ME ę̄ to [ī], at which later stage, of course, it eventually merges with με ẹ̄. Chomsky and Halle (1968), however, assume "that in Cooper's speech ME /ǣ/ and ME /ē/ coalesced into [ī]" (p. 277); that is, they believe that Cooper was mistaken when he thought he could differentiate ME ę̄ from ME ẹ̄. They point out (p. 277) that:

. . . not all reflexes of ME /ǣ/ are treated by Cooper in this fashion; before [r] they are all said to be pronounced with *ee lingual*, i.e. [ī]. The simplest explanation for this choice is to assume that Cooper pronounced the vowel [ī] here but knew, of course, that in the writings of his predecessors the reflex of ME tense /ǣ/ did not coalesce with that of ME tense /ē/.

They quote here the explanation of Zachrisson (1913, p. 204) that Cooper may:

. . . have felt obliged to keep up the old distinction . . . even if this distinction merely consisted in giving the same sound two different names. This assumption may help us to explain the peculiar way in which Cooper treated ẹ, ę, in front of r. Here neither the spelling nor the earlier orthoepistical[28] works gave any clue to the etymology. Hence Cooper confused ẹ and ę in this position, by placing *all* words in which he pronounced *ea* in front of r as ī under *ee lingual*.

First, it must be remarked that it seems rather odd that one whom Dobson called the greatest of the seventeenth-century phoneticians (1957a, p. 280) would erroneously try to differentiate ME ę̄ and ẹ̄ on the basis of spelling if they were indistinguishable in his pronunciation. Second, the account in Chomsky and Halle is factually incorrect. Cooper does not say that all reflexes of ME ę̄ before r are pronounced with *ee lingual*. Chomsky and Halle may here have misunderstood the last sentence in the quotation from Zachrisson;[29] however, Zachrisson says only that Cooper placed in this class "all words in which he pronounced *ea* in front of r as ī." This statement amounts to saying that all words spelled *ea* but pronounced with *ee lingual* were placed in the *ee lingual* class, and does not seem to contribute greatly to the elucidation of the problem.

But in fact many *ea* words are listed by Cooper as being pronounced as *e lingual*, i.e., as μɛ ā; all except one (*scream*) occur before r. Some of the examples are *bear, earl, learn, swear, tear* (= *rend*), *wear* (p. 50). This shows, as Dobson notes (1957a, p. 305), that generally in Cooper ME ę̄ has merged with μɛ ā before r. The examples listed under *ee lingual* are, therefore, only exceptions to the general process, and the development of ME ę̄ before r is shown to have proceeded in two ways, **both** of which are at this stage distinct from the normal development of ME ẹ̄. We notice also that Cooper claimed to differentiate *each* and *seam*, which had long i *lingual*, from *beach* and *steam*, which had *ee lingual*. He does not therefore make a blanket distinction between *ea* words before r and *ea* words elsewhere, but seems to have been classifying genuine differences.

Cooper's list of *ea* words before r pronounced as *ee lingual* seems to have even less value as evidence of the overall pronunciation of ME ę̄ when we compare it with the evidence of some of the other orthoepists and grammarians. Hart has apīr (*appear*), tʃīr (*cheer*), diër (*dear*), and uīri (*weary*). Robinson has tlīr (*clear*), dīr (*dear*), hīr (*hear*), nīr (*near*), and yīrlei (*yearly*). Gil has chiërful (*cheerful*), kliër (*clear*), diër (*dear*), and both nër and niër for *near*, and (as noted above) Coles has many of Cooper's *ea* words with /ī/ before r listed under μɛ ę̄ before *r*. But the most interesting evidence on this point comes from Butler. In his chapter 2, *Of Spelling* (pp. 28-29), we read (spelling emended):

Ea is sometimes abusively written for *æ*; as in *tear* [*lachryma*], *year*, *appear*; for seeing we say *tær'*, *yær'*, *appær'*; why do we not write so, that strangers may read so? as we do in the like; *bær'*, *hær'*, *nær'*, *pær'*, &c. For *ea* hath an other kind of sound: as in *bear*, *fear*, *tear* [*lacero*][30] . . .

He refuses to allow the derivation to be any argument, instancing also *clear* (*clarus*) (p. 29). He then continues:

Dear [*charus*] . . . differs from *dær'* [*carus*, and *dama*,] as well in voice as writing; *ea* being rightly sounded as *e* long, not as *æ*; and *weary* . . . hath the like sound and orthography: and yet some, in pronouncing *dear* and *weary* incline too much unto *æ* . . .

Likewise to *hear* seemeth to be rightly written, and the ancient sound to be according: not only because I find it always so spelled, as well in ancient as modern writings; but also because the *cognata* *heard*, *hearken* and *ear* have the same orthography: although in *hear* and *ear*, some corruptly sound *ea* like *æ*, and in *heard* and *hearken* like *a*.

Butler also has *gær'* (*gear*), *spær'* (*spear*), and twice (pp. 48, 92) notes that *shear* is now pronounced *shær'*.

There seems then to be ample evidence that even in the writings of Hart, Gil, Robinson, Coles, and Butler, in which ME $\bar{e}$ was undoubtedly distinct from ME $\bar{ę}$, ME $\bar{ę}$ before *r* had started to develop in two ways. Generally, $\bar{ę}$ did not raise before *r*, but eventually merged with με $\bar{a}$; in a few items, however, raising occurred to merge these with με $\bar{ę}$ as /ī/, before ME $\bar{e}$ in general raised to /ī/. Dobson (1957*a*, pp. 636-637) discusses this in some detail, and claims that in the South it must have ceased to operate by "at latest about 1400."

This whole matter is complicated by the fact that many words such as *there*, *where*, *were*, *hair*, *bier*, *fear*, *rear* (vb.), *year*, could have either $\bar{ę}$ or $\bar{ę}$ in ME, depending on the dialect, and therefore perhaps /īr/ came in these words from the dialect with ME $\bar{ę}$. There are some words, however, which had $\bar{ę}$ in all dialects, such as *spear*, *shear* (vb.), *ear* (noun and vb.), *beard*, *smear* (vb.), and which yet raised to /ī/.

What is quite clear is that ME $\bar{ę}$ had a different history before *r* than elsewhere. Here it is either raised to merge with με $\bar{ę}$, or remained lower to merge later with με $\bar{a}$, even though in other environments it remained distinct from either. Thus the history of words with ME $\bar{ę}r$ tells us nothing about the sound of ME $\bar{ę}$ in general. Butler in particular shows that this idiosyncratic raising was still an ongoing process (despite Dobson's suggested terminal date; cf. above)—and provides some evidence for the view that sound changes are first diffused lexically (cf. Chapter II)—by his statement that *shear* had only recently come to be pronounced *shær'*, and by his discussion of the alternate pronunciations of *dear, weary, hear*, and *ear*. Cooper certainly provides data illustrating this divergence, but it seems quite valueless as evidence that ME $\bar{e}$ had everywhere raised to /ī/ and was thus in his dialect identical with με $\bar{e}$.

This whole matter has been amply discussed and documented (cf. Wyld (1927, pp. 63-67); Dobson (1957a, pp. 636-637)), and there seems no reason to pursue it further here. I therefore merely reject all words with ME $\bar{e}r$ from further consideration in establishing Cooper's pronunciation of ME $\bar{e}$.

There seems little reason then to disbelieve Cooper when he claims to differentiate ME $\bar{e}$ and $\bar{e}$, except that he equates the vowels of *win* and *wean*. But this does not seem to me to be an insuperable obstacle to accepting Cooper's vowel system. First, he says himself that except for *a* and *o* (i.e., [æ] and [ɔ] or [ɒ]), "in the other the short Vowel hath a distinct sound for its long one" (p. 10). That is, he acknowledges that the long and short varieties of *i* and *e lingual* and *o labial* differ in quality as well as in quantity. Second, as we shall see, what seems to us the rather striking disparity between *i lingual* short and long is matched in the back vowels. Third, this unequal pairing is not new; it has an exact predecessor in Middle English (cf. Chapter V). Fourth, Cooper's analysis is supported by one of the shorthand writers in the eighteenth century (cf. Chapter IV).

There is one more reason, and to my mind a most convincing one, in favor of Cooper's long *i lingual* being [ē], not [ī], and thus in favor of ME $\bar{e}$ and $\bar{e}$ being still distinct in his speech, and, indeed, being generally distinct in the dialects known to him. Cooper records variant pronunciations in his work, for instance the vestigial remains of a diphthongal pronunciation of ME *ai*, even though by far the more common pronunciation was monophthongal. There is ample evidence that even after ME $\bar{e}$ had raised to [ī] and thus merged with με $\bar{e}$, in some dialects the pronunciation [ē], in which it usually merged with με $\bar{a}$, was still heard late into the eighteenth century, and this variation is mentioned by observers much less exact than Cooper (cf. Tuite, below) and is evidenced in rhymes. Yet Cooper mentions only one pronunciation. If we assume this to be [ī], we must assume either that Cooper was unaware of the variant pronunciation with [ē], or that he knew of it and deliberately did not include it in his description. Either assumption seems highly implausible. By far the most plausible explanation for Cooper's describing only one pronunciation of ME ẹ̄ is that at that time only one existed commonly, and if there were only one, it must have been [ē] and distinct from με ẹ̄.

Having therefore indicated reasons for accepting that ME ẹ̄ as in *wean* ≠ ME ẹ̄ as in *ween*, and also the consequence that in all probability the vowel of *wean* is not what we would consider the long equivalent of the vowel in *win*, there seems no reason why we should not assign to *i lingual* the tentative value of [ē]. This avoids the problem, in Jones's analysis, of assigning Cooper a long lax vowel unlike all the other long vowels. Since we cannot at this date determine from the description we have available the exact phonetic quality of the sound, the symbol we assign to it is in a sense immaterial. It should be understood merely as distinct both from με ā and from με ẹ̄, to which (cf. above) we had assigned the values [ɛ̄] and [ī] respectively.

Cooper then discusses his vowel *o labial*, which "is formed by the lips a little contracted, while the breath is emitted Circular, as in *hope*" (p. 7). Other examples of *o labial* long are *go, notary, bone, cloke, know, coach* (p. 40). He notes that the short equivalent occurs in very few words, except for those beginning with a labial consonant, and instances *wolf, wonder,* "the syllable *wor-, pull, full,* not because this is the truest but the easiest pronunciation," *good, stood, hood, wood, wool,* and compounds ending in the noun suffix *-hood* (p. 41). Here again we seem to have two different vowels paired, [u] and [ō], and again, as for *i lingual,* many explanations have been advanced. In the case of *i lingual,* since ME ẹ̄ did eventually raise to [ī] and merge with με ẹ̄, the tendency has been to suggest a high value for the long vowel. In the case of *o labial,* however, since ME ǭ did not raise to [ū] and merge with με ọ̄, the tendency is to equate the pair by suggesting that Cooper's *o labial* short was approaching [o]. But there is no reason to assume that Cooper meant the two vowels to be identical, or to doubt that he is here making the same kind of pairing that he did with the front vowels. In both cases (cf. below) he is left with a high tense vowel which has no lax equivalent; presumably he preferred this to equating *win/ween* and similarly for the back vowels, and leaving the developments of ME ẹ̄, ọ̄, without short alternates.

In the back vowels, then, the counterpart of his *ee lingual* is *oo labial,* which "is formed by the Lips very much contracted; as in *book, boot:* there is very little difference between the short and long sound, for the reason aforesaid under *ee*" (p. 8). He instances *move,*

boar, court (p. 8), *aboard, born, could, force, tomb, worn, look, roof,* and
many others (p. 41). It should be noted that in, e.g., *book, look,* shortening either has not yet taken place, or Cooper knew of variants with
the long vowel; the second explanation seems more likely, since we
find *foot* as an example of both short *o labial* and short *oo labial.*

Cooper next discusses what he calls *o guttural* (p. 8), which ". . . is
formed by the root of the Tongue moved to the inner part of the Pallat,
while the middle of the Tongue is depressed, which causes the greatest
space between the fore part of the Tongue and Pallat; and therefore
it hath the most open and full sound of all the Vowels; as in *loss.*"
Since this sound has no distinct letter, he assigns it the symbol *a.*
Some of his examples are *was, watch, all, halt, awl, cause* (p. 8), from
which we can see that ME *a* has rounded to [ɔ] before *l#* and *lC,* and
also following *w,* and also that ME *au* has monophthongized and rounded. (In his discussion of diphthongs, Cooper gives some examples
in which the diphthong /aw/ is used, but admits it is usually pronounced as *a.*) However, ME *a* did not always round to [ɔ] following
w, since Cooper earlier (p. 7) gives *wan* and *wasp* as examples of short
and long *a lingual,* that is, of [æ] and [ǣ]. It seems then that Cooper's
grammar had two rules for ME *a,* one which usually rounded it after *w,*
and to which there were exceptions, and one which fronted to [æ]
those which were not rounded.

Cooper's last distinct vowel is *u guttural* (p. 9), which ". . . is formed
onely in the throat, by the Larynx striking the Air, causing a naked
murmur, which is the same with the groaning of a man that is sick
or in pain . . ." He notes that there is little difference between this
vowel, as in *nut,* and the related rounded vowel in *pull.* In his later
discussion he notes that *er, ar, or, ur,* and *ure* are all pronounced with
this vowel when unstressed. We may take this to be a sound approximating to /ə/.

Cooper gives the following table of his eight distinct vowels in their
long and short variants (p. 13):

1	2	3	4	5	6	7	8
can	ken	will	folly	full	up	meet	fool
cast	cane	weal	fall	fole	—	need	food

Next Cooper proceeds to discuss the English diphthongs, claiming that "The sounds *ee* and *oo,* which are the closest of all Vowels,
and come nearest to the nature of consonants, can only be set after
other Vowels" (p. 14). He explains then that where he uses *i* or *u* for

the second element in a diphthong, these are to be taken as having
the value *ee* and *oo*.

He recognizes two diphthongs, *ai* and *ei*, as in, e.g., *bait, caitiff,
eight, praise, weight,* and *convey,* but adds that "For the most part
in common discourse we speak *ai* as *a* simple in *cane*" (p. 15). *I lingual*
and *ee* "make the most subtle Dipthong. Never used in the *English*
tongue" (p. 15). Since the first element here may be the vowel of
either *win* or *wean,* we cannot tell whether he is referring to /iy/ or
/ey/. However, it is clear that although Cooper recognizes the theoretical
possibilities of such diphthongs, he is quite certain that they do not
exist in English. He does recognize a diphthong *oi,* as in *joy, coy, coif,*
and also *ai,* which, he says, occurs in only five words, *boil, moil, point,
poison,* and *boy,* which last "is a dissyllable, to wit *boai.*" Cooper's
last diphthong ending with a front glide is *ui* (= /əy/), which "make
a dipthong which we call *i* long" (p. 15). He instances *blind, wind,
pined, beguile, guide, disguise, guidon, injoin, joint-ure, ointment, broil.*

Of the six possible combinations of vowel plus back-glide, Cooper
claims that *a lingual* plus *u* is "never used with us," that *e lingual*
with *u* is not commonly heard, being used only as an affected pronunciation of, e.g., *account, how,* and that *o guttural* plus *u,* spelled *au,*
is more usually monophthongized as *a.* However, a diphthong composed of the vowel of *will, weal,* plus *u* "is very common with us, which
we call *u* long." The examples include *funeral, huge, juice, chew, knew,
true,* and *rheum.* Here we cannot tell whether or not he distinguishes
ME *ēu* and *ęu,* since this diphthong may be either *iu* or *eu* (and cf.
discussion of this sound in section on Webster, below). Cooper never
discusses whether the first element of the diphthong is long or short.
If we assume that he has lax first elements (which seems probable;
it is the general tendency in the works studied), then presumably
ME *ēu* and *ęu* have been leveled under /yu/.

However, if we assign to these first elements the value of the lax
vowel, then we have a problem with reconciling our interpretation
of *o labial* with the diphthong composed of this vowel plus *u,* as in
coulter, mould, soul, ow as in *know,* and before *lC,* as in *bold,* since this
diphthong would then be /uw/, whereas it more probably was /ow/.
In general, it does not seem possible from Cooper's ambiguous descriptions to pin down with any certainty exactly which vowel he intended in the diphthongs consisting of a combination of *i lingual* or
o labial plus an off-glide. However, we note that like many of the
other writers, he describes the glide developed after ME *o* before *l#*
or *lC.* There are many more examples of this in his later discussion

of proper diphthongs (p. 47). Cooper's last diphthong is composed of *u guttural* plus *u*, i.e., /əw/, as in *out, about* (p. 17), *avow, crown, loud, tower* (p. 48).

Cooper then has only five diphthongs which occur freely in his speech: /əy/ and /əw/ from ME *ī* and *ū* respectively, /ew/ from ME *ę̄u* and *ęu*, /ow/ from ME *o* before *lǂ* and *lC*, and from ME *ou* in word-final position, and /oy/. /əw/, /ey/, and /ay/ he recognizes as occurring only very occasionally in formal speech. /ɛə/, which apparently occurred quite freely in Cooper's speech but was probably substandard, he seems not to have recognized as a diphthong.

COOPER'S VOWEL SYSTEM

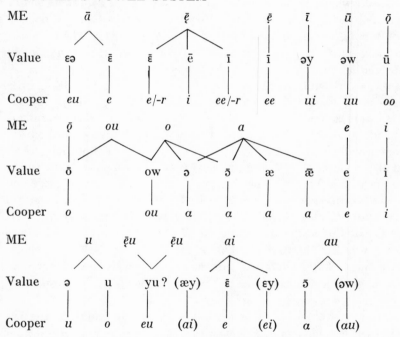

Note that since both *a lingual* and *o guttural* are subject to lengthening before certain consonant combinations, and since the rule rounding ME *a* after *w* does not apply in all cases, ME *a* has four possible realizations in Cooper's dialect, [æ], [ǣ], [ɔ], and [ɔ̄]. Note also that as a result of this lengthening, Cooper now has four distinct vowel heights as the output from the phonological component, [ǣ], [ɛ̄], [ē], and [ī], though he has only three in the underlying forms, namely ME *ę̄*, *ę̄*, and *ī*. We shall not discuss this further here, other than to note that if the data is to be accounted for then it would seem that we have to

allow for four vowel heights. Of course, if we assume that ME ę̄ and
ę are no longer distinct in this dialect, then there is no problem. Unfortunately, it seems impossible to reach this conclusion without dis-
torting the evidence. We cannot, therefore, assume the restructuring
and simplification of Cooper's grammar postulated by Chomsky and
Halle (though obviously this is applicable at a later stage; merely,
it seems unlikely it had occurred as yet). In one respect this makes
Cooper's grammar easier to understand. Part of the hypothetical restructuring concerns ME *a*, which becomes æ in the underlying form.
In most cases this is correct, but Cooper has many cases of ME *a* becoming [ə], e.g. before *l*♯ or *l*C and after *w*. These would presumably
now have to be *ā* or *o* in the underlying form (or perhaps both occur
as *o* if lengthening before certain consonant combinations is a late rule
following rounding adjustment), and there would therefore seem to
be no connection between those examples of ME *a* which had rounded
already (and perhaps lengthened also) after *w* and those which had
not. But since the rule continued to spread until all examples rounded
(except before velar stops, e.g. *wax*, *wag*), it seems probable that they
were still related in the underlying form, and that therefore restructuring is incorrect at this stage.

We see then that in Cooper we have very clear evidence that ME
ī, *ū*, had diphthongized, and that the first element of each had lowered
and centralized to a sound which Cooper identifies with the vowel
of *nut* and *up*. It seems that Cooper was well able to distinguish long
tense vowels from diphthongs, and he provides strong evidence for
the trend toward monophthongization of the original ME diphthongs.
Further, although he recognizes the theoretical possibility of diphthongs
such as /iy/ and /uw/, he is quite certain that they do not exist in
English. Cooper's evidence is, then, very much against the analysis
of EModE long vowels as sequences of vowel plus off-glide.

THE WRITING SCHOLAR'S COMPANION: 1695

We may assume that the author of *The Writing Scholar's Companion*
was a Londoner at least by residence, since he says ". . . at *London*,
where to avoid a broad clownish Speaking, we are too apt to run into
the contrary Extream of an affected way of speaking perhaps too
fine" (p. 12). This makes the more interesting that he clearly shows
coalescence of ME ę̄ and ę. In his discussion of the sound of (e), he
notes that the long sound, which he indicates by (ee), may be shown
orthographically by a final silent *e*, as in *here*, *mete*, *sincere*, but that

"most commonly the sound of long (e) is supplied with a diphthong
[= digraph], either (ee) as in *need*; (ie) as in *brief*; (ea) as in *read*" (p. 24),
and he directs the reader to the various tables for further examples.
Further, in his discussion "*Of the Diphthong* (ea)" (pp. 39-40), we find
the pronunciation for *ea* words to be (a) long, as in *hear, swear*; (a)
short, as in *hearken, heart*; (e) short, as in *already, bread* (examples
from the table on p. 114); disyllabic, as in *creation, reality*; and (e)
long. He gives an extensive list (pp. 113-114) in his "Table XII (ea)
Sounding (ee) *or* (e) *long*," including *break* and *great*; the pronunciation
of *steak* and *yea* is not mentioned.

ME $\bar{e}u$, $\bar{e}u$, have also coalesced in this dialect, and are said to be
pronounced (iw) (p. 36). The digraph (oi) is given two pronunciations,
/oy/ and "(i) long" (presumably /əy/), but, as we would expect from
the orthoepistical writings, the differentiation in pronunciation does
not follow the etymological *oi/ui* distinction; e.g., *moist*, which has
/oy/ in Gil and Hodges, has /əy/ here, whereas *hoise* has /oy/. ME
ai and *ā* are not distinct. ME *ou* has apparently monophthongized
and merged with ME $\bar{\varrho}$, since the author tells us that *w* is silent in,
e.g., *snow, own, fellows* (p. 28), and that "(ow) sounds like (o) long
in *blow, bow, row* . . ." (p. 39); but it seems possible that the glide was
preserved before *l*, since "The sound of (ou) is sometimes expressed
by (o) long, before (l) . . . as *droll, knoll*, . . . but *soul* and *souldier*"
(p. 39). There is the rather confusing statement that "(ou) and (ow) keep
their full sound, in *boul, coulter, flout, gout, grout, house, moulter, poul-
tice, poultry, pout, our, out, rout; shoulder, shout, stout: Mould* . . ." (p. 38).
We cannot tell here whether the writer has several words in which
ME *ou* has merged with ME $\bar{u}$, or whether he is indicating two distinct
pronunciations, με $\bar{u}$ (whatever it may be) and his *ou* before *l*.

As indicated above, we are given no information which would enable us to identify the quality of με $\bar{u}$; the writer refers merely to the
diphthong (ou) and (ow), and, as we have seen, does not distinguish
between the sounds in *poultry* and *pout*. Similarly, he refers to με $\bar{\imath}$
simply as "(i) long," but from the description of some of the *oi* words
we may infer that the pronunciation was probably /əy/.

There is evidence of *a* rounding to [ɔ] after *w*, as in *wart, warm, was,
wash, water*, and before *l‡* and *lC*, as in *scald, all* (p. 23). *Far, part,
blast*, and *past* are listed among the words with (a) short (p. 23), which
suggests that lengthening before certain consonant combinations has
not taken place in this dialect; however, *o* is said to be "commonly
long" before (ld), (ls), (lst), (rm), (rn), (rt), (st), as in *frost, consort,
scorn, form* (p. 27).

THOMAS TUITE: 1726

The description of pronunciation in *The Oxford Spelling-Book* by Thomas Tuite is not sufficiently exact to afford us much help. Nevertheless, there are points of interest which make it worth including.

First, note that to Tuite diphthong simply means any digraph which is pronounced as one syllable; the only digraphs not considered diphthongs are those consisting of two separate vowels, as in *reiterate* (p. 36). Because of this, we cannot tell from Tuite the difference between ME *ai*, which had probably monophthongized, or, at any rate, which is generally shown by other writers to be monophthongal, and ME *oi*, which is presumably diphthongal.

Tuite equates the *a* in *made* with *ai* as in *fail, pain*. In addition, he recognizes a short *a* as in *bat, land*, and a "broad" *a* like *au* when *a* is followed by *ll, ld, lk, lt, lm*, or when *w* precedes *a*, as in *bald, all, war, want* (pp. 12-13). We may assume Tuite's short *a* to be [æ], *ā* to be [ē], and *au* to be [ɔ] and [ɔ̄]. Tuite does not distinguish between long and short variants of his *au* sound.

Tuite then discusses the sound *é*, as in *bed*, and *ee*, as in *here, be, glebe* (pp. 13-14). Presumably since he is concerned with the various pronunciations of the letter *e*, he makes no comparison between the vowel of *bed* and that of *made*. However, when he distinguishes two pronunciations of *i*, he gives the name *ee* to the short pronunciation as in *bit*, thus making it the short equivalent of the vowel in *glebe* (p. 19). But he apparently does not recognize "long *i*" as a diphthong.

Three pronunciations are assigned to the letter *o*: *o* as in *robe, holy*; *oo* as in *who, tomb, lose, move*; and *au* as in *storm, fond, for, folly*. Here it is not at all clear whether he means all the *au* sounds to be short, since he has never discussed the question of length with reference to this sound. There is also a problem with *o* and *oo* short. Some of the examples of *o* short are *cover, mother, money*, from which we would assume that *o* long is [ō] and that *o* short is [ə]; however, Tuite includes *poverty* in this list, and this certainly does not have [ə] today. Further, *dost, doth*, are given as examples of *oo* short, and *conjure, constable, conduit, London, Monday, month, Monmouth, attorney, sponge, conger, wonder* (p. 28), are all given as examples of *oo* without any mention of length. Also, in the discussion of *u*, Tuite assigns it two sounds, *u* long as in *cure, muse, fume*, and *oo* short as in *cut, study, frustrate, but, drum*. It is thus not clear whether *o* short or *oo* short = [ə]; whichever it was, it is clear that Tuite still used, or at any rate knew of, [u] in many words which have [ə] today.

Perhaps the most interesting passage in Tuite is his discussion of the varying pronunciation of *ea* (pp. 40-41). He differentiates four variants:

1. as in *bread, dead,* etc.
2. as in *bear, tear, break.*
3. as in *appear, clear, clean, weasel.*
4. as in *heart, hearth, hearken.*

He then goes on to say:

Ea in most other words has the second sound according to some, and the third sound according to others, especially *Londoners,* as in the following words: *flea, plea, pea, sea, tea, pease, beans, please, veal, meat, eat, ear, fear, neat, reason, season, seam, stream, lean,* to *breath, creature, feature, beat, beast, beard, feast, beadle, speak, shear, spear, seat, conceal, deal, glean, reap,* to *steal, meal, wheat, sheaf, leaf, cease, ease, easy, clean,* to *lead, cheap, cheat, heathen, preach, teach, each, peach,* &c.

We thus have a fairly extensive list showing that the pronunciation of ME $\bar{e}$ varied between με $\bar{e}$ as /i/ and με $\bar{a}$ as /ē/, even in some words, e.g., *spear, shear,* which in much earlier works had been shown to raise to /ī/ to merge with με $\bar{e}$, though at that time με $\bar{e}$ was generally distinct. Tuite also indicates that the tendency in Standard English was to use /ī/, that is, that ME $\bar{e}$ and $\bar{e}$ had merged (contrary to the claims made by Wyld; cf. Chapter I).[31]

Tuite apparently does not distinguish ME $\bar{e}u$ and $\bar{e}u$. He says "u long" sounds "somewhat like *French* u" (p. 131), that "Eu sounds like *u* long, as *feud, deuce* . . ." (p. 36), and that "Ew, though no diphthong, is us'd instead of *eu* in the end of a word, as *few, new, blew, Jew* . . ." (p. 37). In the case of *oi,* he claims that "*boil, broil, spoil,* have a finaller sound" (whatever that may mean) than the *oi* of *toil, oil, hoise,* etc., and that "Oy sounds like *i* in *voyage.*" /oy/ seems to be the general pronunciation, to which he has a few exceptions.

ME *ou* is, he says, pronounced as "*o* long" in *blow, flow, crow, know* (p. 39). Of ME $\bar{u}$ he says only that *found, bound, house,* etc., have "the proper sound of *ou.*" Before *ld, lt,* as in *bold, hold, colt, bolt,* Tuite has *o* long, with no mention of a glide. This lends support to the claim that ME *ou* had monophthongized, since these two sounds fall together.

JAMES DOUGLAS: c1740

James Douglas's treatise is undated, but the editor, B. Holmberg, assigns the date of ca. 1740 to it, since in it Douglas's address is given as Red Lion Square, Holborn, and he was living there 1732-1742, when he died. Holmberg considers it more probable that Douglas wrote the work towards the end of this period, when he was less active in professional life.

Douglas was born in Scotland but left when he was eighteen. In London he was very successful professionally, being at one time physician to the Queen. Although we cannot tell to what extent his own pronunciation remained Scottish, there seems no reason to doubt his ability to recognize and describe Standard English, since for most of his life he apparently associated with people who spoke this dialect. That he was aware of the difference is shown by his occasionally comparing the English pronunciation with the Scottish.

His treatise confirms the merger of ME *ẹ̄*, *ę̄*, as /ī/, since he gives numerous examples of *ea* being pronounced as "*E* long," e.g., *ease, mean, plea, sea, appeal, beard, bleak, gleam, reach, steal, treat* (pp. 200-202). *Break, great,* are, however, listed with *pear, wear,* etc., as having "*A* long" (p. 203). This then confirms Tuite's claim that ME *ẹ̄*, *ę̄*, had merged for most Londoners.

Douglas shows lengthening of ME *a* to [ā], as in *chaff, alms, chance, arm* (pp. 121-122). He describes it as "a kind of Middle Sound between the broad Scotch *A* [= [ɔ]] & the Short Guttural *A* [= [æ]] which may be call'd the Scotch *A* short" (p. 112). This is perhaps the earliest unequivocal indication of [ā], since earlier authorities such as Cooper claim that the lengthened vowel is qualitatively identical with the short.

Finally, it seems that Douglas differentiated [ʌ] and [ə], though it does not seem possible to predict the occurrence of one as opposed to the other; e.g., the second syllables of *gammon* and *bacon* are said to have [ʌ] and [ə] respectively (cf. p. 183, and Holmberg's discussion of the phonology).

NOAH WEBSTER: 1789

Webster's second dissertation is worth considering for a few points. First, he notes that "Most of the vowels in English are capable of being prolonged at pleasure, without varying the positions of the organs" (p. 82). He claims that English has five vowels which have long and short variants, one which has no long equivalent, and one which has no short equivalent. These are: [i], [ī], as in *fit, feet*; [e], [ē], as in *let, late*; [æ], [ǣ], as in *carry, cart* (he claims (p. 84) that these are qualitatively the same); [ə], [ɔ], as in *folly, fall*; [u], [ū], as in *full, fool*; [ō], as in *coal*; and [ʌ], as in *tun*. He also cites four diphthongs, which he defines as "two simple sounds, closely united in pronunciation or following each other so closely that the distinction is scarcely perceptible" and notes that "In pronouncing a diphthong, two positions of the parts of the mouth are required" (pp. 82-83). His examples are first, a diphthong "composed of the third or broad *a*, and *ee*" (p. 85), i.e., [ɔi]; ᴍᴇ *ī*, which has for its first element "nearly the same aperture as we do the broad *a* but not quite so great," plus *ee* (p. 85); *e* plus *oo*, spelled *u*, as in *salute, salubrious*;[32] and ᴍᴇ *ū*, which, like ᴍᴇ *ī*, has as its first element a sound approaching the broad *a*, plus *oo* (p. 86). These descriptions seem to indicate that ᴍᴇ *ī, ū*, had reached the usual present-day value, since Webster very definitely does not equate or even compare the first element with the centralized vowel of *tun*. He seems quite clear on the distinction between vowels and diphthongs, and offers no evidence of an off-glide in *feet, late, cart, fall*, or *fool*.

CONCLUSIONS

First, none of the English orthoepists show any merger of ME *ę̄* and *ā* in Standard English. Tuite mentions ᴍᴇ *ā* as a possible pronunciation of ME *ę̄*, but says that ᴍᴇ *ę̄* is the more usual pronunciation for Londoners. *The Writing Scholar's Companion* is the first work to unequivocally show coalescence of ME *ę̄* and *ẹ̄*; prior to this ME *ę̄* is distinct from both ME *ẹ̄* and ME *ā*, and after this Tuite, Douglas, and Webster all give ᴍᴇ *ẹ̄* for ME *ę̄* words.

Hart and Bellot both show a merger of ME *ai* and *ę̄* as monophthongal [ē] or [ɛ], and Gil and Butler describe this as a current nonstandard pronunciation of ME *ai* of which they disapprove. Robinson shows optional monophthongization of ME *ai* to merge with ᴍᴇ *ā*, and the coalescence of ME *ai, ā*, is shown by the later grammarians and orthoepists such as the author of *The Writing Scholar's Companion*, Cooper, and Tuite, though many of the writers, such as Wallis and Wilkins, still describe a diphthongal pronunciation for ME *ai*. ME *ou* is early described as a diphthong, and Hart, Gil, and Butler show it as a diphthong differing from ᴍᴇ *ū* only by having a tense first element. Hodges, Hart (sometimes), Wilkins, Coles, *The Writing Scholar's Companion*, Tuite, and Webster all show it as a monophthong identical with ᴍᴇ *ọ̄*. ME *au* is described as a diphthong by Hart, Mulcaster, and Daines, but is usually described as a monophthong approximating to [ɔ]. In general, then, ME *ai, au, ou*, are often described as diphthongs, particularly by the earlier orthoepists, but later are more often described as monophthongs, ME *ai*, *ou*, merging with με *ą̄*, *ǭ*.

ME *ę̄u*, *ẹ̄u*, are kept distinct by many writers, e.g. Hart, Robinson, Gil, Butler, Daines, Wallis, Wilkins, Holder, and Coles, but are merged in Cooper, *The Writing Scholar's Companion*, and Tuite. This corresponds with the merger of ME *ę̄* and *ẹ̄*, except for Cooper. No conclusion can be drawn as regards the development of ME *oi*, *ui*, except that there seem to have been at least two pronunciations, originally /oy/, /uy/, later /oy/, /əy/, which did not correspond in distribution with the etymological distinction.

As noted in the sections on the individual writers, several seem to have been quite capable of distinguishing a diphthong from a monophthong, Gil giving a particularly good description of an off-glide in *ai*, and Cooper outlining in some detail the theoretical possibilities for diphthongs in English. They certainly perceived some sounds as long tense vowels and others as diphthongs, and it would seem unwise to assume that their perception was necessarily faulty.

The first suggestion of the lowering and centralization of /u/ to /ə/ is in Daines, but Hodges is the first to clearly distinguish two pronunciations of ME *u* and /u/ < /ū/ < ME *ǭ*. After Hodges all writers show this distinction (except perhaps Holder, who is not clear on this subject), though there is considerable disagreement about which words belong in which class, and occasionally the same lexical items are shown in both classes, as in Wilkins. Hodges does not identify the pronunciation of με *ī*, but με *ū* is given as /ow/, without centralization of the first element.

The orthoepists offer no support whatsoever for the claim (cf. Chapter I) that centralization preceded lowering. It has, however, been suggested that the descriptions of the orthoepists of με *ī*, *ū*, as /ey/, /ow/, respectively, should be interpreted as indicating /əy/, /əw/, and often this is done without any explanation or acknowledgment at all (cf. Kökeritz's remarks on Wodroephe, Chapter I). The usual explanation for the discrepancy between the early transcriptions and descriptions and the desired interpretation is that the early orthoepists could not recognize a centralized vowel, and that they were handicapped by the English alphabet's having no symbol for /ə/. One argument against this is that Robinson invented a completely new set of symbols, even giving different ones for long and short vowels, yet he did not show /ə/ as a variant of ME *u*, and he still gave /ey/, /ow/, for με *ī*, *ū*. Second, all orthoepists before Hodges give /ey/, /ow/, while those after Hodges show /əy/ /əw/. Assuming that all the earlier orthoepists really heard /əy/, /əw/, we then have to explain: (*a*) why none of the orthoepists writing before Hodges could recognize /ə/, while those writing later all could; this seems to indicate a sudden and surprising improvement in phonetic perception; (*b*) why all of the pre-Hodges orthoepists were handicapped so badly by the English alphabet (including Robinson, who didn't even use it), while the post-Hodges orthoepists were not; here we have a sudden and surprising increase in ingenuity; and (*c*) why the early orthoepists, at least some of whom seem well able to distinguish front from back vowels, all distinguished different first elements in με ī, ū, and equated them with /e/, /o/, respectively, whereas the later writers heard the same first element in both (except Wallis, who claimed to distinguish two centralized vowels) and equated it with the vowel in, e.g., *nut*; here we have an early tendency to hear nonexistent differences, and to make erroneous equivalences, which ended abruptly with Hodges.

These considerations seem to me to make very improbable the assumption that με ī, ū, are always to be interpreted as being /əy/, /əw/. A much simpler and more straightforward interpretation is that there was an actual sound change, and that Hodges (or possibly Daines) is the first to show any trace of this.

Note that even if it could in some at present unimaginable way be shown that Hart, Gil, Robinson, and Bellot in fact heard /əy/, /əw/, this would not prove that centralization preceded lowering. It would show simply that the diphthong first recorded had both centralized and lowered, and it would still be possible to claim that lowering was the first rule. On the other hand, centralization can be shown not to have preceded lowering if there are dialects with /ey/, /ow/, earlier than those with /əy/, /əw/. It therefore seems that those who support lowering before centralization have a possibility of proving their case, whereas the best the advocates of centralization before lowering can hope for is a verdict of "Not proven."

All orthoepists illustrate the shortening of /ū/ < ME ǭ, though again there is variation in the words assigned to each class, and often words are shown with /u/ which have /ū/ in ModE. Hart and Mulcaster both show a back-glide after *a*, *o*, before *l‡* or *lC*; later writers show this /aw/ monophthongized to [ɔ], presumably by the same rules rounding and monophthongizing the original ME *au* (cf. discussion in Chapter VI). Cooper also shows lengthening of ME *a*, *o*, before certain consonant combinations; *The Writing Scholar's Companion* confirms this for *o*, and Douglas for *a*. Rounding of *a* to [ɔ] following *w* is not shown in Hart, but occurs sporadically later. It is not shown as a general rule, comparable to the rounding before *l*. The early writers all show ME *o* as the short equivalent of µε *ǭ*; however, Hodges and later writers show ME *o* as the short equivalent of µε *au*. The lowering of ME *o* to /ɔ/ thus seems to correspond diachronically with the lowering and centralization of ME *u* to /ə/.

CHAPTER IV

In this chapter the evidence from rhymes, from occasional spellings, and from shorthand systems will be considered. Except for some rhyme evidence from Middle English, primary sources have not been consulted; I am only reporting the findings of earlier workers in these areas.

THE EVIDENCE FROM RHYME

We may consider the evidence of rhymes as coming from three sources: from rhyme lists in orthoepists such as Cooper, Hodges, and Coles, from rhyming dictionaries, and from rhymes used naturally in poetry. We shall see that these three sources do not yield the same kind of evidence. I am concerned here with the evidence of rhyme only as it affects vowels participating in the Vowel Shift, not with consonants or vowel changes other than those of the Vowel Shift.

Neither Dobson (1957a) nor Zachrisson (1913; 1927) concern themselves with rhymes in poetry. Zachrisson notes that of three possible criteria by which we can ascertain the pronunciation of English at any particular period, namely othoepistical description, occasional spellings, and rhyme, "the rhymes afford us the least assistance, particularly when it is a question of dating the sound-changes" (1913, p. 3), and that Wyld's work on rhymes (1927, p. viii) ". . . does not settle the difficult question to what extent the early rhymes reflect the actual contemporary pronunciation or to what extent they are traditional, influenced by the spelling, or due to poetic licence . . ." Wrenn

(p. 34) believes that "The orthography of rhymes as a criterion for pronunciation ... has been used far too confidently," and describes five kinds of rhymes "especially likely to become sources of erroneous conclusions about pronunciation." The only rhymes Zachrisson takes into account are lists in, e.g., Cooper. In addition to these lists, Dobson uses the rhyming dictionaries of Thomas Willis (1651) and Joshua Poole (1657), and he includes the first table from Coles (1674) in this kind of evidence. He includes this evidence while excluding the rhymes of poets on the grounds that "a rhyming dictionary should ideally include only exact rhymes," and in particular "such rhymes as are good in correct educated speech" (Dobson (1957a, p. 422)). However, Dobson admits that rhyming dictionaries for many reasons often fall short of this standard (p. 423). Kökeritz claims (1953, p. 31) that:

As a criterion of early NE pronunciation, Shakespeare's rhymes and, for that matter, the rhymes of any 16th- or 17th-century English poet are not so dependable as the reliable phonetic spelling or homonymic pun. The reason is, of course, that already in the 16th century, and probably earlier, there had apparently developed a rhyming tradition that was to some extent independent of the contemporary pronunciation.

Possibly for this reason, Kökeritz lists rhymes alphabetically, but gives no analysis or statistical breakdown of them. He gives no justification for his claim that phonetic spellings and puns are more reliable evidence.

In Willis με ai and με $\bar{a}$ are never rhymed, even before r. Willis also distinguishes με $\bar{e}$ and με $\bar{e}$; Dobson assumes the pronunciations of these to be [ɛ] and [ī] before r respectively, though the second pronunciation has some examples of words which in ME had $\bar{e}$ which had apparently raised to με $\bar{e}$, as we would expect. There is no evidence that με $\bar{a}$ and με $\bar{e}$ are alike. Willis does not distinguish /u/ and /ə/, although at this date we would expect him to; Dobson suggests that he regarded them as free allophonic variants. ME $\bar{e}u$, $\bar{e}u$, are not distinguished.

Dobson regards Poole as the least reliable of the dictionaries used. Poole shows identity of ME $\bar{u}$, ou, and /ow/ < /o/ before l; since these words are not shown to rhyme with ME $\bar{o}$, we may assume that they were diphthongal. Dobson assumes that this is a dialectal pronunciation. Since in, e.g., Gil and Butler the only difference between με $\bar{u}$ and με ou is in the length of the first element, the simplest explanation seems to be that Poole has shortened the /ō/ in ME ou, and that all three word classes now have /ow/. However, this is pure speculation.[1] Poole does not distinguish between ME *ai* and *ā*, nor between /u/ and /ə/. Like Willis, ME *ęu*, *ęu*, are merged. ME *ę̄* and *ę* have merged before *r* (except, I assume, though Dobson does not say, for those words in which ME *ę̄* before *r* merged with με *ā*), but generally Poole distinguishes ME *ę̄* and *ę*.

Coles's rhyme list occurs as part of *The Compleat English Schoolmaster*, and the evidence from this was therefore discussed earlier (cf. Chapter III).

The evidence of rhyme in poetry is presented and discussed in Wyld (1923), and from this he draws (and states as categorical facts) some rather surprising conclusions about the merger of ME *ę̄*, *ā*, and *ai* in educated English (cf. discussion in Chapter I). He lists many examples showing their merger in poetry, such as *please/days* (Surrey), *break/betake* (Sackville), *mead/braid* (Drayton), *sea/way* (Waller). However, Wyld notes: (*a*) that such rhymes are not common in sixteenth-, seventeenth-, and early eighteenth-century poets; (*b*) that some poets, e.g. Milton, never used them at all; and (*c*) that they are rare in any poet except Swift (who perhaps had an Irish pronunciation here, and in ModIr ME *ę̄* is /ey/). Wyld's explanation of these facts is that poets don't like rhyming words which are not spelt alike. Like Dobson, Wyld assumes (1923, pp. 51-52) that merger of ME *ę̄* and *ę* came from a nonstandard dialect.

Wyld next adduces evidence from occasional spellings to support his conclusions, such as *maid* (*made*), *saive* (*save*), *pane* (*pain*), *credyll* (*cradle*), *bare* (*ber* = *bier*), and *discrate* (*discreet*) (p. 54). He then brings forward his confirmatory data from grammarians. First, he says that Cooper gives *mate/meat* the same vowel. This is, however, not true; the word Cooper equates with the *ea* class is *mete*, not *mate* (Sundby, pp. 10, 12), as noted by Zachrisson (1927, p. 39), and indeed Wyld himself at one point gives the correct pairing (Wyld (1936, p. 172)). Next, Wyld claims that in Cooper *praise*, *convey*, have the same vowel as *cane*, and that Cooper generally merges ME *ę̄*, *ā*, and *ai*. Again this is incorrect; Cooper merges ME *ā*, *ai*, but keeps ME *ę̄* distinct. Dobson (1957*a*, pp. 291, 298 n. 1) points out that Wyld has misunderstood Cooper. Finally, Wyld says that Wallis describes English *ei*, *ea*, as having the sound *é clarum*. Wallis's *e* masculine, when short, is the sound represented orthographically by *e*, and when long the sound represented by *ea*, and occasionally by *ei*. But (as pointed out by Dobson (1957*a*, p. 241)) the examples are *seize*, *deceit*, *receive*, all of which varied in ME between *ei* and *ę̄*. In addition, it should be remembered that rhyme lists in, e.g., Cooper, Hodges, Coles, all have ME $\bar{e}$ distinct from με $\bar{a}$. Therefore, Wyld's statement (p. 55) "Thus the testimony of the Occasional Spellings and that of the Grammarians agree, and both are in accord with the usage of the poets . . ." is simply not correct.

Further, when one does get data on a merger of ME $\bar{e}$, $\bar{a}$, ai, the evidence indicates very different conclusions about Standard English from those Wyld draws, since it was shown that Tuite (1726) notes that ME $\bar{e}$ may be pronounced either like με $\bar{e}$ or like με $\bar{a}$, but that the majority of Londoners pronounced it as με $\bar{e}$. It should be noted also that we have no English orthoepistical evidence of any merger of ME $\bar{a}$ and $\bar{e}$ prior to the eighteenth century—two hundred years after Wyld claims they became identical.

Gabrielson seems to show approximately as many rhymes of the ME $\bar{e}/\bar{e}$ type as of the $\bar{e}/\bar{a}/ai$ type, but for some reason dismisses the $\bar{e}/\bar{e}$ rhymes in Spencer and Pope as being "purely traditional" (pp. 118-119), and inspection of Kökeritz's index to Shakespeare's rhymes shows similar results (1953, pp. 399-495). Kökeritz adduces a great many homonymic puns which depend on the identity of ME $\bar{e}/\bar{a}/ai$, but since he assumes this identity as a method of discovering the puns (p. 62), these examples cannot then be used as independent evidence for the merger. Conversely, since he rejects suggested $\bar{e}/\bar{e}$ puns on the assumption that these sounds were **not** identical (p. 88), his failure to list such puns cannot be construed as evidence against such a merger. Kökeritz (1965) notes that Wyatt often spelled both ME $\bar{e}$ and $\bar{e}$ with i, y, and that his rhymes show that the two had completely fallen together as [ī]. He takes this to be a dialectal trait in Wyatt indicative of his Kentish origins. However, since Wyatt was a member of the court, it can equally well be taken as illustrating court dialect.

Wyld notes (1923, p. 58) that rhymes of ME $\bar{e}$, $\bar{e}$, are rare before the eighteenth century, which is what we would expect, since even as late as Cooper they are apparently distinct.[2] Wyld does cite a few early occasional spellings (p. 61) and rhymes (p. 60) of this kind, and points out also that Gil denounces this as an advanced pronunciation. Wyld does not seem to have noticed other examples of such raising, e.g. Hart's $kl\bar{i}n$ ($clean$), which show that idiosyncratic raising, anticipating the later general rule, occurred quite early.

Wyld devotes four pages (63-67) to the discussion of ME $\bar{e}$, $\bar{e}$, before r, noting that generally ME $\bar{e}$ did not raise to με $\bar{e}$ so often in this environment as it did otherwise.[3] He shows that this divergence in the grammarians is reflected in the rhymes, but does not say that this is the **only** environment in which ME $\bar{e}/\bar{a}/ai$ are shown as triplets in rhyme lists, e.g. *pair/pare/pear*. He notes that both occasional spellings and rhymes support rounding of *a* following *w* (pp. 67-69), and also the unrounding of *o*, as criticized by Gil (Wyld (1923, pp. 70-72)). He cites examples (pp. 73-75) of ME *oi, ui*, rhyming with ME $\bar{i}$, and seems to think that all ME *oi, ui*, words originally rhymed this way, and that /oy/ is a "restored pronunciation"; he says that [oi] is "apparently the present pronunciation based on the spelling" (p. 74). He illustrates the utter confusion of writers on the subject, which is certainly evident enough in Dobson and in the primary sources.

The merger of ME *oi/ui/ī* is usually taken to indicate a pronunciation /əy/. However, according to Zachrisson (1927, p. 55) there are also instances of ME $\bar{i}$ rhyming with ME *ai/ei* (though he cites none and gives no references), which indicates lowering without centralization. *Athelstan*, a medieval metrical romance, has the rhymes *prayer/choir* (lines 429-430); *prayer/fire* (lines 631-632); and *said/tied* (lines 801-802) (Sands, pp. 143, 148, 153). The dialect of this poem is usually taken to be Midlands, with some Northern features, and the date of composition 1350-1400. Other examples are *laid/pride* from *Floris and Blancheflour*, the language of which is late fourteenth century East Midlands (Sands, p. 296, lines 577-578), and *byse (grey)/preyse (appraise)* from *Sir Gawayn and the Carl of Carlisle*, the manuscript of which is late 15th century, and the language a mixture of Northern and Midlands (Sands, p. 370, lines 609, 612). Rhymes which may perhaps indicate /ey/ for ME $\bar{i}$ are *might/said, milde/feld* (/ey/:/ē/), *Carlisle/well* (/ey/:/e/), *ende/kinde* (/ē/:/ey/), and *maner/shire* (/ē/:/ey/), all from *The Wedding of Sir Gawayn and Dame Ragnell* (Sands, pp. 326-347, lines 52-53, 112-113, 127-128, 167-168, 557-558); the only manuscript is dated ca. 1500, and the language is East Midlands. Gabrielson (p. 52) cites *repine/slain* from Spenser. Similarly, rhymes between ME $\bar{u}$ and ME *ou*, e.g. *avow/flow* (Palladius, ca. 1420, cited by Zachrisson (1927), p. 59), and *town/atone*, from *The Wedding of Sir Gawayn and Dame Ragnell* (Sands, p. 335, lines 381-382), evidence lowering of the first element of ME $\bar{u}$ without centralization.

From rhyme evidence Wyld documents the *flood/good/food* differentiation (pp. 75-82) and assumes (pp. 76-77) that words which did not unround all shortened later, and therefore missed unrounding, though he documents the fluctuation between two variant pronunciations in many instances (p. 78). He says that "before -**k** as in *hook, shook*, etc., we invariably have the later shortening" (p. 77). But we know from, e.g., Bellot that words like *book* shortened quite early, so that all Wyld can really deduce is that lowering and unrounding of /u/ < /ū/ < ME ǭ did not occur before *k*, although all ME *u* > [ʌ] in this environment, even after labials.

Like the occasional spellings, rhyme evidences the widespread lowering of ME *i* to /e/.

THE EVIDENCE OF OCCASIONAL SPELLINGS

Occasional spellings are used as evidence by Zachrisson (1913; 1927), and by Wyld (1923; 1927; 1936), but not by Dobson (1957*a*), who points out that we have no way of telling whether the person writing spoke Standard English or not, and comments rather acidly (p. 197) that it seems ". . . unreasonable and unscientific to prefer the accidental mis-spellings of imperfectly literate people, however well born, to the intentionally phonetic transcriptions of intelligent and well-educated men who understood phonetic principle." Wrenn also criticizes what he terms "an exaggerated belief in the significance of the evidential value of spelling" (p. 167), and asks: "How many of the spellings of what we call in common parlance an illiterate person have really anything to do with his pronunciations?" A distrust of occasional spellings has also been expressed by Wilson (1963, p. 206), who says that ". . . it must be emphasized that only when the number of examples is large enough to be statistically significant is it safe to use them as evidence. Occasional spellings may or may not be significant; no use can be made of them because it can never be certain that their explanation is linguistic and not psychological." My own feeling is that anyone who has corrected many high school essays will be reluctant to ascribe much if any phonetic accuracy to occasional spellings.

This kind of evidence is, however, valued highly by Zachrisson, who accepts it while rejecting that of rhymes. Zachrisson (1913) relies partly on original letters of the fifteenth century, but uses also collections of official documents, of literature of the fifteenth century, and of letters and printed works of the sixteenth century. He distinguishes between *irregular spellings*, which arise through various kinds of orthographic confusion, *phonetic doublets*, which show alternate forms arising from different dialects, and *phonetic spellings*, which alone "can be used as evidence on the contemporary pronunciation." However, it is not always easy to understand Zachrisson's discussion of these categories. Thus, when discussing irregular spellings, he instances the spelling of ME *ū* as *ou*, where, he claims, "this

use of ou might be *analogically transferred* also to other words, where
ou has no historical justification" (1913, p. 54). He discusses other
such variations as *er/ar* and *au/a*, and then goes on to state: "On the
other hand, I do not believe that an orthographic vacillation between
two symbols could be transferred under any circumstances to words
where only one of the two symbols was historically justified (mechanical
transference)." Yet this is, it would seem, the same process he has
just been claiming can occur, and has discussed as analogical transference. Further, he says (1913, p. 55) that if ". . . irregular forms
are used independently by two or more than two writers, we may be
fairly certain they represent two different pronunciations, i.e. they
should be looked upon as phonetic *doublets*, not as phonetic *spellings*."
It seems strange to reject evidence when it is confirmed by more than
one source, and would seem logically to lead one to accept as reliable
phonetic spellings only those which occur infrequently. This cannot
be what Zachrisson means, since he quotes many examples from different sources (as does Wyld). Possibly he means that if the same
word turns up more than once in the same variant spelling it should
be excluded as evidence. In any case, it is not easy to decide just
what Zachrisson's principles of discrimination are.

Wyld also makes great use of occasional spellings, and, indeed,
believes that this kind of evidence should be preferred to orthoepistical.
He believes that if the statements of grammarians seem to oppose
"the plain facts, as revealed again and again by the occasional spellings" (1936, p. 116), then the grammarians should be disregarded.
We shall consider his evidence along with Zachrisson's, noting here
only that it is not always as easy to determine "the plain facts" from
the spelling as Wyld seems to think. Unlike Zachrisson, who considered
the orthographical evidence separately from the orthoepistical, and
gave his conclusions from this evidence alone, Wyld considers orthoepistical, orthographical, and rhyme evidence together and gives a combined conclusion.

Zachrisson (1913) gives many examples of *e* spellings for ME *ā*,
and from these concludes that ME *ā* had raised to [æ] or [ɛ] as early
as the fifteenth century (p. 56). He has very few spellings of *e* for
a or of *a* for ME *ę̄*. Zachrisson finds some examples of *o* for *a* following
a labial consonant, which he takes to indicate rounding in this environment. He cites a few examples of *ai* for ME *ā* and several of
a for *ai*, concluding "that as early as the 15th century *ā* and *ai* had
been levelled under the same sound or at least were very much alike"
(1913, p. 65). Zachrisson also quotes examples of an *e* spelling for

ei, ai, and states that these "corroborate my previous conclusion as to the great approximation in sound between *ā* and *ai, ei*" (1913, p. 67). Wyld cites spellings of *e* for ME *ā,* and of *e, ea,* and *a* for ME *ai,* from the beginning of the fifteenth century on (1927, §§ 225, 268; 1936, pp. 248-249). He notes also a few inverted spellings of *ai* for *a,* e.g. *maid (made), tayking (taking).* Because of this, he assumes that ME *ai, ā,* had merged, and that both were identical with ME *ę̄,* although the spelling evidence he quotes for a merger of ME *ę̄, ā,* is very sparse (e.g., the reverse spelling *discrate* for *discreet* (1927, p. 196)), since he appears to depend mainly on rhymes to support this claim.

Zachrisson (1913) does not claim that ME *ę̄* merged with ME *ai, ā,* but, discussing ME *ẹ̄,* notes that although ME *ẹ̄* is frequently spelled with *i, y,* indicating that it has been raised to /ī/, this spelling is never used for ME *ę̄,* and that the two sounds are always kept distinct. However, in his later work he concludes that in some dialects ME *ę̄, ā,* and *ai* had merged (Zachrisson (1927, p. 43)), and, from the occasional spellings, that in other dialects ME *ę̄, ẹ̄,* had merged (1927, pp. 43-44). Wyld quotes several examples of *i, y,* for ME *ę̄,* e.g. *prych (preach), spyking (speaking),* and concludes that in some dialects ME *ę̄, ẹ̄,* had merged (1927, p. 172).

ME *ī* is frequently spelled *ei, ey,* sometimes *e,* and occasionally *ai* and *oi.* Zachrisson states (1913, p. 73): "In my opinion, *ei* is a phonetic spelling, used to symbolize the diphthong into which ME *ī* had developed." He feels that it could be meant to represent either /ey/ or /əy/, and that the instance of *ai* and *oi* suggests that /əy/ is the more likely value, since if ME *oi* and *ī* were alike, "this common pronunciation must have been (əi)" (1913, p. 89), which agrees with Wyld's conclusion (cf. below). Zachrisson (1913, p. 76) believes that "the spelling *ai* for *ī* . . . points to a pronunciation (əi) or even (ai) . . ." and he notes that this spelling is often used to denote a broad, Northern pronunciation. But it seems that another interpretation is possible. To believe that the spellings *ai, ay,* meant /ay/ accords with modern phonetic representation, but not with what the spellings indicated to speakers of ME or of EModE. At that time με *ai* was probably /ɛy/ or /ey/, and the rhymes between ME *ai* and ME *ī* (cf. above) suggest that occasional spellings of *ai, ay,* for ME *ī* may in fact represent /ey/. It is not very likely that ME *ī, ai,* rhymed as /əy/, since there is no evidence that ME *ai* was ever /əy/ (except in Wallis (1765, p. 36); cf. Chapter III, n. 21). Wyld also cites several examples of *ey* for ME *ī,* and claims that "the stage [ai] [by which he means [əi]] was reached before the end of the 15th century" (1927, § 254, p. 187) since spellings like *oi, oy* for ME *ī*, as in *defoyled*, show that ME *ī* and *oi* had merged.

ME *ǭ* is frequently spelled *ou, ow* (the normal spelling for ME *ū*) and sometimes *u*, indicating that με *ǭ* is /ū/. Examples of this are cited by both Zachrisson (1913, pp. 77-78) and by Wyld (1927, § 236). Zachrisson cites some examples of *au, aw*, for με *ū*, concluding that this indicates a diphthongal pronunciation, and, from the use of *au* rather than *ou*, that (1913, p. 79) ". . . the first element of the diphthong thus represented was neither (u) nor (o), but either (a) or a mixed sound (ə) not differing much from the one used in modern pronunciation." Wyld adds nothing to this, merely citing Zachrisson's examples.

Zachrisson first believed that the spellings of *a* for *o* indicate an attempt to render graphically the new sound /ə/ that had developed from ME *u* (1913, p. 81). He does not explain why, if /ə/ was a reflex of ME *u*, this spelling is used for ME *o* words (which became [ɒ], not [ə]) rather than for ME *u*. It seems more likely that such spellings represent an unrounding of *o* to something like [ɑ] (cf. discussion of Gil, Chapter III). This is the interpretation of Wyld, who cites many examples, e.g. *yander* (*yonder*), *hars* (*horse*), *caffin* (*coffin*) (1927, § 244; 1936, pp. 240-241). Later (1927, p. 70) Zachrisson also simply says that this is evidence of unrounding, and cites Gil's remarks on the Mopsey dialect.

Both Wyld and Zachrisson cite spellings of *o, ow*, for ME *au*, and also the reverse, i.e., *au, aw*, for ME *ǭ* and *o*, which seems to show that με *au* was a rounded monophthong. Zachrisson thinks that ME *au* > [ɔ] "as early as the second half of the 15th century" and says that there is some suggestive but not conclusive evidence from the first half (1927, pp. 65-68). He takes the use of *o, oo*, for ME *ǭ* and for *o* before *l*C to indicate that ME "*ow* and *ǭ* were pronounced alike, or very nearly so," though, as he observes, even if they had merged "the spelling is no very safe guide as to the exact development of this sound" (1913, p. 83). He points out that since a diphthongal representation is often given where the conventional spelling has a simple vowel, e.g. *old*, then the evidence seems against believing that the orthoepists and grammarians described the sound as diphthongal simply because they were influenced by traditional spelling (1927, p. 75). For some reason, Wyld does not discuss the development of this diphthong.

Zachrisson believes that ME *ēu* and *u* < Fr. [y(:)] had merged, since *u* is used as a spelling for both, that ME *ēu* was distinct, since this is never spelled *u*, and that the first element of ME *ēu* had raised to

/ī/ contemporaneously with ME ę̄ becoming /ī/, since we find the spelling *iw* also. He concludes that the pronunciation was [ju:] in 15th-century Standard English. Wyld (1927, §§ 265-267) notes that all eventually merge as /yuw/, but does not give any date for this.

Wyld documents in some detail the lowering of ME *i* to /e/ in some dialects, citing, e.g., *gresly* (*grisly*), *merour* (*mirror*), *fenyshe* (*finish*) (1936, pp. 226-229). This is important both for one possible explanation of a problem connected with shortening and lengthening in ME (cf. Chapter V) and also for paralleling the change ME *ī* > /ey/. If ME *ī* did first diphthongize to /iy/, then there seems no reason to regard the lowering of the first element to /e/ as improbable when this parallel change in the short vowels is accepted by so many writers and supported by numerous spellings.

In general, there is great agreement between Wyld and Zachrisson (which is not surprising, since Wyld seems to use a lot of Zachrisson's examples); however, there are some differences. First, whereas Zachrisson differentiates the development of ME ǭu, ọu, Wyld does not. Similarly, Zachrisson first appears to postulate a value for ME ę̄ distinct from both ME ẹ̄ and ME ā; Wyld, on the other hand, suggests two developments for ME ę̄, in one of which it merges with ME ẹ̄ and in the other with ME ā, apparently believing that it lost its distinct identity quite early, and Zachrisson later seems to agree with this. In Zachrisson's earlier interpretation, ME ę̄ could follow the same path both in isolation and as the first element of the diphthong ę̄u; Wyld's interpretation would allow this only in the dialects which merged ME ẹ̄, ę̄. Wyld provides a more convincing explanation of the spellings *a* for *o*, which agrees with the rhyme and orthoepistical evidence. Zachrisson does not comment on the lowering of ME *i* to /e/, and Wyld does not discuss the development of ME *ou*.

THE EVIDENCE FROM WRITERS OF SHORTHAND SYSTEMS

The works of writers of shorthand systems have been treated by Dobson (1957*a*), Kökeritz (1935), and Matthews (1936 and 1943). The evidence is most conveniently summarized and clearly presented in Matthews (1943), but Kökeritz's article is valuable in that it reproduces some sections of the works which discuss the pronunciation and articulation of the various sounds, rather like the orthoepistical works; I shall therefore depend mostly on Matthews (1943), but will also make use of the sources as cited by Kökeritz. Since Dobson does not treat of any writers later than 1700, many of the sources used by Kö-keritz and Matthews are necessarily not mentioned at all in his account.

All these scholars point out that phonetic shorthand has only lim-ited value for establishing the pronunciation of vowels and diph-thongs, since it was then (as it still is) standard practice to omit the vowels in shorthand. Further, digraphs were often represented as single vowels, since a common way of shortening the representation was mechanically to ignore one of the orthographic letters and use the other only, regardless of whether the pronunciation was diphthongal or monophthongal, and if the latter, regardless of which letter more nearly represented the pronunciation. Further, as Matthews (1943, p. 137) points out, no phonetic shorthand consistently follows pro-nunciation; all systems compromise between phonetic representation and conventional orthography. Matthews notes, for example, that in Pitman shorthand the /ə/ in *sir, surd, certain*, is represented as short *i*, short *u*, and short *e*, respectively, and that the system does not pro-vide at all for /ə/. For this reason, the evidence provided in the dis-cussion of the vowels, as distinct from that provided by the transcrip-tions themselves, is particularly welcome.

Matthews lists (1943, p. 143) some points on which he feels the shorthand writers provide some help. Those with which I am here concerned are: (*a*) the merging of ME $\bar{e}$ as in *steal* with ME $\bar{a}$, $\bar{e}$; (*b*) the variant pronunciations of *oi* as in *loin*; (*c*) the pronunciation of ME $\bar{\imath}$, as in *life*; and (*d*) the pronunciation of ME $\bar{u}$, as in *house*. I shall, never-theless, summarize what evidence there is for all vowels and diphthongs, but will first present the evidence from the Appendix in William Tiffin (1751): *A New Help and Improvement of the Art of Swift Writing*, and W. Holdsworth and W. Aldridge (1766): *Natural Shorthand*.

Tiffin, whom Matthews (1936, p. 97) calls "the best of the early phoneticians," claims that there are nine distinct vowel sounds, five of which may be either long or short, and gives the following table (Kökeritz (1935, p. 91)):

	1	2	3	4	5	6	7	8	9
Long	arm	Ale	eat	eel	all	O		ooze	herb
Short	am	ell	it		of		up	good	

He very specifically claims that the long and short variants are iden-tical in quality, and says that though some people may be misled, e.g. by spelling, to think them different, if they pronounce them "clear-ly and with deliberation" then his claim will be found to be correct.

He gives several examples for the beginner to practice with, in which we may observe that *great* is assigned to 2, not 3, and that whereas *George, sort,* are assigned to 5, *fort* is listed under 6. Later he gives articulatory descriptions for all of these sounds (Kökeritz (1935, pp. 95-96)):

1. Lay the upper Side or Surface of the Tongue, all the Way, level (or nearly so) to the under Lip, with it's Edges just high enough to lie against the upper Jaw-Teeth, unclose the Lips quite to the Corners of the Mouth: and in that Position you may sound the Vowel that is represented by an a in *Bar, bad, Father,* &c.

2. Begin at the hinder Part to swell up the Ball of the Tongue as far forward as the hinder Part of the Bone of the Roof, and let it's Edges feel the upper Jaw-Gums; and the Vowel sounded in that Figure will be that intended by the a in *Ale,* and by the E in *Ell.*

3. Advance the Swelling of the Tongue about half Way forward under the Bone of the Roof, and let the Edges press the upper Jaw-Gums a little; and there you meet the Vowel spelt with *ea* in *eat*; and as I think, that spelt with *i* in *it.*

4. Bring the Swelling as near as ever to the Roof of the Mouth and fore Gum, hold the Edges of the Tongue somewhat stiff against the upper Jaw-Gums; and so you pronounce the fourth Vowel, as in *see, seen, Eel,* &c.

N. In these forename'd Vowels, the Lips were to be unclose'd quite to the Corners of the Mouth, or very near; in the five following they must be close'd a little, and to be sure a little more than they shou'd in the first four.

5. Sink the upper Surface of the Tongue all the Way below the Level of the under Lip, as low as ever you do (supposeing you to be an Englishman) when you speak, and (the Mouth being close'd a little at the Corners) the fifth Vowel will be sounded, as in *all, saw, Saul, trott,* &c.

6. Let the hinder Part of the Tongue rise a little, draw the Tip of it down inward, close the lips about one third Part at each Corner, and form a roundish Hole in the remaining third Part in the middle, and this will give the Sound of the sixth Vowel, ô, *Toe, sole.*

7. Advance the Rising of Swelling of the Tongue somewhat forwarder, let the lips open again towards, but not quite so near to the Corners of the Mouth as in the first four Vowels, the Tip of the Tongue stand slopeing downward with some little hollow Space under it: and the Vowel so sounded will be the seventh, as in *up, but, curl, come,* &c.

8. Do but advance the Lips forward from the fore-Gums, affecting the Form of the Spout, and you can't miss sounding right the eighth Vowel in *ooze, too, Shoe, shoot,* &c.

9. The ninth Vowel being of small Concern in swift Writing is therefore the less necessary to be nicely describe'd; however if the Learner is willing to give so much Attention, he may hit upon the true Pronunciation of it, by placeing his Lips and Ball of his Tongue as for the first vowel, and the Tip of his Tongue as for the seventh.

Tiffin also comments on the various vowels, giving in the process much interesting information on the various dialects—for instance, that in the Midlands *great* is often pronounced with vowel 3 or 4. But his vowel chart and subsequent annotation are perhaps most interesting in the confirmation they give to Cooper's analysis of ME ẹ̄. Like Cooper, Tiffin equates the vowel of *eat* with that of *it,* but claims that the vowel of *eat* is not the same as that of *eel.* Since this is considerably later than Cooper, it seems to suggest that in some dialects at least ME ẹ̄ long remained distinct from both με ę̄ and με ā. Further, in his discussion he notes that a friend of his believes that the vowel of *it* is the short equivalent of the vowel of *eel,* and that "the third Vowel doe's not occur short" (Kökeritz (1935, p. 93)), but Tiffin is confident that when this short vowel is prolonged, e.g. "In Melody, Scorn, Reproach, Expostulation and such Emphatical Expressions, the third I think is manifestly sounded in them, and not the fourth" (Kökeritz (1935, p. 93)). Note that his friend did not object to the distinction between *eat* and *eel,* but only to the identity assigned to the short vowel of *it.* Tiffin does not make a similar distinction in the back vowels; he was, then, not misled by any desire for symmetry, nor was he merely copying Cooper.

Tiffin's accuracy of discrimination is illustrated by his distinguishing the vowel 7, the [ʌ] of *but,* from vowel 9, the [ə] or [ɜ] of *herb, bird, sir.* He admits that his ninth vowel rarely occurs except "before an r accented" (Kökeritz (1935, p. 94)), but includes it because the sound is in his opinion different from 7. But he assigns the vowel of *curl* to 7, so in his opinion two different centralized vowels could occur before *r.* This should encourage us to believe him when he claims his long and short vowels differ only in quantity, since otherwise he would have had no reason for not counting 9 and 7 as long and short variants of one vowel.

Tiffin is particularly clear on the difference between simple vowels and diphthongs, claiming (Kökeritz (1935, p. 91)) that "A simple Vowel may be distinguish'd from a Diphthong by the Ear, by this Rule. The

Sound of a single Vowel continu's the same from first to last if drawn out never so long; therefore, if before you have done you hear yourself making a different Sound from what you begun with, then you have sounded at least a Diphthong, which makes two Sounds into one Breath . . ." He notes that, e.g., *ea* in *great, head, oa* in *road* ". . . if examine'd by the foregoing rule will be found to be simple Vowels. In like manner the common English Sound of i long and u long, will be found to be Diphthongs, though not commonly so reputed."

Tiffin considers ME *ai* to be most agreeably pronounced with 2-4, i.e., [ɛi], but notes that it sometimes is defectively pronounced with 2 only. He thinks the most agreeable pronunciation of ME *au*, as in *raw*, to be 5 only, i.e., [ɔ], but states that a 1-8 diphthong also occurs, though only in Suffolk. "3-8 is the genuin English of u long," he claims; he does not distinguish ME *ęu, ẹu*. I presume this to be [iu], since he differentiates it from ME *ū*, in his dialect 2-8, or [ɛu]. Kökeritz believes that Tiffin probably heard [əu] for ME *ū*, but if so there seems no reason why he should not have been able to hear, identify, and describe it correctly. He may have had a substandard pronunciation, but it should be remembered that Cooper recorded this variant as an ultrafashionable pronunciation. For ME *ou*, he gives the most common pronunciation as 5-8, i.e., [əu], but the most agreeable as 6-8, or, by some speakers, 6 only, namely [ou] or [ō]. ME *ī* he apparently pronounces as [ʌī], since he insists that the first element should be "as short as possible" and that the off-glide is "4 long." He also documents the existence of pronunciations 1-4, 5-4, and 4 only, "as for *Christ, Chraist, Chroist, Chreest*" (Kökeritz (1935, p. 97)). For ME *oi/ui* he gives the common pronunciation as [ɔi], but acknowledges also [oi] and [ʌi].

Tiffin is, of course, much too late to add anything to the question of the relative order of centralization and lowering; his evidence is, however, definitely against the analysis of the long tense vowels as vowels plus off-glide. Further, it is interesting to see that as late as the mid-eighteenth century he confirms the survival of the ME diphthongs; the sixteenth- and seventeenth-century grammarians and orthoepists are often condemned for describing these pronunciations, which supporters of the superior evidential value of rhymes and occasional spellings believe had disappeared much earlier. Description of diphthongal pronunciations is therefore usually held to indicate how artificial and outdated the pronunciation advocated by the orthoepists is. Tiffin's evidence confirms the accuracy of these earlier observations.

Finally, we note that it is possible that Tiffin, like Cooper, has a vowel system with four vowel heights. This depends on the value

assigned to the long and short variants of his vowel l. Since Tiffin
insists on their qualitative identity, they can only be [æ]/[ǣ] or [a]/[ā].
Kökeritz suggests that the flat tongue mentioned by Tiffin in his account of the articulation suggests a value of [ā] rather than [ǣ]; however, this is a much less likely value for *bat, am*, etc. Matthews (1943,
p. 148) assumes [æ]/[ǣ], but in his earlier study appears to think Tiffin
may have had [æ]/[ā] or [ā] (1936, p. 101).

Holdsworth and Aldridge give only six distinct vowels, each of
which may be either long or short. They give a table, which they
later expand with additional examples (Kökeritz (1935, pp. 102-103)).
Their vowels are then:

	1	2	3	4	5	6
Long	be	base	calf	bawl	bone	bloom
	cheese	fail	grant	call	comb	fool
	grief	great	half	malt	fort	goose
	leave	may	laugh	Paul	Noah	moon
	plea	laid	staff	tall	sole	room
Short	live	debt	am	cough	but	book
	rich	head	at	God	come	root
	sieve	well	that	what	love	took

They make no claims as to the qualitative identity of the vowel pairs,
and in the case of 5 the vowels are almost certainly not the same. We
are therefore free to conclude that the vowels in 3 are [æ]/[ā], but it is
possible that they are meant to be [æ]/[ǣ]. ME ę̄ is merged with με ę̄,
but here, too, *great* is an exception, being listed with με ā. Holdsworth
and Aldridge note "that the long *i* as in *thine*, and the long *u* as in *mute*,
are not inserted among the vowels. The reason is they are both diphthongs" (Kökeritz (1935, p. 102)). Like Tiffin, they assign to ME ī a
pronunciation compounded of 5 short and 1 long, i.e., [ʌī]; ME ę̄u, ę̄u,
apparently both have [iū].

According to Matthews, the shorthand evidence generally indicates
both diphthongal and monophthongal pronunciations of ME *ai*, even
in the eighteenth century, but "uniformly supports the monophthongic
pronunciation" of ME *au* (1943, p. 152). Both monophthongal and
diphthongal pronunciations of ME *ou* are shown; the shorthand transcripts more often show a monophthong, but this may be partly due
to the wish to shorten mechanically wherever possible. Tiffin's discussion clearly documents both types of pronunciation. Tiffin also
has the interesting comment that a monophthongal pronunciation of

ME *ou* in *thought, brought,* etc, "seems to be a modern Fashion" (Kökeritz (1935, p. 93)), and that there are people everywhere who still pronounce such words with a diphthong. It will be recalled that this was the only environment in which Robinson did not monophthongize ME *ou* to /ō/. Shorthand shows [iu] for both ME *ẹu* and *ęu* in the seventeenth and eighteenth centuries. Shorthand also supports the view that [ui], [ʌi], and [ɔi] were all possible pronunciations for words spelled with *oi*, e.g. *coin, poison.* Matthews notes that here again there is no clear distinction between words with ME *oi* and those with ME *ui*; it seems that the stenographers sometimes transcribed ME *oi* with *i,* and that ME *ui* is often given as *o* or *oi* (cf. Matthews (1943, p. 164)). This confirms the evidence of the orthoepists, rhymes, and occasional spellings, where the confusion seems to work both ways. Dobson often goes to great lengths to try to explain why ME *oi* words appear with /uy/ or /əy/.

ME *a* seems to have been fronted to [æ] before the seventeenth century, and by this date ME *ā* has been fronted too. The degree of raising varies for ME *ā*, [æ] being a probable value in the seventeenth century, while [ɛ] or [ē] are possible in the seventeenth and the more usual value in the eighteenth century. Matthews (1943) notes that the lengthening of ME *a* before, e.g., *r, f, st,* though attested by seventeenth-century orthoepists, is not indicated by shorthand before the eighteenth century, and that [ā] as opposed to [æ] is first shown in 1762. Again, there is no reliable shorthand evidence of the rounding of *a* following *w* until the eighteenth century, and even then Tiffin notes that *warn* and *war* are often pronounced with his first vowel, i.e., with [æ]. Matthews concludes that the rounded vowel was less common than the unrounded. However, all the shorthand evidence confirms the rounding of *a* before *l‡* or *lC.*

There is little indication of the exact quality of ME *e*. ME *ẹ* is uniformly given as [ī]. Most of the earlier stenographers indicate that ME *ę* was [ɛ] or [ē,] but in the eighteenth century there are indications that ME *ę* has raised to merge with με *ẹ*; however, it appears that [ē] for ME *ę* was still used.

ME *i* is usually (except for Tiffin) given as the short equivalent of με *ē*. Shorthand evidence indicates that there were four pronunciations of ME *ī* current in the seventeenth and eighteenth centuries: [əi] varying with [ī] in the North, [æi]/[ei], [ɔi], and [ʌi].

Most stenographers give ME *o* as the short equivalent of ME *au*; it was therefore probably [ɔ] or [ɑ]. There is very little evidence of unrounding. ME *ǭ* is generally indicated as having raised to [ū], but

Matthews notes that shorthand evidence supporting shortening to [u] and [ʌ] is "rather unsatisfactory" (1943, p. 162). For ME ǫ, "the best evidence favours the pronunciation [ō]" (p. 163), but a lower variant may still have been used.

There are some indications that even in the seventeenth century [u] was retained for ME u where today we have [ʌ]; but the normal pronunciation seems to have been an unrounded vowel similar to [ʌ]. Pronunciations of [ʌu] and [əu] are both attested for ME ū, and there are some indications of [əu], [ɛu], and perhaps [ou].

CONCLUSIONS

Let us now briefly review the various limitations of the different kinds of evidence considered in this chapter.

First, with reference to rhyme in poetry (as opposed to rhyme lists in, e.g., orthoepists, where quite definite claims are made), we have no knowledge of how exact any particular rhyme is, or was ever, meant to be. Danielsson (1959, p. 280) quotes the discussion from Walker (1775, pp. 669-670) on the imperfect rhymes used by Pope and Addison. Since this dictionary is dated only thirty years after Pope's death, Walker's testimony should not be dismissed lightly, though it should be remembered that at that time ME ẹ̄ and ẹ had certainly merged as /ī/. Even so, it seems improbable that he would not have known that, e.g., Waller's *sea/way* had once been good, if in fact it had ever been an exact rhyme in Standard English. Pope, a poet much praised for his technical ability, rhymes *God* with *rod*, *abode*, *woods*, and *unawed*. We must therefore accept either that his rhymes were sometimes inexact or approximations, or else that he used a great variety of dialectal pronunciations, or both. In any case, we can draw no firm conclusions about Pope's own dialect from such rhymes.[4]

Further, Labov's research casts serious doubt on the claims of untrained observers that certain sounds are the same, since he found minimal pairs, e.g. *sauce/source*, which were consistently differentiated in use although the speakers insisted they were identical. He remarks (n.d., p. 10) that:

. . . these results serve to explain a number of unsolved anomalies in historical linguistics. In London English of the 15th century, it is reported that *mate* and *meat* were homonyms, but at a later date, *meat* appeared as distinct from *mate* and merged with *meet*. We would now question the original intuitive remarks of observers that *meat* and *mate* were "the same." In the eighteenth century, it is reported that *line* and *loin* were merged in England and America, but afterwards separated—a totally incomprehensible event, in the light of the concept of "merger." Our results suggest that *line* and *loin* were never merged in actual use.

For occasional spellings, it must be remembered that (as noted by Kökeritz (1953, pp. 21-22)), Wyld does not always distinguish phonetic doublets from phonetic spellings, and that both Wyld and Zachrisson relied on printed sources which often reproduced the letters inaccurately. Dobson's remarks (cf. above, p. 115) are also apposite here; even if the spellings are reproduced accurately, we do not know whether the writer spoke Standard English or a dialect, or how nearly the representations approximated phonetic accuracy. The folklore that people from Brooklyn say *oil* for *earl* and *earl* for *oil* is relevant here as a reminder of the inaccuracy of amateur observations on pronunciation. Kökeritz (1953, pp. 20-21) also points out that to deduce the pronunciation indicated by an occasional spelling it must always be related to the norm, and that therefore the value of the same orthographical spelling will vary with the period and regional dialect. It is of course impossible to do this with the examples as given in Wyld and Zachrisson. Further, it is possible that the spelling of even a personal letter may be the product of two distinct dialects, and there be no way to separate out the different features. Wrenn (pp. 24-25) points out that the Paston letters are often used as if "they were first-class evidence," but it has been shown that "Margery Paston (whose spellings have been widely cited as evidence for contemporary pronunciation) nearly always employed a secretary; and she, probably, was a lady of East Anglia with some local characteristics of pronunciation, dictating to a scribe who came from a different area whose ear for the finer points of pronunciation was not good." Further, it is impossible to tell from the data in Wyld and Zachrisson how frequently the misspellings occurred as a percentage of the total, both generally and within the dialect of a particular individual, and therefore we cannot tell how significant they are; indeed, even if we knew how frequent they were, I do not see any principled way of deciding what would count as a significant number or percentage of misspellings.

Another problem occurs with Wyld's three-way merger of ME $\bar{e}/\bar{a}/ai$. First, it is obvious that all of Wyld's examples of these vowels before *r* should be removed from consideration in the general discussion, since the development of ME $\bar{e}$ is quite different in this environment. Zachrisson (1913, p. 3) acknowledged this and therefore excluded it from his study, but Wyld was not so discriminating and apparently considered this evidence of equal value in determining the development of ME ẹ̄. But the biggest problem with the way the data is given is that even though we may have scattered examples of the same spelling for all three sounds, we have no way of telling whether all three were merged in the speech of any one person. From the grammarians we have evidence of the merger of ME *ai* and ME ẹ̄ (Hart, Bellot, Gil, Butler), and of the merger of ME *ai* and ME *ā* (Robinson, Cooper), but none at all of the merger of all three sounds (except much later, e.g. Tuite, who offers it only as a nonstandard variant to the more usual merger of ME ẹ̄/ẹ̄). If it were possible to separate out the evidence and the different sources, we might find that only two of the three sounds had merged in any one person's speech. But again, even if one individual did write *e* to represent all three sounds, he might still have a two-way distinction.[5] Suppose he has, e.g., [ɛ̄] for ME *ai*, *ā*, and [ē] for ME ẹ̄; presumably he would still spell them all with *e*. Wyld seems not to have noticed how inconsistent his position is, since he accepts that in Middle English orthographic *e* indicated two distinct sounds ẹ̄ and ẹ̄ (which he certainly does not wish to consider identical), yet when orthographic *e* is used in EModE for ME *ai*, *ā*, and ẹ̄ he wants to claim that it indicates that all three were pronounced exactly alike.

Indeed, one big drawback to both rhyme and orthographic evidence is that one never gets a detailed investigation of an individual's phonology (except for Kökeritz (1953)), and it seems improbable that one could get enough information for a reliable study from these sources. We cannot therefore tell what the contrasts were in any one person's speech, or what rules have been added to the grammar. In fact, we cannot tell whether **any** rules have been added, since the data is so fragmentary that any spellings suggestive of sound change may in fact simply be idiosyncratic lexical items. Because of this, we also cannot tell whether any changes are related—that is, whether the addition of one rule may be responsible for several changes which on the surface seem quite independent. Luick claims (1900, pp. 94-98) that dialects with /oy/ from ME ī often have /ew/ from ME ū, which suggests the possibility of an *e/o* switch (cf. Chapter V). But this is exactly the kind of information which is not recoverable from the data as presented in Zachrisson and Wyld.

The limitations of shorthand transcriptions have already been indicated—namely, that vowels are usually omitted, that words are often shortened quite mechanically and without any phonetic basis, and that the conventional spelling is never disregarded completely. These limitations do not, of course, apply to the very detailed and insightful analyses found in the discussion of some of the shorthand writers, e.g. Tiffin.

Finally, for rhymes, occasional spellings, and shorthand transcriptions, even if we can conclude that two sounds are the same (and it would seem that only in the case of rhyme is it possible for us ever to consider them identical, and that even here they may be merely similar), we usually have no way at all of telling what the sound they have merged as is. A merger of ME $ai/\bar{a}$, or of ME $ai/\bar{\varrho}$, is no help in trying to decide whether the vowels traditionally interpreted as long and tense were in fact diphthongs. A merger of ME $\bar{\imath}/oi/ui$ probably indicates /əy/, but there are dialects with /oy/ < ME $\bar{\imath}$.

Summing up, we may say that the evidence from these sources generally agrees with that given by the grammarians and orthoepists. The greatest general difference is that occasional spellings perhaps indicate an earlier date for some of the changes, e.g. monophthongization of the ME diphthongs, but against this the analyses (though not the transcriptions) of the stenographers confirm that nevertheless diphthongal forms survived for some time, and that the observations of the grammarians are correct. We are given evidence of great dialectal variation, but this is also true of the work of, e.g., Cooper and Gil. On the other hand, occasional spellings do not help us at all to identify the forms of Standard English. Values of /ey/, /əy/, and /oy/ for ME $\bar{\imath}$, and of /ow/, /əw/, and /ew/ for ME $\bar{u}$, are indicated, but there is no evidence to bear on the relative order of centralization and lowering, or to suggest that we are wrong to believe the grammarians when they attest to lowering before centralization. Nor do we have any additional information from which to judge whether the long tense vowels were in fact diphthongs, except for Tiffin's testimony, which is directly opposed to this analysis.

The main difference is the claim (made by Wyld but accepted by Kökeritz (1953), by Dobson (1957a), and by Weinreich, Labov, and Herzog) that ME $ai/\bar{a}/\bar{\varrho}$ merged quite early in Standard English, which is completely at variance with the orthoepistical evidence (though Wyld seems unaware of this discrepancy, as does Kökeritz). But despite this acceptance by Kökeritz, Dobson, and Weinreich, Labov, and Herzog, Wyld's conclusions do not follow incontrovertibly from his evidence, which is quite insufficient to prove the point he wishes to make. His major argument for the three-way merger seems to be Cooper's testimony (Wyld (1936, pp. 210-211)), which, as we have indicated, he has completely misinterpreted. Once this is removed, Wyld has very little evidence left at all. He himself remarks that (1936, p. 211)

"It is rather strange that the evidences of the [ē] pronunciation of the old [ɛ] words should be so comparatively rare as they are."

The inadequacies of Wyld's evidence were noted by Ekwall (1958, pp. 308-309), who concludes that Wyld was wrong. I concur with this conclusion. Since it does not seem that Wyld has proved his claim for the merger (and Kökeritz offers no additional evidence, merely using Wyld's assumptions as a basis for his analysis), it follows that the more specific claims for the social distinctions indicated by the dialect difference are also unattested. In fact, neither Wyld nor Kökeritz even attempts to support this part of the claim, and much of the evidence cited seems to oppose it. The evidence Wyld gives for the ẹ̄/ę̄ merger is from speakers such as Queen Elizabeth I, which does not make the equation of this merger with lower class speech very credible. Kökeritz (1953, p. 9) notes that in the South Eastern and East Midlands dialects ME ę̄ had raised from [ē] to [ī], whereas in the Southern dialect the change was from [ɛ] to [ē]. Since Standard English is usually presumed to be based on the East Midlands dialect, it would seem that [ē] for ME ę̄ was certainly a more conservative variant (cf. Kökeritz (1953, p. 10)), but a mark of rustic rather than of either fashionable or educated speech.[6] Because of this, I cannot at all understand the remarks of Weinreich, Labov,[7] and Herzog (pp. 147-148) about the:

. . . rich evidence brought forward by Wyld (1936) and Kökeritz (1953), which shows that the Systems I and II [i.e., merger ẹ̄/ā/ai vs. ẹ̄/ę̄] alternated in London for a considerable period, and that the social significance of the conservative and innovating rules must have been known to most Londoners. In Shakespeare's texts, for example, Kökeritz finds ample support for the notion that the conservative system was identified with refined and conservative speech . . .

This particular problem is discussed in more detail below (Chapter VI).

CHAPTER V

In this chapter various kinds of evidence are discussed in relation to different questions, such as the possibility of /ī/, /ū/, becoming /ey/, /ow/, without prior centralization of the first element, the impairment of intelligibility when vowels are interchanged, the analysis of the English long tense vowels as diphthongs consisting of a vowel plus off-glide, the introduction of exchange rules into a grammar, and the possibility of explaining the English Vowel as resulting from the introduction of such a rule into the grammar.

/ī/, /ū/ → /ey/, /ow/: EVIDENCE FROM OTHER LANGUAGES

McCawley (following Stockwell) has suggested (1969, pp. 8-9 & n. 5) that the Vowel Shift is dependent upon the prior diphthongization of the high vowels, and that diphthongization is followed by centralization. However, there exists evidence from other languages to show that centralization is not universally necessary as a consequence of diphthongization or as a prerequisite to vowel shift.

As described in Kučera (1958; 1961), Czech speakers have available to them today two more or less common dialects, and a number of local dialects. The Literary Language (LL) is used in the schools, and is predominant in literature, the theatre, church sermons, etc. Its use was established during the nineteenth century as part of the Czech Nationalist Revival, and it is in some respects archaic—e.g., its phonology ignores some earlier sound changes. The Czech Common Language (CC) is based on the dialects of Bohemia and is a kind of interdialect. Many speakers have substituted this for their own dialect and are bilingual, using CC and LL. Other speakers may use CC in addition to their own dialect and LL, being thus trilingual. There are other speakers who use only LL and their own dialect, not CC.

I shall ignore here all changes involving consonants and/or short (lax) vowels. The relevant alternations between LL and CC are:

LL		CC
/ī/	~	/ey/
/ē/	~	/ī/
/ū/	~	/ow/

Some examples of these changes are (Kučera (1961, p. 88)):

LL		CC	
/tīden/	~	/teyden/	*week*
/krutī/	~	/krutey/	*cruel*
/mīdlo/	~	/meydlo/	*soap*
/mlēko/	~	/mlīko/	*milk*
/nēst/	~	/nīst/	*carry*
/dobrē/	~	/dobrī/	*good*
/ūrat/	~	/ourat/	*office*
/ūdolī/	~	/oudolī/	*valley*

It is obvious that these changes are (with one gap, cf. below) exactly those illustrated in the dialect described by Hart, Bellot, Gil, and Robinson.

These alternations are the synchronic reflex of a historical sound change which occurred in the Central Bohemian dialect in the fifteenth century, LL being the older, pre-Vowel Shift dialect. The historical change parallels the synchronic alternations, namely, /ī/ → /ey/, /ē/ → /ī/, and /ū/ → /ow/ word-initially. I understand that this is exactly how the change is reflected in the documents of the period. If one wishes to claim that the high and mid vowels did not switch, but that some other factor such as centralization played a role, then one must do so purely on theoretical grounds, unsupported by any documentary evidence. In fairness, it should be pointed out that all documents apparently make use only of the standard orthography and therefore only *a e i o u y* are available to the scribes. There seem to have been no orthoepists or grammarians interested in phonetic alphabets. But it should also be remembered that any such factor has disappeared without leaving any trace, since in Czech today centralization is not present; the CC variant of LL /ī/ is /ey/, not */əy/. Of course, /ey/

and /ow/ are precisely the variants of /ī/, /ū/, respectively, which are reflected in Hart, Bellot, Gil, and Robinson.

A similar situation in Old Prussian has been described by Schmalstieg, who refers to the variants as the Conservative System (CS) and the Innovating System (IS). Here we find all possibilities:

CS		IS
/ī/	~	/ey/
/ē/	~	/ī/
/ū/	~	/ow/
/ō/	~	/ū/

Examples are:

CS		IS	
gīwan		geiwan	*life*
semmē	*earth*	sīdons	*sitting*
weddēdin	*she brought*	īdis	*food*
būton		bouton	*to be*
nūmas		noumas	*us*
nōseilis		nūseilin	*spirit*

It can be seen that here the change applies generally, rather than being limited as in Czech. Czech has no underlying /ō/ to become /ū/, and /ū/ → /ow/ is restricted to word-initial position. Neither of these restrictions applies here. The variants are apparently unpredictable. The following examples are taken from the three versions of the Catechism, the first two of which are dated 1545 and the third 1561:

(i)	nusen rickis	
(ii)	nouson reykeis	*our Lord*
(iii)	nouson Rikijs	

Note that the first text has all CS, the second IS, while the third has IS followed by CS. We also find:

(i)	noumans nuson	
(ii)	noumans nousan	*(forgive) us our (trespasses)*
(iii)	noumas nousans	

Here the first has IS followed by CS, whilst the other two have all IS. Another combination of CS and IS, this time involving also the lowering of lax /i/ to /e/, is:

(i)	wīdekausnan	CS	IS	
(ii)	weydikausnan	IS	CS	*evidence*
(iii)	wīdikausnan	CS	CS	

These alternations appear to be the reflex of a historical sound change at a time when the change was still optional. It should be noted that there is no progression from the earliest to the latest text; in some instances the latest text is the most conservative.

We have only a spelling change to base our conclusions on here, and therefore can make no exact claims about the phonetic nature of the alternations. Further, since Old Prussian is dead we have no current pronunciation to check against. But certainly we have no evidence in support of centralization as a stage in the shift, and certainly the first elements in the diphthongs are clearly distinguished one from the other and identified with /i/ and /e/.

Both contemporary Czech and Old Prussian, then, seem to provide evidence that it is possible for these changes, i.e., /ī/→ /ey/ and /ū/→ /ow/, while at the same time /ē/→ /ī/ and /ō/→ /ū/, to occur without any centralization.

/ī/ → /ey/: EVIDENCE FROM ENGLISH DIALECTS

Stockwell (forthcoming) also claims that the Chomsky and Halle formulation of the Vowel Shift is lacking in historical validity in that it postulates certain forms, namely /ey/ and /ow/, which are not attested in any English dialect today. McCawley (p. 8) makes the point that if a dialect were discovered in which ME ī were /ey/ and still had /i/ alternating with it, as in *divine/divinity*, then this "would provide evidence that a rule interchanging high vowels with mid could be part of the grammar." But Kökeritz notes that Staffordshire has [ei] for ME ī (this being what leads him to postulate two separate lines of development for ME ī in the Vowel Shift) (1953, p. 216 n. 4), and Carter (1967) notes that Wright's *English Dialect Grammar* gives /ey/ as the value of ME ī in parts of Northern Scotland, Northern Ireland, Yorkshire, and Northumberland (p. 2). Neither mentions any dialects with /ow/ for ME ū, but Kökeritz makes the corresponding claim that if it existed it could never have passed through the stage /əw/ (1953, p. 245).

It has been objected that evidence of this kind, based on Ellis or on Wright, is not reliable, for much of the data was gathered by people who were not competent phoneticians. Orton comments (Preface, p. viii):

For the linguistic conditions of the Twentieth Century, I have preferred to depend almost entirely upon the publications of those specialists who have studied particular areas at first hand. Indirect investigation, carried out through the medium of helpers unschooled in Phonetics, can hardly produce results of real scientific value. Accordingly, I have not felt obliged to take into account much of what has previously been written upon the history of Northern vernacular English from medieval times onwards.

Later (p. 201, § 351) he cites the following present-day variants of ME $\bar{\imath}$: [ai], [ei], [ɑi], [aⁱ], [ɑⁱ], [ɑɑ], [əⁱ], [ɑⁱ], [ɑɑⁱ], [εⁱ], [ɑ̄], for various areas, and says that:

In the case of Northumberland, the recent investigations of the Armstrong College Survey[1] show that the various representatives of old $\bar{\imath}$ are as follows:—

(1) [ɛi] (= m.f.s. + h.f.t.) medially.
(2) [æi] (= l.f.s. + h.f.t.) finally and before [v]
          (e.g. *sky* and *five* respectively).
(3) [aⁱ] (= fully *open front* + i) when preceded by the uvular
          r and followed by [v] (as in *drive*).

Further, at Coxhoe (Du.) ME $\bar{\imath}$ appears regularly as [ai] (= fully *open front* + h.f.t.).

For ME $\bar{u}$, he records the variants (p. 235, § 387): [ʉu], [ū], [əu], [uu], [oʉ], [au], [öu], [oᵘ].

Even more striking examples can be found in Orton and Halliday. Here only the basic materials are given, the actual responses of the informants, with no attempt to tabulate or even group the data. But the results are quite clear. ME $\bar{\imath}$ is usually a diphthong but occasionally a monophthong, ranging through [ei], [əi], [ɛi], [ɛ̈i] ([ɛ̈] = a centralized variant of [ɛ]), [æi], [ɐ̈i], [ɐ̣i], [ɐ̣i], [ai], [ɑi], [ā], to [ɑ̄]. Examples with a retracted vowel are progressively more common as the vowel lowers;[2] that is, [əi] is quite rare, [ɛ̈i] fairly common, while [ai], [ɑi], and the monophthongal [ā] and [ɑ̄] are very common indeed. I saw no examples of [ɪi]. A typical example is *knife* (p. 107, I.7.18), which has the variants [neif], [nɛif], [nɛ̣if], [nɛ̈if], [nɛ̣if], [næif], [nɐ̈if], [nɐif], [naif], [näif], [nɑif], [na:f], [nɑ:f]. Note that this example has no centralization higher than [ɛ̈i]. The realizations of *cow(s)* demonstrate very clearly that although variants with centralization do occur, the majority of present-day developments of ME $\bar{u}$ are scattered around the periphery of the vowel triangle. There seems to be some overlap with the development of ME $\bar{\imath}$ in the first element of the diphthong, and in some versions it may be that we have a development from the old mutated plural, or perhaps a blend of the two plural forms.[3] The present-day realizations of *cow(s)* seem to be (p. 210; III.1.1.): [ku:z], [ku:], [kᵊu:z], [kᵊu:], [kəu:z], [kəu:], [kəuz], [kᵊuz], [kəʊz], [kᵓu:z], [kᵓu:], [kᵓʊ], [kʊu:z], [kʊu·z], [kʊu·], [kʌuz], [kʌu], [kaʊz], [kaʊ], [ka:z], [ka:], [kja:z], [kæəz], [kæə], [kæ·az], [kæ·a], [kǣüz], [kǣü], [kæʊz], [kæʊ], [kæuz], [kæu], [kᵆuz], [kᵆu], [kæ:], [kæ:], [kɛaz], [kɛa], [kɛä], [kɛ:z], [kɛi], [kea], [këuz], [këu]. *Lice, louse* (pp. 417-418, IV.8.1. (*a*), (*b*)), and *mice, mouse* (pp. 384-385, IV.5.1. (*a*), (*b*)), are also good examples. In both *mice* and *lice* the highest centralized nucleus is [ɛ̈], while in *dry* (p. 218, III.1.9) there is no centralization higher than [a] and the highest nucleus is [ɛ], the relevant variants being: [ðrɛi], [dræi], [drai], [drɑi], [drɑi], [dra:], and [drɑ:]. It seems that (as noted in Orton, cf. above) the environment may have some bearing on the development of the vowel. Any conclusions must of course be very tentative pending a full analysis of the data, but it is clear that there are many variants attesting lowering without centralization.

Luick gives many instances of both /ey/ for ME ī and /ow/ for ME ū, including the Swabian dialect of German (1900, p. 95). This also shows then that Stockwell's criticism is ill-founded, and provides some of the confirmatory evidence suggested by McCawley. Note that these diphthongs have a lax first element; again this is parallel to the dialect indicated by the early orthoepists. McCawley's centralization constraint is then apparently not necessary.

/ī/ → /ey/: EVIDENCE FROM SOUND CHANGES CURRENTLY IN PROGRESS

In a recent account of current research into sound changes in progress Labov describes how his recent research has modified his own earlier view that centralization preceded lowering. He says (n.d., pp. 9-10) that:

The more precise view of phonological space which we obtain with spectrographic studies shows us that the raising of tense vowels, in front and in back, takes place along a peripheral route, with relatively extreme second formant positions. The falling of the short vowels and diphthongal nuclei takes place along a less peripheral path, well separated from the raising track, but still distinctly front and back rather than central. . . . Thus we see diphthongs or short vowels passing downward in close proximity to the long or tense vowels, but preserving a distinct separation. One might believe that such narrow distinctions cannot be preserved by speakers. But evidence from our research in New York City shows that vowels can maintain such distances—even though native speakers do not consciously hear them as "different" when they reflect consciously about them.

Diagram showing the paths followed by the vowels in chain shifts.

Thus the evidence provided by current instrumental research also supports the traditional view of the Vowel Shift.

EVIDENCE FROM OTHER LANGUAGES FOR THE ADDITION OF EXCHANGE RULES TO A GRAMMAR

As discussed in Chapter II, another objection which has been raised to the Chomsky-Halle formulation of the Vowel Shift is to their use of an exchange or switching rule to effect the change. Neither Chomsky and Halle nor Halle and Keyser claim that the Vowel Shift was added as an exchange rule; Halle and Keyser suggest an alternate way of effecting the change (Rule 16, p. 775) but point out that in a synchronic grammar describing a dialect such as Hart's an exchange rule must be used since it is simpler to state. Similarly Chomsky and Halle note that Hart's rule may be the result of restructuring, and that the language may have changed by the addition of something like their Rule (15) (1968, p. 258). In the case of the English Vowel Shift this is possible because the environment for raising /ē/, /ō/, to /ī/, /ū/, is distinct from the environment in which original /ī/, /ū/, are lowered to /ē/, /ō/. However (cf. Chapter II, pp. 17-18), Kiparsky and Wang have presented cases in which an exchange rule seems the only plausible way of explaining the sound changes.

A third example[4] comes from a discussion of drum signaling. Herzog (1964, p. 312) notes that "The few studies we have establish beyond doubt that in Africa this signaling . . . is based on a direct transfer into a musical medium of spoken language elements." It is therefore not an arbitrary code, and evidence from such a system is relevant for the study of natural languages.

Herzog documents a tone switch in the signaling of a West African tribe. He reports that when listening to a particular drum he "observed that what I expected to sound as high tones sounded rather consistently as low, and vice versa" (p. 320). When he mentioned this to the natives, they insisted that the drum was fine. He then discovered that the drum, which was rather old and had become quite worn down in places, especially in the favorite spot for hitting a final tone 1, had at some time been turned round. Since the drummer kept his normal hitting patterns, this "meant that henceforth many low tones were higher, and many high tones lower, than the central tone 2" (p. 320). This exchange was not completely predictable, however, since there are several ways of producing any particular tone; therefore, high tone was often realized as low, but sometimes as high, and conversely low tone was often high, but sometimes low. In this way the linguistic situation rather resembles that of Czech. Herzog suggests that in fact "the pitch contrast is merely one phase of a complex contrast"; that is, that (as was pointed out in Chomsky and Halle (1968, pp. 256-257)) the exchanged items, whether vowel segments or tones, do not occur in isolation, and therefore that a switch in these is not in itself enough to impair intelligibility. Note also that in this case the change must obviously have been discrete, and can only be described as a switch. Herzog remarks (p. 320) that ". . . the comparative lack of disturbance at the reversal of the pattern . . . may shed some light on the curious phenomenon that in neighboring languages of the region groups of low-tone words of one language may be found to have high tone in another, and vice versa." It seems possible that some detailed study of the lexicon and of interdialectal relationships might reveal several instances of exchange rules.

EVIDENCE FROM ENGLISH DIALECTS FOR THE ADDITION OF EXCHANGE RULES TO A GRAMMAR

In some dialects of English a sound change connected with the Vowel Shift occurred which can most plausibly be described and explained by means of a switch.

Luick (1896, p. 20) noted that a symmetry existed in certain dialectal variants of ME *ī*, *ū*: "Eine symmetrische Ausgestellung der Lautwerte zeigt sich insofern, als einem *eu*-Dipthong als Wiedergabe des *ū* gern ein *oi* als die des *ī* entspricht . . ." He later remarks on the unusual nature of this symmetry, pointing out that although the development of ME *ī*, *ū*, is rarely exactly parallel, /oy/, /ew/, offer the only exception to this, since dialects with one normally have the other also (1900, p. 100): "Wie unsicher schlüsse aus dem heutigen bestande an sich sind, zeigt auch der umstand, dass die behandlung von *ī* und *ū* oft ganz verschieden ist. Nur *oi* and *eu* gehen viefach [*sic*] hand in hand."

Tiffin (1751) also records /oy/, /ew/, as dialectal variants of ME
ī, ū, and Matthews (1936) points out in his discussion that the *English
Dialect Grammar* records /oy/ for ME ī in the Midland, Eastern, and
Southern areas, and /ew/ for ME ū in the South Midland, Eastern,
and Southern areas. Luick's claim then seems to be essentially correct in that the two variants tend to cooccur. Luick believed that
this development was subsequent to the lowering of the first element
of the diphthongs to [a], that is, that the development of ME ī was
/ī > ey > əy > ay > oy/, and that of ME ū was /ū > ow > əw > aw
> ew/. Since we know from Tiffin that these variants existed in the
mid-eighteenth century, before /əy/, /əw/, had lowered to /ay/, /aw/,
and when some dialects still had /ey/, /ow/, it seems improbable that
Luick is correct on this point. A much more plausible explanation
is that there was an *e/o* switch, so that /ey/ → /oy/, and /ow/ → /ew/.
Further, if this were an exchange rule it would provide an explanation
of why the two variants occur together. In fact, there is no other way
of offering an explanation for this correlation, since, although the
two vowels could easily be raised or lowered together without using
a switching rule, for this particular change /e/ has to be retracted to
/o/, whereas /o/ has to be fronted to /e/, and the only way of effecting
these two different changes in one rule is by using an exchange rule.
Variables were first introduced as a means of treating assimilation
and dissimilation (Halle (1962*a*)) and it seems possible to consider /ey/
→ /oy/ and /ow/ → /ew/ as a case of dissimilation of backness from
the following off-glide. That is, the change can be both described and
explained by assuming that the dialects concerned added a rule of
the form:

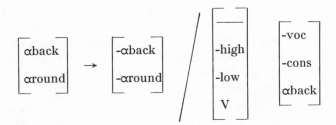

It has been suggested recently that it is very questionable whether it
is linguistically possible for an *e/o* switch such as this to occur (Langacker
(1969*a*, p. 11 & n. 14)). But it would certainly seem the most natural
way of explaining the change described above.

EVIDENCE FROM NORTHERN DIALECTS AGAINST THE VOWEL SHIFT RESULTING FROM THE ADDITION OF AN EXCHANGE RULE

Carter (1967) has presented arguments against the initial stages of the English Vowel Shift having been effected by the introduction of an exchange rule. Carter pointed out that in Northern England and in Scotland με *ū* is still /ū/, that is, it remains unchanged, and that the areas in which this occurs coincide with areas in which ME *ǭ* did not raise to /ū/ but followed another path, such as fronting to [œ]. Carter suggests that the Vowel Shift was effected by the introduction of some kind of schema which raises the mid vowels and diphthongizes the original high vowels, providing that enough phonetic mid vowels are raised (p. 9): "If at the point of the grammar at which the rule is being added there are few or no morphemes containing a mid vowel which will be raised to the position of that high vowel which it differs from only in height, then that high vowel will not be diphthongized. The number qualifying as 'few' would have to be empirically determined." This theory is by no means new; exactly the same data was noted by Luick (1896, § 142) and similar conclusions drawn (§ 587): "1. das gemeinenglische vorrücken von *ę̄*, *ǭ*, zu *ī*, *ū* . . . Bei dieser bewegung stossen sie auf me *i*, *u*, und verdrängen sie aus ihrer stellung: *ī*, *ū*, werden zu diphthongen." However, Luick was not, of course, concerned with whether the change had been effected by the introduction of an exchange rule, but with attempting to determine the "primary impulse" of the Vowel Shift.

One would certainly not wish to dismiss this evidence as coincidence. But it should be remembered that in all areas ME *ū* did not participate in the Vowel Shift as generally as did the other long vowels. In particular, ME *ū* did not shift before labials or velars or following initial *w* or *y*, with the result that we have *wound*, *youth*, with /ū/, and that we never have /aw/ before labials or velars. Further, King (1967) has investigated the theory of "functional load" and shown that in general "functional load, if it is a factor in sound change at all, is one of the least important" (p. 848); he notes that the particular hypotheses formulated predicted less "than half of the facts." The particular hypotheses relating to functional load which King formulated and investigated in detail do not correspond exactly to Carter's hypothesis, though they relate to the general requirement that sound change not impair intelligibility, and that this requirement (King (1967, p. 834)) ". . . should help prevent the merger of two phonemes whose opposition bears a high functional load, while such a therapeutic factor need not assert itself to prevent the eradication of an opposition whose functional load is very small." It seems to me that this is exactly the basis from which Carter wishes to predict whether a high vowel will diphthongize or not, and from King's results one would not wager much for Carter's chances of empirically determining a value for "few." And in fact Western long ago pointed out that, contrary to Luick's claims, dialects exist in which ME *ū* is diphthongized and lowered even though ME *ǭ* does not raise to /ū/, and at least one in which ME *ū* did not shift even though ME *ǭ* did raise to /ū/ (Western (1912, pp. 3-4)). It seems, then, that this provides confirmation of King's reservations regarding the value of functional load even with regard to this particular piece of data, and that since King has shown that the predictive value of hypotheses based on measures of functional load is in general not very high, there seems no reason for requiring that the Vowel Shift rule generally be changed to incorporate Carter's schema or that it be considered "as part of the child's innate linguistic capacity" (Carter, p. 10). This does not, then, provide evidence against the possibility that the Vowel Shift resulted from the introduction of an exchange rule into the grammar.

EVIDENCE FROM OTHER LANGUAGES AGAINST THE VOWEL SHIFT RESULTING FROM THE ADDITION OF AN EXCHANGE RULE

There are implications from the Czech evidence suggesting that perhaps the English Vowel Shift was not the result of adding an alpha-switching rule. It is clear that the alternations in Czech can be accounted for if the vowel system of LL is adopted for the underlying forms and the phonological component contains three of the rules postulated by Chomsky and Halle (1968) for Hart's dialect, namely:

Diphthongization   (Chomsky and Halle (1968, p. 256))

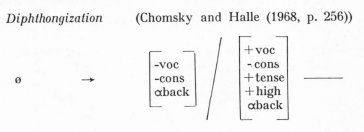

$$\emptyset \rightarrow \begin{bmatrix} -voc \\ -cons \\ \alpha back \end{bmatrix} \Big/ \begin{bmatrix} +voc \\ -cons \\ +tense \\ +high \\ \alpha back \end{bmatrix} \underline{\hspace{2cm}}$$

Vowel Shift   (Chomsky and Halle (1968, p. 256))

$$\begin{bmatrix} \alpha\text{high} \\ \text{-low} \end{bmatrix} \quad \rightarrow \quad [\text{-}\alpha\text{high}] \quad \Big/ \quad \begin{bmatrix} \rule{0pt}{1em} \\ \text{+tense} \\ \text{+stress} \end{bmatrix}$$

Diphthong Laxing   (Chomsky and Halle (1968, p. 265))

$$[\text{-low}] \quad \rightarrow \quad [\text{-tense}] \quad \Big/ \quad \underline{\hspace{2cm}} \quad \begin{bmatrix} \text{-voc} \\ \text{-cons} \end{bmatrix}$$

If these optional rules are applied throughout whenever possible, then CC results; when (as, it appears, is usually the case) the rules are sometimes applied and sometimes not, we get the normal type of conversational utterance which is termed Colloquial Czech (CL). Although the incorporation of this sequence of rules would seem to make a faulty prediction with regard to Czech, namely, that LL /ō/ → CC /ū/, which is not one of the alternations described above (p. 132), it should be noted that this formulation of the rules will not produce incorrect outputs, since there appear to be no underlying /ō/'s in LL. /ō/ occurs as an expressive variant of /o/ in casual or emotional pronunciation, and is also found in some loanwords. However, Kučera notes that it is usually only the native vocabulary which participates in these alternations; loanwords, particularly if of a learned nature, in general do not switch, even those with /ī/, /ē/, or /ū/, and these would presumably have to be marked as not undergoing any of these rules. The unpredictability of the occurrence of a particular variant (cf. below, p. 147) would seem to militate against the possibility that we postulate separate lexical entries for each variant, and lends further support to the claim that, rather, we have one underlying form and a set of optional rules.

Note that, in both Czech and Old Prussian, though the rules are optional, they are not individually so; the condition is all or none:

$$/\bar{\text{i}}/ \rightarrow /\text{ey}/ \nrightarrow /\text{iy}/ \nrightarrow /\bar{\text{i}}\text{y}/ \nrightarrow /\bar{\text{e}}\text{y}/ \nrightarrow /\bar{\text{e}}/$$
$$/\bar{\text{u}}/ \rightarrow /\text{ew}/ \nrightarrow /\text{uw}/ \nrightarrow /\bar{\text{u}}\text{w}/ \nrightarrow /\bar{\text{o}}\text{w}/ \nrightarrow /\bar{\text{o}}/.$$

It seems therefore that this whole sequence must in effect operate as one rule. The only slight evidence against this is that, in both Old Prussian and Czech, /ī/ is occasionally spelled *ij*; this is usually considered a spelling variation only, but, in any case, doesn't vitally affect the rules, since we wish to diphthongize the high vowels before switching.

However, there remains the question of how we are to express this interdependence of rule within the current formalism. We can imagine something like:

$$
\begin{bmatrix}
\text{Diphthongization} \\
\text{Vowel Shift} \\
\text{Diphthong Laxing}
\end{bmatrix}
$$

optional .

The decision whether or not to enter the block is optional, but once in, all applicable rules must be applied. But this seems rather a strange condition to impose on a grammar, and is certainly an extension of the formalism.

If this is not possible, then it seems that one must break up the Vowel Shift rule, since it **must** apply to the high vowels if diphthongization has already applied, and **may not** apply if it has not, whereas it is completely optional for the mid vowels. That is, one must instead use Rule (15) in Chomsky and Halle (1968, p. 258):

$$
\begin{bmatrix}
\text{-low} \\
\text{+tense} \\
\text{+stress}
\end{bmatrix}
\rightarrow
\left\{
\begin{array}{l}
[+\text{high}] \\
\\
[-\text{high}]
\end{array}
\middle/
\ \underline{\quad\quad}\
\begin{bmatrix}
\text{-voc} \\
\text{-cons}
\end{bmatrix}
\right\}
\begin{array}{l}
(a) \\
\\
(b)
\end{array}
$$

Part (*a*) would be optional and part (*b*) obligatory.

If, then, we assume that the English Vowel Shift originated as an optional change, it would seem that these arguments would hold against explaining that development as resulting from the introduction of an exchange rule as formulated in Chomsky and Halle (1968). Against this Halle (personal communication) has pointed out that rules of this kind ". . . are really abbreviations of whole sets of rules and the main purpose of writing these sets of rules in the abbreviated form is to evaluate the degree of generalization that has been achieved. It is only the latter rules that contain no abbreviations whatsoever that function to explain the phonological processes of the language." Optionality would then be a feature not of the abbreviated rules but "of the maximally specified rules of which the complex rules are special notational abbreviations." Halle would consider the obligatory application of some unabbreviated rule if another unabbreviated rule had already applied as similar to the obligatory nonapplication of an unabbreviated rule if another had applied, which is of course the interpretation of the parenthesis notation.

This point of view has also been argued in Langacker (1969*b*), in this instance with specific reference to the formalization of the obligatory vs. optional status of parts of a rule. It is here claimed (pp. 578-579 n. 4) that ". . . it is NOT important whether a certain notational convention like the braces or the asterisk allows the information that some subrules are optional and others obligatory to be represented neatly when the rules are written out in collapsed form on paper. One can interpret the collapsing notations as measures of generality applied to representations given in full, non-collapsed forms." But one may surely question here the validity of such a concept of generality. Of this point of view, it has been observed (Hyman, p. 75 n. 9), that "if the collapsed form of a phonological rule does not exist, then there is no point evaluating it." It should also be noted that if we, following Halle and Langacker, consider the Vowel Shift Rule postulated by Chomsky and Halle for the synchronic grammar of present-day English in its full, unabbreviated form, we will discover that one of the subparts is self-contradictory (Wang (1968, p. 704, § 17)):

$$
\begin{bmatrix}
V \\
+\text{high} \\
+\text{mid} \\
+\text{high} \\
-\text{mid} \\
+\text{velar} \\
-\text{velar} \\
-\text{labial} \\
-\text{long}
\end{bmatrix}
\rightarrow
\begin{bmatrix}
-\text{high} \\
-\text{mid}
\end{bmatrix}
$$

Halle's own argument would then invalidate the rule he has himself given for contemporary English.

The question is not whether certain notational conventions such as the use of variables should be allowed at all, but whether it is valid to use this method of collapsing several rules into one when the product does not in fact behave as a unit rule. This has also been discussed by Zwicky, who concludes that if two processes behave differently (in his example, with respect to exceptions to the rule), then they should be considered different rules rather than subparts of the same rule. Further examples from the rapidly changing phonological system of a young child acquiring a grammar have been discussed by Smith, who feels that some of the rules postulated capture a psychological and linguistic generalization whereas others, in which the subparts of the rule developed differentially, do not.

Kiparsky has also argued that linguistic notation should not be considered merely as an abbreviatory device, but should rather correspond to some psychological reality, and that there should be some empirical basis on which to decide this. Kiparsky suggests that linguistic change can provide evidence bearing on this question, and discusses several diachronic changes in relation to this, concluding that (Kiparsky (1968*b*, p. 182)) "One answer, then, to the question concerning the empirical basis for the notational conventions of linguistic theory is that these conventions are an essential part of any attempt to characterize what is a possible linguistic change and what is not a possible linguistic change." It seems to be the case that current notational conventions will not easily allow us to incorporate the facts concerning the interdependence of parts of this change into an exchange rule. Halle notes that at present not enough is known of cases of this kind, where a part of a rule is obligatory if another, optional, rule has applied, but must not apply if the optional rule has not. If there are many such cases, then perhaps the theory should be extended to accommodate them.

In fact, even within the current theory all the facts can be incorporated into one rule of the form:[5]

$$
\begin{bmatrix} V \\ +\text{tense} \\ -\text{low} \\ +\text{high} \end{bmatrix} \rightarrow \begin{bmatrix} 1 \\ \langle -\text{high} \rangle \\ \langle -\text{tense} \rangle \end{bmatrix} \Big\langle \begin{bmatrix} 1 \\ -\text{tense} \\ -\text{voc} \end{bmatrix} \Big\rangle
$$

which expands into the two following rules:

$$
\begin{bmatrix} V \\ +\text{tense} \\ -\text{low} \\ +\text{high} \end{bmatrix} \rightarrow \begin{bmatrix} 1 \\ -\text{high} \\ -\text{tense} \end{bmatrix} \begin{bmatrix} 1 \\ -\text{tense} \\ -\text{voc} \end{bmatrix}
$$

$$
\begin{bmatrix} V \\ +\text{tense} \\ -\text{low} \\ -\text{high} \end{bmatrix} \rightarrow \begin{bmatrix} 1 \\ +\text{high} \\ +\text{tense} \end{bmatrix}
$$

This will perform the changes /ī/ → /ey/ and /ū/ → /ow/, while at the same time /ē/ → /ī/ and /ō/ → /ū/, in one fell swoop. But then we must ask whether we wish to postulate that an adult can add a rule such as this to his grammar (and cf. discussion on constraints on sound change, Chapter II). At first sight this seems counterintuitive, and one would prefer to claim that such a rule could result only from re-structuring. But against this I think that intuition, however valuable in telling us which sentences are or are not grammatical, related, para-phrases, etc., is not the right basis on which to attempt to decide what has psychological reality. Following Kiparsky, we should look for empirical evidence. And in both English and Czech we seem to have evidence of a unitary process—a fact which is certainly not captured in the Chomsky-Halle analysis, in which the three rules are quite separate and their cooccurrence apparently fortuitous. This seems another weakness in the formulation, and Lass has suggested certain implicational rules to capture the interdependence of the changes, in particular, that the raising of mid vowels implies diphthongization of the high vowels.[6] Whatever the correct formulation may be, the ex-traordinary fact that exactly the same complicated change appears to have occurred in three unrelated languages, and that we have no evidence of any intermediate steps, suggests that we should treat this as some kind of unitary operation, rather than as three distinct processes.

LOSS OF INTELLIGIBILITY WITH VOWEL EXCHANGE:
EVIDENCE FROM OTHER LANGUAGES

A further objection, more particularly to the type of rule formulation in Chomsky and Halle (1968), was that to alternate segments in this way would impair intelligibility. But with regard to the variation in Czech, Kučera stresses that in fact Czech speakers usually speak in CL, that is, in a mixture of LL and CC, and that the use of any particular alternation in any specific utterance is unpredictable. He points out that (1961, p. 19) ". . . the frequency and the combination of LL and CC elements in CL may be inconsistent even in sustained conversation of a single speaker, or, not infrequently, even within a single utterance." He states again (1961, p. 107) that "the phonological utterance of the two codes may thus coexist not only in the same utterance but even in the same micro-segment." The following are, for instance, all possible:

LL	CC	CL	
/ūskī/ ∼	/ouskey/ ∼	/ouskī/ ∼	/ūskey/	*narrow.*

There are some morphological and other constraints on these variations, and any attempt at a complete phonology of these dialects of Czech would, of course, have to incorporate all these. For the purpose of this argument, however, it is sufficient to note that although these constraints exist, it is still true to say that in many instances the variation is optional. It seems probable that work of the type done by Labov would result in greater understanding of the precise nature of the nonlinguistic factors which trigger the use of one or other of the variants. But it seems clear that in most instances these factors are nonlinguistic, or, at any rate, nongrammatical (ignoring the question of how far stylistic alternation may be considered grammatical—that is, the use of one form rather than another merely for variation, or to intensify the force of a word). Further, it does not seem that these factors would provide cues for the hearer, enabling him to predict the occurrence of any particular variant. In Old Prussian also the variation seems quite unpredictable. We are therefore left with almost exactly the situation described by McCawley (cf. Chapter II), namely, that /peyl/ will alternate with underlying /pīl/, and /pīl/ with underlying /pēl/, though in the case of Czech most speakers have both variants. Further, there is no evidence, either historical or in Czech today, to suggest that this caused any inconvenience whatsoever to the speakers or readers of Czech or Old Prussian.

EVIDENCE FOR THE ANALYSIS OF EARLY ENGLISH LONG VOWELS AS DIPHTHONGS

I now turn to the question of whether we should more properly consider the long tense vowels in early stages of English as consisting of a vowel plus off-glide, as suggested by Stockwell (1961; 1964; 1969; forthcoming). He bases his claim mainly on two phenomena in diachronic English phonology. First, in OE -*ig*, as in *stig*, comes to be spelled *i*, *y*, *ii*, and merges with *ī*, and similarly -*ug*, as in *bugan*, comes to be spelled *u*, *ou*, *ow*, falling in with *ū* (1961, p. 533). He suggests that what had actually happened was that the palatal and velar fricatives lost their friction and fell in with /y/, /w/, respectively. If original /ī/, /ū/, are analyzed as /iy/, /uw/, then the merger is easily explained. But although we may accept that -*ig*, -*ug*, became /iy/, /uw/, it is not necessary to assume that *ī*, *ū*, were diphthongs also. We have already seen a great deal of evidence to suggest that ME *ai*, *ou*, *au*, monophthongized, the first two falling in with με *ā*, *ō*, and the third becoming [ɔ]. It is equally possible that OE -*ig*, -*ug*, first became sequences of vowel plus glide and then monophthongized. A third possibility is that -*ig*, -*ug*, became /iy/, /ow/, and that OE *ī*, *ū*, previously monophthongal, then diphthongized and merged with the reflexes of -*ig*, -*ug*. There is no proof either way.

Stockwell's second piece of evidence concerns vowel alternations in ME. Normally when vowels lengthened or shortened in OE there was no indication of any qualitative change. That is, /ī/ > /i/, /ē/ > /e/, /ū/ > /u/, /ō/ > /o/, and vice versa. But in ME we find exceptions to this (Stockwell (1961, pp. 530-531)): "/ẹ/ (long close *e*) and /ọ̄/ (long close *o*) when shortened during ME times fell in with /i/ and /u/, and, conversely, /i/ and /u/ when lengthened during ME times fell in with /ẹ/ and /ọ/." He suggests that we interpret the ME vowel system as being (1961, p. 534):

$$\left.\begin{array}{l} \text{/iy/} \\ \text{/ih/} \end{array}\right\} \text{/i/} \qquad \text{/u/} \qquad \left\{\begin{array}{l} \text{/uw/} \\ \text{/uh/} \end{array}\right.$$

$$\text{/eh/} \quad \text{/e/} \qquad\qquad \text{/o/} \qquad \text{/oh/}$$

rather than the traditional:

$$\left.\begin{array}{l} \text{/ī/} \\ \text{/ẹ̄/} \end{array}\right\} \text{/i/} \qquad \text{/u/} \qquad \left\{\begin{array}{l} \text{/ū/} \\ \text{/ọ̄/} \end{array}\right.$$

$$\text{/ẹ̄/} \quad \text{/e/} \qquad\qquad \text{/o/} \qquad \text{/ọ/.}$$

In this interpretation, ME *ī̜*, *ę̄*, differ not in the quality of the vowel but of the off-glide, and similarly ME *ū̜*, *ǭ*: "Now if we rewrite /ę̄/ as /ih/, when it is shortened it must yield /i/ . . . Similarly, /ǭ/, if it is /uh/, must give /u/ when it is shortened—as it does. Conversely, if an /i/ is lengthened, it must fall in with /ih/, and /u/ with /uh/— as they do." First, note that the second part of this statement is not true, since it would seem equally possible for /i/ to lengthen either to /ih/ or to /iy/, and similarly for /u/ to lengthen to /uh/ or to /uw/ —unless, that is, there is some kind of constraint to the effect that only centralizing off-glides may be added. Stockwell does not mention such a constraint here, and it is difficult to see what justification could be offered for it. In an earlier work this constraint is assumed simply by definition (1952, p. 90): ". . . the term 'lengthening' is used to mean 'the development of a lengthening central off-glide,' phonemic- ally /h/ . . ." No justification is offered, and it should be noted that shortening is defined as the loss of any glide, not restricted to /h/. Further, such a constraint cannot have been generally true, since both *a* and *o* added a back-glide before *l♯* or *lC*, later merging with ME *au*, *ou*, respectively, as evidenced by many of the orthoepists.

And alternate explanations can be found for this phenomenon. Dob- son (1962) points out that lengthening in open syllables was much less common for ME *i*, *u*, than for *e*, *o*, and *a*, that geographically it was limited (occurring mainly in the North, but also to some extent in the East or Northeast Midlands, especially Norfolk, and in some of the South), and that it was later in date. Dobson notes that in the dialects in which /i/ became /ē/, there is much evidence to show that ME *i* had lowered to /e/, and that therefore the change to /ē/ involved only lengthening. Similar evidence for ME *u* is hard to find since *u* often was rendered orthographically by *o*, as in *son*, *come*, but he claims that there is some evidence for dialectal lowering of ME *u* to /o/. Further, Dobson suggests that whereas in OE /i/ and /u/ had been tense and close, in ME they were lax and more open, and in fact approximated much more closely to /ē/, /ō/, than to /ī/, /ū/. It should be remembered that Cooper, faced with a vowel system which offered a choice of two long vowels with which to equate one short one, paired /ē/:/i/, and /ō/:/u/, not /ī/:/i/, and /ū/:/u/, and that Tiffin did the same with /ē/:/i/.

It seems clear that the rule of lengthening in open syllables origin- ally applied only to [-high] vowels, and that later, in some areas only, this rule was simplified by the deletion of this feature so that it ap- plied to all vowels in the relevant environment. We have ample evidence that ME *ī*, *ū*, at some period diphthongized; it is possible that, at the time when the lengthening rule was generalized, ME *ī*, *ū*, were in fact /iy/, /uw/ (or even that they had lowered to /ey/, /ow/), and that ME *ę̄*, *ǭ*, had raised to /ī/, /ū/ (which is the explanation advanced in Bliss (pp. 41-42), this explanation having the advantage of combining neatly with the development of the diphthongs derived from OE *ēg*, *ōg*). It would then be natural for the lengthened /i/, /u/, to be spelled with the same orthographic symbols as the existing /ī/, /ū/, namely *e* and *o*. Stockwell's explanation rests on a similar assumption that ME *ę̄*, *ǭ*, had raised, and that their developments were in some way distinct from ME *ī*, *ū*.

We have little external evidence for this. We know that ME *ī*, *ū*, did diphthongize and lower. It is usually assumed that ME *ę̄*, *ǭ*, had become /ī/, /ū/, at least before the end of the fifteenth century and probably much earlier, judging from the *i*, *y*, spellings for ME *ę̄* cited by Wyld (1927, §§ 162, 229). ME *ę̄*, *ǭ*, are paired with ME *i*, *u*, in the earliest orthoepistical writings, and are described as having the pronunciations /ī/, /ū/. There does not, however, seem to be any evidence that would indicate that με *ę̄*, *ǭ*, were phonetically diphthongal, and clearly it is not necessary to assume this to explain the phenomenon.

A rather different explanation has been advanced by Lass (pp. 19-21). Here it is claimed that **all** vowels lower when lengthened in open syllables, /i/ > /ē/, /e/ > /ǣ/, /u/ > /ō/, /o/ > /ɔ̄/. Such an explanation, however, involves (as was noted by Bliss) a rather improbable assumption. For words such as OE *wicu* we must postulate a lowering to /we:kə/ followed by a raising to /wi:k/ in the Vowel Shift; that is: "it is necessary to suppose that a sound change was followed within a comparatively short period by a directly opposite change" (Bliss, p. 41). Since it is possible to explain the orthographic facts more simply, there seems no reason to accept this rather complicated solution.

It would seem then that there are three explanations other than that proposed by Stockwell (1961) for the ME alternations, and since there does not seem to be any external evidence in support of analyzing all the long tense vowels as diphthongs at this date, there certainly do not seem to be any very compelling reasons to choose Stockwell's analysis in favor of the more traditional one.

CHAPTER VI

THE DEVELOPMENT OF ME ī, ū

In Chapter I three scholarly positions on the development of ME ī, ū, were outlined: (1) that centralization of the first element of the resulting diphthongs took place only after lowering was complete; (2) that centralization occurred before any lowering took place; and (3) that centralization occurred after the first element of the diphthongs had been lowered to a mid vowel, that is, that we have (chronologically) lowering to a mid vowel, then centralization, and then lowering to a low central vowel. The three lines of development (after diphthongization) may be represented as follows:

(1)
$$
\begin{array}{ccc}
\text{iy} & & \text{uw} \\
\downarrow & & \downarrow \\
\text{ey} & & \text{ow} \\
\downarrow & & \downarrow \\
\text{æy} \longrightarrow \text{ay} & \text{aw} \longleftarrow \text{ɔw}
\end{array}
$$

(2)
$$
\begin{array}{ccc}
\text{iy} \longrightarrow \text{ɨy} & \text{ɨw} \longleftarrow \text{uw} \\
\downarrow & \downarrow \\
\text{əy} & \text{əw} \\
\downarrow & \downarrow \\
\text{ay} & \text{aw}
\end{array}
$$

(3)
$$
\begin{array}{ccc}
\text{iy} & & \text{uw} \\
\downarrow & & \downarrow \\
\text{ey} \longrightarrow \text{əy} & \text{əw} \longleftarrow \text{ow} \\
\downarrow & \downarrow \\
\text{ay} & \text{aw}
\end{array}
$$

In Chapter III the evidence of the early phoneticians, grammarians, and orthoepists showed quite clearly that before Hodges (1643) the first elements of the diphthongal realizations of ME $\bar{\imath}$, $\bar{u}$, were perceived as distinct from each other and as being the same as με e, o, and that in stressed syllables ME u had only one sound. But in Hodges's description we find for the first time that ME o appears to have lowered, perhaps to [ɔ], and that ME u now has two realizations, [u] and [ʌ]; he does not, however, provide any evidence for centralization of the first elements of με $\bar{\imath}$, $\bar{u}$. In Wallis (1653) we find centralized first elements for both of these (though Wallis insists that there is a slight difference between them; cf. discussion in Chapter III), and from this point on the descriptions given (where clear and precise enough to identify the sound meant) indicate that με $\bar{\imath}$, $\bar{u}$, now begin with the same centralized vowel, which is identified with one of the developments of ME u and is distinct from [e], [æ], [o], and [ɔ].

There is then no support for position (1), that is, for the view that centralization occurred after lowering had been completed, as far as Standard English is concerned (for Northern English this may be the correct hypothesis), since centralization about mid-seventeenth century is very clearly attested. There is one interesting point about Wyld's discussion of ME $\bar{u}$ (1936, p. 230), which should perhaps be mentioned. Wyld wished to claim that the line of development was [ū] > [ŭ^u] > [ou] > [au] > [a^u]. He believed that the description of the orthoepists could indicate either [au] or [əu], but preferred the former, stating that "it may well be that Wallis and Cooper are really referring to a diphthong to all intents and purposes identical with that now in use" (1936, p. 231). If Wallis and Cooper (to say nothing of the other writers) did really mean /aw/, it seems strange they should have identified the first element with the vowel of, e.g., *cut*, *dull*. It is difficult to see why Wyld is reluctant to accept centralization of ME $\bar{u}$ as an intermediate stage, before its final lowering to /aw/, but this is, of course, parallel with his analysis of the front vowel, in which also he does not allow for centralization. This seems quite unjustifiable on the basis of the available data.

Similarly, the evidence of Chapter III does not support position (2) either, and (as noted at the end of Chapter III) it seems improbable that one ever could discover evidence of this kind that would unequivocally support position (2) over (3), since one would need a description accurate enough to distinguish [ɨ] from [ə]. There were however theoretical arguments advanced for position (2) and against position (3).

It was noted in Chapter I that Dobson and Stockwell believe the possibility of intersection with ME *ai* to be an insuperable objection to any theory of the Vowel Shift which proposes lowering before centralization, since they assume that intersection would inevitably produce merger of the two sounds. But the objections raised seem far from conclusive.

First, even if the paths of ME *ī* and ME *ai* were to cross, it does not necessarily follow that they would merge. As Chomsky and Halle (1968) point out, Dobson's conclusion is based on his view that sound change is a gradual process. But if we believe that sound change is discrete, and is produced by the addition of rules to the grammar, then Dobson's conclusion does not follow; ME *ī* and *ai* could have crossed without merging, like the mid and open vowels in Corsican and the high and low tones in Chinese (cf. Chapter II). Stockwell and McCawley (cf. Chapter II) have objected to the use of exchange rules in this way, claiming that either loss of intelligibility and/or merger would result. But in Chapter V I presented evidence from English dialects and from other languages to show that this claim is ill-founded, and that exchange rules cannot be ruled out on those grounds.

But even accepting Dobson's assumptions about the gradual nature of sound change, since ME *ai* was monophthongized in most dialects (even though a less common diphthongal variant coexisted for some time), and since ME *ī* was certainly a diphthong, the two could have been kept distinct. The claim that ME *ai* did not monophthongize (as advanced by Jesperson (1907), Sarrazin), or that all long tense vowels were in fact diphthongs (Stockwell), is here irrelevant; the orthoepistical evidence shows very clearly that ME *ī, ū*, were **perceived** as diphthongs, whereas ME *ẹ̄, ę̄, ọ̄, ǭ*, were **perceived** as pure long tense vowels, as were ME *ai, au, ou*, after monophthongization. It is therefore obvious that they were perceptually distinct in some way, and this distinction, whatever its phonetic basis, would have kept them from merging. Note that, since ME *ai* is perceived as a long tense vowel similar to ME *ā, ẹ̄, ę̄*, there is no reason to pick on this one diphthong as likely to merge with ME *ī*. If ME *ī* could merge with what the orthoepists heard as and called a long vowel, or if, alternatively, the long tense vowels were all diphthongal, then in a theory of gradual change ME *ī* could have merged with any one of them, since it had to cross the path of each (in the line of development attributed to the "usual" view, i.e., position (1)), and I cannot see why ME *ai* is chosen as the particular villain of the piece.

Third, Ekwall (1958, p. 311), rejecting Dobson's justification for his analysis of the Vowel Shift, says there is no need to assume merger would necessarily result even if ME *ai* were [ei] when ME *ī* diphthongized, since many kinds of *ei*-diphthongs are possible which could very well have been kept distinct. This claim is supported by the instrumental evidence presented in Labov (n.d.) which was cited in Chapters IV and V.

Fourth, even assuming a theory of gradual change, and that ME *ai* did not monophthongize, there is no motivation for wishing to exclude the traditional line of development, position (3), which would seem to offer a way of combining Kökeritz's dual lines of development and also to obviate the possibility of ME *ī* merging with ME *ai*. Indeed, Jespersen certainly believed in gradual change and also that ME *ai* did not monophthongize, yet his theory on the development of ME *ī* led to no problems of merger in his mind.

It would seem, then, that a line of development which supposed first diphthongization and then lowering one stage followed by centralization, i.e., position (3), would account for all the attested stages and would cause no difficulty in anyone's theory except Stockwell's (and the noncentralized version, position (1), but this is so much at variance with the data for Standard English that I propose to ignore it henceforth). In this one theory, since ME *ī* and *ę̄* are both diphthongal, and since exchange rules are not allowed, there is no non ad hoc way of getting ME *ī* to /ey/ and ME *ę̄* to /iy/ without merger. But it should be recognized that this difficulty is a product of the conditions imposed by this particular theory, and is not inherent in the evidence. Some arguments regarding the evidence for the vowel plus glide analysis and the validity of exchange rules have already been discussed in Chapter V, and some further difficulties with the diphthongal interpretation of ME long tense vowels are discussed below. Let me just note here that whatever the phonetic facts may be, we have to explain why the orthoepists all perceived a difference in structure between ME *ī*, *ū*, and the long tense vowels. If we believe (as Stockwell in part does) that the long vowels were diphthongs ending in a centralizing off-glide, then the difference in glide would keep /eə/ and /ey/ apart. But Cooper at least differentiates /eə/ from /ē/ as variants of ME *ā*, and in any case Stockwell believes that ME *ę̄* raised to /iy/, and ME *ǭ* to /uw/. Further, to assume a diphthongal analysis removes some of the motivation for Stockwell's analysis, since he then has to postulate an overall change to homorganic glides where the traditional analysis postulates a change from long vowels to diphthongs, and remove the constraint on lengthening that only centralizing glides may be added. Viewed in this way, there is no great gain in simplicity in stating the historical changes.

It should be noted that in his discussion of various possible lines of development Stockwell (1969, p. 30) instances only:

$$(a) \quad [ɪ^ɪ] \; > \; [ə^ɪ] \; > \; [a^ɪ]$$
$$(b) \quad [ɪ^ɪ] \; > \; [ɨ^ɪ] \; > \; [ə^ɪ] \; > \; [a^ɪ]$$
$$(c) \quad [ɪ^ɪ] \; > \; [ɛ^ɪ] \; > \; [æ^ɪ] \; > \; [a^ɪ]$$

Only (b) and (c) are well formed under Stockwell's constraints (1952; 1969; and cf. discussion in Chapter II), and Stockwell would disallow (c) because of intersection with ME *ai*, assuming that this would cause merger, though, as discussed above, this seems doubtful. But Stockwell seems not to have considered position (3), namely:

$$(d) \quad [ɪ^ɪ] \; > \; [e^ɪ] \; > \; [ə^ɪ] \; > \; [a^ɪ]$$

which would be perfectly well formed even under his conditions and which would avoid the "problem" of merger with ME *ai* (though not, of course, the problem of merger with ME *ẹ̄*, if that is interpreted as a diphthong). In his discussion here (1969) Stockwell does not include as one of his constraints the exclusion of exchange rules as additions which switch existing vowels.

The above arguments seem to me to suggest that it is difficult to insist on the priority of centralization over lowering on any of the grounds generally advanced. The only possible justification remaining is the belief that /iy/→ /ey/ is not a possible change, or perhaps that /iy/→ /ey/ while /ē/→ /ī/ is not a possible change. But the evidence from Czech establishes without any doubt that this alternation is not only possible but actually exists in the synchronic grammar of a contemporary language. There cannot then be a universal constraint against this change, or even a serious claim that it cannot occur without impairing intelligibility or leading to a merger of the exchanged segments. Further, there is the evidence from German and English dialects for /iy/→ /ey/, so there can be no constraint against /ey/ being the reflex of older /ī/ in synchronic grammars. Since the simplest and most plausible interpretation of the orthoepistical evidence (Chapter III) is that diachronically lowering preceded centralization, and since this is in no way contradicted by anything in the rhyme, orthographical, or shorthand evidence (Chapter IV), then there seems no reason to reject position (3), the traditional interpretation supported by Ekwall, Horn, Luick, Jespersen, and Chomsky and Halle, which, after all (as pointed out by Ekwall (1958, p. 311)), is only very slightly different from Dobson's position.

But although there seems to be evidence from both English dialects and other languages to support exchange rules, there are arguments against the Chomsky-Halle formalization of rules for a dialect which has /ey/, /ow/, for earlier /ī/, /ū/, and /ī/, /ū/, for earlier /ē/, /ō/, two of which were discussed in Chapter V. One is that the subparts of the Vowel Shift Rule do not function alike with regard to their optional vs. obligatory status. At present, opinion is divided on whether this invalidates the rules; in my view this certainly militates against the possibility of claiming any psychological reality for such a rule. The second weakness in this analysis is that the whole change is represented as the result of the accidental cooccurrence of three separate rules, Diphthongization, Vowel Shift, and Diphthong Laxing, rather than as the unitary process it seems to be. And if English were to be analyzed in terms of four rather than three vowel heights, as Wang (1968) has suggested (an analysis which some of the evidence discussed in Chapters III and IV would seem to support; cf. discussion below), then this would be a third reason for rejecting the present form of the Chomsky-Halle rules for the historical change.

THE DEVELOPMENT OF ME ẹ̄

The claim that ME ẹ̄/ā/ai merged in educated upper-class speech, but that this dialect was displaced by one in which ME ẹ̄/ę̄ had merged, was outlined in Chapter I, and the evidence presented and discussed in Chapters III and IV.

Note first that for both Kökeritz and Dobson, to abandon the pronunciation of [ē] in favor of [ī] for ME ẹ̄ is not a sound change only because they assume that all sound changes must occur gradually. But note also the difficulties entailed by their acceptance of Wyld's claims.

Dobson accepts Wyld's suggestion that the pronunciation was borrowed (not as a rule, but from the surface form of each individual item) from a dialect which had already raised ME ẹ̄ to merge with με ẹ̄. In most words, then, he wishes to explain the Standard English pronunciation of /ī/ by borrowing. But this will not solve all his problems, since he also has to explain why ẹ̄ raised to /ī/ in foreign loanwords adopted as ME ẹ̄ during the EModE period. For Latin, Greek, and Hebrew he gives an explanation based on the difference between the "reformed" and "unreformed" pronunciation of Latin, and for loanwords from other languages he explains that since fifteenth-, six-teenth-, and seventeenth-century Standard English had no [ē] sound but only [ī] and [ɛ], speakers had to assign [ē] to one or the other, and "they might often identify the especially tense foreign [ē] with the rather lax English [ī] from ME ẹ̄ . . ." (1957a, p. 617). This last has the disadvantage of claiming that ME ẹ̄ remained completely unchanged from its ME value until the seventeenth century, and of making rather precise phonetic judgments on what seems to me quite sufficient evidence, and, finally, of saying it was just arbitrary choice that assigned these words to /ī/ rather than to /ē/. Further, Dobson's whole account has the disadvantage of requiring a triple explanation for the raising of ME ẹ̄ to /ī/.

Also, as Dobson himself discusses at some length, the assumption of borrowing merely uncovers the same problem in the dialect borrowed from, since in this dialect (Dobson suggests probably the Eastern dialects of Essex, Norfolk, and Suffolk (1957a, p. 611)) an explanation has to be found for the raising of ME ẹ̄ to merge with με ẹ̄, and again there is no single solution. The basic assumption is that "'all ME ẹ̄ words' had a ME variant in ME ẹ̄. How is this variation to be explained?" (Dobson (1957a, p. 612)). Here again the scholars quoted by Dobson have all been forced to make multiple explanations. Kökeritz's (1932) view is that in Suffolk ẹ̄ generally raised to /ī/, ẹ̄ for OE æ¹ being borrowed from the Anglian area and ẹ̄ for OE æ² being borrowed from Kentish. By some unexplained means ME ai, ā, also raised to /ī/, and when it was realized that Standard English had /ē/ for many of these sounds, /ē/ was substituted for /ī/ in all classes of words, i.e., ME ai, ā, ẹ̄, ẹ̄. Alternate explanations by other scholars are also quoted by Dobson. However, it seems quite clear that synchronically the situation in Suffolk was that a series of rules had been adopted raising ME ai, ā, ẹ̄, ẹ̄, to /ī/, and that these rules were optional. In fact, so far as I can tell this is essentially the view advanced in three of the accounts described by Dobson (though not, of course, in those terms). The differences in explanation seem to center largely around which dialect Suffolk is supposed to have borrowed the rules from, and the extent to which the rules were not all borrowed but were partly extended by analogy within Suffolk. But since all agree that there was a raising process in operation, and that there is (largely unpredictable) fluctuation as to whether this process applies or not, there seems nothing to conflict with the view that certain optional rules were added to the grammar of this dialect, and that it is not now (if it ever was) possible to determine what motivated the adoption of the rules. This should not surprise us, since the question of why sounds change is still unresolved (cf. Introduction). Dobson (and the scholars whose explanations he quotes) seems satisfied if he can discover a dialect from which the rule has been borrowed; but this, of course, merely pushes the question one stage further back (and also, as is natural considering the theory they work in, these scholars do not discuss either the mechanism of or constraints on adding rules to a grammar).

But Dobson seems not to have noticed that two of the Latin borrowings he cites, *supreme* and *sincere*, have the related forms *supremacy* and *sincerity* (Sundby, p. 35). Since /ē/ is here alternating with /e/, it would be surprising indeed if these words merged with με *ā*, which alternated with /æ/ (underlying /a/) as in *fable/fabulous*, *nature/natural* (all from Cooper). Further, these alternations suggest that even if the surface phonetic forms of ME *ẹ̄*, *ā*, had merged, in many instances the underlying forms must still have been distinct, so that it would have been possible to add a rule raising ME *ẹ̄* to /ī/ before the rule raising ME *ā* to /ē/.[1] It would then be possible to separate out a large number of ME *ẹ̄* words without assuming the speakers to have conscious knowledge of their etymology.[2] Thus the raising of ME *ẹ̄* to /ī/ in these loanwords, which for Dobson presents an extra problem, can in a generative phonology be explained by exactly the same mechanism as the general raising.

However, the surprising fact is that Dobson accepted Wyld's claims at all, particularly since he comments on Wyld's misinterpretation of the orthoepistical evidence. He admits himself that the authors of a few homophone lists are the only orthoepists to give any evidence of the merging of ME *ẹ̄* and *ā*, and they clearly distinguish between them in their general discussion. He notes with surprise that the rhyming dictionaries distinguish the sounds, as do the lists of "phonetically spelt" words, and that the two sounds are shown to be identical only in lists published after 1650, only in the careless lists, not the careful ones, and that there are in any case many exceptions. When we recall that Dobson does not consider the evidence of rhyme or of occasional spellings to be as reliable as that of the orthoepists, that the only orthoepist to identify the sounds is Tuite (and then only as a non-Standard English variant), and that Kökeritz, though accepting Wyld's claim, adduces no independent evidence to support it, Dobson's acceptance of Wyld's hypothesis seems singularly ill-motivated.

CONDITIONED DEVELOPMENTS OF ME *a, o*

Many orthoepists (e.g., Mulcaster, Hart, Robinson, Gil, Cooper) document an off-glide following *o* or *ō* before *l⧣* or *lC* (in fact, the environment differs slightly in the various orthoepists), as in *fold, gold, control*, etc., but not in, e.g., *solid, follow*. Dobson (1957a, p. 211) would explain this as being caused by lengthening of all /o/ in this position, followed by a raising of /ō/ to late ME *ū*, so that the /ū/ thus created participated in the Vowel Shift, producing /ow/. There are several disadvantages to this explanation.

First, note that if this were so, there is then no explanation for the failure of the lexical items affected by the change to fall in with με *ū* and thus to have /aw/ today, but we do not have */awld/ *old* */kəntrawl/, etc. Second, this analysis offers no explanation for Gil's /ōw/ in this environment, as in *göuld, föuld, höuld* (Jiriczek, p. 18). Third, Mulcaster, Hart, and Butler note a glide following ME *a* in the same environment; in later writers this is usually realized as /ɔ/. In Dobson's interpretation, this is a completely unrelated development.

A much more satisfactory explanation seems to be that /a/ was lengthened in this environment, and /o/ also in some dialects, and that then a rule was added inserting a back-glide before the /l/; we thus have /ow/, /aw/, with the length of the nuclei varying. For /a/, this stage is attested only in Hart, Mulcaster, and Butler, since the /āw/ produced by this rule in general falls in with original ME *au*. /ā/ is rounded before the glide /w/, and then the glide is deleted. /āw/ thus becomes /ɔ/. In fact, the derivation is more complicated than this, since although this change seems to have been quite general at first, and is illustrated in, e.g., Hodges, later /ɔ/ seems to have unrounded before labials, as in *calf, balm*. /ow/, on the other hand, falls in with με *ū* in Robinson's dialect, but more usually with με *ou*, as in Gil, and the two are later monophthongized to /ō/ together. There is also another rule which deletes /l/ following /ā/, /ō/, or /ɔ/ before labials and velars, as in *psalm, balm, yolk, holm, walk, chalk*, but not before dentals or word boundary, as in *ball, scold*. There seems to be little external evidence of the ordering, but simplicity would require us to order deletion of /l/ before original /ɔ/ had raised to /ō/, so that it applies to /l/ following low back tense vowels. Vowel raising must apply before rounding, since /ɔ/ from /āw/ does not raise to /ō/, and glide deletion must follow both, since it is the following glide which conditions rounding. We must then have the following ordering:

(1) vowel lengthening   (a, o)
(2) back glide insertion   (a, o)
(3) deletion of /l/   (a, o)
(4) vowel raising   (o)
(5) rounding   (a)
(6) monophthongization (both, but /āw/ much earlier than /ow/).

Note that this cannot be considered a case of /l/ "vocalizing" to /w/ (in traditional terms) because the glide and the /l/ cooccur in, e.g., *ball, fold.*

THE MIDDLE ENGLISH DIPHTHONGS AND
LONG TENSE VOWELS

The examination of the orthoepistical data led to the conclusion that ME *ai, au,* and *ou* were monophthongized to /ē/, /ɔ/, and /ō/, respectively, the first and last thus merging with με *ā* and *ǭ*. Further, there is nothing in the orthographic, shorthand, or rhyme evidence to conflict with this view. However, Sarrazin, Jespersen (1907), and Stockwell (1952; 1961; 1964; 1969; forthcoming) would claim that ME *ai* never monophthongized and that the present-day diphthong is a survival of the ME one. Sarrazin's opinion and evidence were disputed by Luick (1900), and Jespersen's by Horn (1912). In support of his theory, and against the orthoepistical evidence, Jespersen argued that even some modern phoneticians are unable to hear off-glides, and adduced the example of Ellis who (though acknowledging the existence of such glides both in general and in certain instances in his own speech) claimed that *say* was monophthongal when he said: *I say so,* even though phoneticians listening to him could invariably hear the off-glide there (Jespersen (1907, p. 42)). Stockwell (1969) would claim that all diachronic phonological descriptions and reconstructions are greatly conditioned by the "assumptions about the nature of sound-change which are presumably imposed by the historian on his data," and that although he may have reasons for his reconstructions, "these reasons are to be found not in data-based inferences but in theory-based inferences." No one will seriously dispute that a phonologist's analysis will be to a large extent (and, in the absence of data for certain stages, completely) determined by his theory, but it surely does not follow that theories should be advanced which directly conflict with the available data, particularly when there are alternative explanations which do not thus conflict.

Further, if Sarrazin, Jespersen, and Stockwell are correct, then we still have to explain why so many orthoepists heard the ME diphthongs as simply long tense vowels, while recognizing that ME $\bar{\imath}$, $\bar{u}$, were diphthongs. Why, for instance, does Hart hear ME $\bar{\imath}$, spelled with a single orthographic symbol, as /ey/, while perceiving ME *ai*, normally spelled with the digraphs *ai*, *ay*, as /ē/? Here one can neither claim that he cannot hear a diphthong nor that he is influenced by the spelling—and similar instances can be adduced from the other orthoepists.

Stockwell would also claim that all the sounds usually described as long tense vowels were then, as normally today, diphthongs consisting of a vowel plus off-glide. The arguments were outlined in Chapter I, and the evidence presented and discussed in Chapters III, IV, and V. In general it seems that the data does not support this analysis, and the claim that such an interpretation provides a solution to problems of ME which a more traditional analysis cannot does not seem to be true. The only difference is whether we believe that, after the high vowels had diphthongized (or, in Stockwell's formulation, after the glides on the high vowels had become homorganic), the system was:

/iy/	/uw/
/eh/	/oh/
/æh/	/ɔh/

or:

/iy/	/uw/
/ẹ̄/	/ọ̄/
/ę̄/	/ǭ/.

In the first system, after the mid vowels had raised, and the high vowels perhaps also centralized or lowered, depending on which occurred first, we have (Stockwell (1961)):

/iy/ (or /ɨy/)	/uw/ (or /ɨw/)
/ih/	/uh/
/eh/	/oh/

or, in the other system:

/iy/ (or /ey/)	/uw/ (or /ow/)
/ī/	/ū/
/ē/	/ō/ .

In either case there is a contrast between με *ī*, *ę̄*, and με *ū*, *ǭ*, which will account for the lengthening and shortening problems in ME. This seems to suggest that the Vowel Shift had started quite early, but does not indicate whether ME *ę̄*, *ẹ̄*, *ǭ*, *ọ̄*, were diphthongal or monophthongal.

Similarly, it was noted in Chapter V that the merger of OE *-ig*, *-ug*, with OE *ī*, *ū*, indicates nothing of the quality of the sound they merged as. *-ig*, *-ug*, could have become /iy/, /uw/ and then monophthongized to /ī/, /ū/. But even if we assume they fell together as /iy/, /uw/ (which later developments make more likely), this still offers no proof that OE *ī*, *ū*, were originally /ih/, /uh/; they could equally well have been /ī/, /ū/, and still have diphthongized to /iy/, /uw/, to fall in with the reflexes of *-ig*, *-ug*.

Further, let us consider some of the individual vowel systems described by the orthoepists. Gil, for instance, has /o/, /ō/, /ow/, and /ōw/, all in contrast. In Stockwell's theory, these would transliterate as /o/, /ow/, /ow/, and /oww/. Thus we are quite unable to represent one of Gil's contrasts, and have only a three-way distinction, with ME *ǭ* and *ū* merged. Further, we claim in this analysis that in Gil's dialect με *ū*, *ou*, were distinguished by the length of the glide, whereas Gil claims them to be distinguished by the length of the first element. It seems that given Stockwell's assumptions, /ō/ < ME *ǭ* can only be represented by either /ow/ or /oh/, and the second interpretation would yield worse results, since we would then assign to Gil the sounds /o/, /oh/, /ow/, and /ohw/. Here the distinction between με *ǭ* and *ū* is preserved, but the analysis of με *ou* seems rather unfortunate.

This is no straw argument, invented for the purpose of being demolished. Stockwell (1952) interprets Orm's dialect in just this way. Orm's *trewwess*, *strawwenn*, *trowwe*, are analyzed as /trewis/, /strawin/, and /trowe/, respectively. But Stockwell notes that Orm also has forms (1952, p. 136):

. . . which, in traditional terms, represented a 'long diphthong'—those which consisted of a vowel graph plus a single *w* or a single *ʒ*. Examples of these are *cnāwen*, *sāwle*, *sāwen*, *āʒhenn*, *wāwenn*, *shāwenn*, *halīʒ*, *manīʒ*. In this analysis they are interpreted as follows: *āw* = /oww/ or /ohw/; *āʒh* = /owg/ or /ohg/; *æw* = /eww/ or /ehw/; *īʒ* = /iyy/ or /iyj/. The alternates given here are possible alternate interpretations; they do not indicate that the spellings sometimes represented one, sometimes the other, of the alternates given.

Stockwell notes that he is interpreting a spelling such as *-oww* as representing VG, whereas a spelling *-āw* is interpreted as VGG; that is, superficially he seems to have reversed the values. He justifies his interpretation on the basis that Orm correctly heard that one complex nucleus had greater overall length than the other, but erroneously assigned this length to the vowel whereas in fact the glide was lengthened. The doubled semivowel merely indicates that the preceding vowel is short, which is Orm's normal practice. Stockwell claims that (p. 137) "It is completely consistent with the rest of Orm's orthography that he should have written the phonetically longer nucleus, /Vww/, as Vw, and the shorter nucleus, /Vw/, as Vww, so long as one recognizes that he was indicating the length of a *total nucleus*, not merely of a vowel alone."

First, the use of the term "recognize" seems rather to prejudge the issue; we have here a particular interpretation made in the framework of a specific linguistic theory, not an obvious fact. Next, it seems that Stockwell is himself not completely happy with this interpretation, or, rather, with the ambiguity of interpretation, since he points out (pp. 137-138) that:

The *ā* spelling in Orrm normally represented /oh/, just as *æ* normally represented /eh/. But in the complexes *āw* and *æw* there is some possibility that /oww/ and /eww/ are better interpretations than the more obviously consistent /ohw/ and /ehw/. The sound law . . . which stated the assimilation of /VSw/ to /Vww/ was predicated in willful disregard of Orrm's spellings of the reflexes of these nuclei.

These are, then, the two interpretations offered for Orm, which parallel the interpretations I suggest for Gil. But the lines of development suggested in Stockwell's outlines of English historical phonology (n.d.; 1959) would assign the values of /o/, /oh/, /əw/, and /ow/, to Gil's /o/, /ō/, /ow/, and /ōw/, respectively. We have then **three** possible interpretations of this notation, and there seems no principled way of predicting the interpretation to be assigned to the symbols. This in itself seems to me to be a flaw in the theory, since there seem to be no constraints on the values to be assigned to what native speakers hear as "long" and "short" diphthongs. We must then ask what justification there is for rejecting the analysis given by Orm and Gil. The only one offered in Stockwell (1952) is (p. 135): "An analysis which includes 'long' and 'short' diphthongs is to be avoided if the initial postulates of this study are to be followed without inconsistency." This is of course true, but the problem is the product of the theory on which the postulates of the study are based. The fact that an analysis which adheres more closely to Orm's description (and, of course,

to that of Gil and many other orthoepists) contradicts the postulates
of the study does not necessarily mean that such an analysis is wrong.
Rather, it seems to cast doubt on the postulates, particularly when
the interpretation seems counterintuitive (as it does here to me) and
not even definite since, as noted above, we are offered two analyses
here, both of which differ from that which Stockwell would offer for Gil.

Another possible justification which has been offered is the claim
that no existing language uses both long and short diphthongs, since
a principle generally accepted in historical linguistics is that reconstructions and descriptions of earlier languages should not violate the
constraints apparently obtaining in observed languages. Stockwell
and Barritt (1951), having defined four possible types of vocalic nuclei
CVC, CVLC, CVSC, and CVLSC (where L = a length phoneme and
S = semivowel, i.e., an off-glide), state (p. 5):

> We think it is an accurate statement that no languages have been
> found that utilize more than three of these four theoretically possible
> distinctions, or of any other four that might be set up; i.e., three types
> of syllabic nuclei seem to be a generalizable maximum. . . . The modern
> American English dialects of the writers have but two: V and VS.
> We know of some speakers who appear to have, in rare sets, three:
> V, VS, and VLS; but we know of none with four.

Tonkawa is an example of a language which appears to use all four,
that is, to have /e/, /ē/, /ey/, and /ēy/. Apparent instances of /ey/
contrasting with /ēy/ (which is what Stockwell particularly objects
to in some reconstructions of earlier stages of English, though admit-
ting this kind of contrast in the quotation above) in Tonkawa are
/mʔēyca/ *to urinate*, and /he-mʔemʔeyca/ *to urinate continuously*;
/heylapa/ *to stand up*, and /xēylapa/ *to stand way over there* (Hoijer,
p. 14, nos. 137.1, 137.4; p. 43, nos. 531.3, 531.11). I am further in-
formed that Welsh has [man] *place*, [ma:n] *small*, [maịn] *thin*, and
[ma:ịn] *stone*.[3]

A further objection is that modern dialect work shows very clearly that an analysis of English which allows only for short vowels and
diphthongs is inadequate. Some dialects make extensive use of pure
long tense vowels without off-glides (cf. the data in Orton and Halliday). One of Stockwell's arguments for preferring the diphthongal
analysis of ME (cf. Chapter I) was that it would make possible simpler
diachronic statements, but this was based on the assumption that
the output in ModE would be diphthongal. This is the case for Standard English, but it is possible that the Northern dialects represent

the kinds of sounds more common throughout England at earlier periods (as the orthoepistical evidence suggests), and that Modern Standard English is an innovation in this respect.

It seems that the only way to interpret the data by Stockwell's theory, incorporating his constraints, is to claim that the data is wrong, since on the face of it it is impossible to describe either earlier stages of English or contemporary dialects without using long vowels as well as diphthongs. And once we have the feature [±tense] (or [±long]) in addition to the possibility of adding an off-glide, it seems awkward to exclude arbitrarily one of the possible combinations—and perhaps incorrect, since we need them all for Tonkawa. Similarly, if we agree that, e.g., Gil is describing his dialect accurately, then we need all four types again. I would therefore prefer to believe that at this time English did have long tense vowels in contrast with both short vowels and with diphthongs, since this has the advantage of being able to interpret and explain the existing data rather than requiring one to reject it. It therefore seems possible to account for the changes in EModE without postulating underlying diphthongs except for the traditional ME diphthongs, or surface diphthongs except με ī, ū, and for the ME diphthongs not yet monophthongized. On the other hand, there seems no way of accepting and accounting for the data without using a tense/lax (or long/short) distinction.

A further, more problematic point concerns the general nature of change. The claims of Sweet (1888), Labov (n.d.; forthcoming), and Labov and Wald (1969) (cf. Introduction) seem to be supported by the development of the original long vowels involved in the Vowel Shift, and of the back short vowels, since ME u lowers and unrounds to [ʌ] while ME o lowers to [ɒ] and, dialectally in Britain and generally in America, unrounds to [ɑ]. But ME i, e, in general do not lower in British English. If, then, the theory of Sweet and Labov can be substantiated, it would help to explain why Czech, Old Prussian, English, and German all underwent such a similar sequence of shifts quite independently. But it would be impossible to make any use of this claim with Stockwell's theory, since there we have only short vowels, and could not explain why some raise while others lower. Labov's recent research into sound changes in progress certainly seems to support this hypothesis, and, therefore, to afford additional support for the traditional analysis of the Vowel Shift.

I now summarize my conclusions from the various kinds of evidence examined with regard to Stockwell's analysis. There is no evidence that to analyze the long tense vowels as diphthongs consisting of a vowel plus off-glide is a more accurate description of the phonetic output either for earlier stages of the language or for contemporary dialects, and there is some evidence against this (Chapters III, IV, V). The merits of such an analysis with regard to theoretical simplicity may be claimed, but they have yet to be demonstrated; the only synchronic description we have (in Stockwell (forthcoming)) is so much less detailed and explicit than that in Chomsky and Halle (1968) that the simplicity of the two cannot really be compared.

I have attempted to apply and extend the analysis to the data I have found, and encountered some difficulty in the attempt. I realize that many of these problems may stem from my imperfect understanding and use of the analysis, but the value of the analysis should consist in the help it gives us in describing and explaining the facts. It did not seem to me to make this in any way simpler. Finally, it entirely removes any possibility of explaining the Vowel Shift in the manner attempted by Sweet and Labov.

It is possible that all these difficulties might be overcome, or, alternatively, that Gil and the other orthoepists are incorrect in their observations. But this seems to be the best evidence there is, and one tends to be suspicious of a theory which forces one to reject the evidence rather than enabling one to describe and explain it. Another possible claim, of course, might be that although there were historical and are synchronic dialects of English having long tense vowels in the phonetic output, yet a simpler grammar can be written postulating diphthongal underlying forms. Such a claim has, for instance, been made for Korean (Kim, 1968), but in the absence of an overall analysis of English phonology within this theory, it is impossible to determine what the explicit rules might be, or what generalizations might be revealed. Therefore, one cannot tell whether such an analysis would be sufficiently superior to any presently available to outweigh the disadvantage of its apparently conflicting with much of the available data.

THREE- VERSUS FOUR-VOWEL-HEIGHT SYSTEMS

As noted in Chapter III, Cooper, although having the normal three long front vowels from ME $\bar{\imath}$, $\bar{e}$, and $\bar{e}$ in his underlying forms, has four in contrast at the systematic phonetic level: [æ], [ɛ], [e], and [i], and this is confirmed by Tiffin's evidence (Chapter IV). In the discussion on Cooper it was suggested that in order to describe his vowel system it would be necessary to allow for four distinct vowel heights.

Wang (1968) and Kiparsky (1968*b*) have already suggested that this is probably necessary in a universal system. The system suggested by Kiparsky is (p. 186):

	æ	ɛ	e	i
High	-	-	+	+
Mid	-	+	+	-

One advantage of adopting this system is that it would enable us to express a difference not capturable within a theory with only three distinctive vowel heights. From the evidence it seems probable that in the dialects of Gil and Holder, while there are only three heights in contrast, they are not the same three heights; that is, it seems likely that while Gil has basically [æ], [ɛ̄], [ī], Holder has [æ], [ē], [ī]. Wang has suggested that in ModE there would be a redundancy rule that raised all [-high] [+mid] vowels to [+high]; this rule apparently did not exist in EModE, and therefore both systems were possible, though not, of course, in contrast. Within a four-vowel-height system the difference is quite plain:

	æ	ɛ	e	i	
High	-	-		+	
					Gil
Mid	-	+		-	
High	-		+	+	
					Holder
Mid	-		+	-	

A further advantage is that this might help us to provide some explanation for the merger of ME ẹ̄, ę̄. Dobson claims that one weakness of considering the raising of ME ę̄ to merge with με ẹ̄ to be a normal sound change is that it destroys the parallelism of development between ME ǭ, ę̄, which had existed up to that point (Dobson (1957*a*, p. 609)). But once it became possible for there to be four distinctive vowel heights for the front vowels, as against three for the back, the situations were no longer parallel. Kiparsky has suggested that "systems of four vowel heights are unstable because of their complexity" (1968*b*, p. 186); this would then lead us to expect a simplification, and the most likely way would be for ME ę̄ to merge with με ẹ̄, since they both alternated with lax /e/.

Adoption of a four-vowel-height system would then enable us to describe the contrasts in the speech of Cooper and Tiffin, the non-contrastive difference between, e.g., Gil and Holder, and to provide a tentative explanation for ME ę̄ ceasing to be a distinct entity. It is possible to describe Cooper and Tiffin's system without a four-height system, by giving /æ/ the features of /ā/, which would mean that the rule lengthening ME *a* would have to apply after the rule fronting the original ME *ā* and before the fronting of ME *a*. ME *ā* and *a* could therefore not be fronted by the same rule. Further, since these distinctions exist at the systematic phonetic level, then if features have any empirical validity, any correlates in the real world, it is a little difficult to see how one would then translate these features of a back vowel into the real sound of [æ].

LEXICAL DIFFUSION OF SOUND CHANGE

In the data discussed there is a great deal of evidence for the lexical diffusion of a rule, as discussed in Wang (1968, p. 699; 1969). First, Dobson, when rejecting the theory that ME ę̄ raised to merge with με ȩ̄ by "phonetic change," cites as evidence the fact that "During the whole of the sixteenth and seventeenth centuries there is evidence of [i:] pronunciations in 'ME ę̄ words'" (1957*a*, p. 611). The spread of rules lowering and unrounding /u/ to /ə/ also supports this concept, and for this alternation we have seen evidence that the same word may have either pronunciation in different orthoepists or even be assigned both by the same writer. What is even more interesting is that in this case it seems never to have become a "major rule" (cf. Wang (1968, p. 699 n. 8)), since even after three hundred years both vowels are quite common, though there is virtually no fluctuation with regard to the pronunciation of any one specific lexical item. Similarly, the rule lengthening ME *a, o*, before certain consonant combinations seems to illustrate lexical diffusion. Finally, the rounding of *a* following *w*, which was still far from common in the eighteenth century, has now spread through British English and in some areas, though not universally, in American English to cover almost all instances except before velars, e.g. *water, war, swan*, vs. *wax, wag, swam*. Another interesting point is that the rounding of *a* **before** *w* seems to have been quite general. If this is true, then we may ask why some changes are generally effective and others gradually diffuse lexically. Is there any principled way of differentiating the two classes?

EXTENSION OF SOUND CHANGE BY
RULE SIMPLIFICATION

In Chapter II I discussed how a sound change can spread by simplification of the environment, so that it applies to a wider class of
lexical items. The data relating to the Vowel Shift provides some
instances illustrating this.

It will be remembered that Hodges has in his grammar /ə/ in stressed
syllables, resulting from the lowering and unrounding of /u/. This
appears in words like *buck*, but με *ū* is still /ow/. Therefore, Hodges
has added a rule lowering /u/ to /o/,[4] and then another rule unrounding
/o/ to /ə/ before consonants only:

$$
\begin{bmatrix} +\text{back} \\ -\text{tense} \\ -\text{low} \\ -\text{high} \end{bmatrix} \rightarrow [-\text{round}] \;\Big/\; \underline{\hspace{2cm}} \; \begin{bmatrix} +\text{cons} \\ -\text{voc} \end{bmatrix}
$$

Note that the first rule will change ME /uy/ to /oy/, but that the second
rule will not apply to change /oy/ to /əy/. This may explain why
ME /uy/ words often seem to be realized as /oy/, a phenomenon which
puzzles Dobson and which he can explain only as analogy.

But in the dialects of Wallis and subsequent writers we find /əw/
for με *ū*; that is, the constraint on the environment has been removed,
and the simplified rule is now:

$$
\begin{bmatrix} +\text{back} \\ -\text{tense} \\ -\text{low} \\ -\text{high} \end{bmatrix} \rightarrow [-\text{round}]
$$

as in Chomsky and Halle (1968, p. 269), and the rule is now generalized to apply in many more cases including, of course, not only με
ū but also ME /uy/, which, as we would expect, turns up in Wallis's
dialect as /əy/. Further, ME /oy/ can also be unrounded to /əy/ by
this rule, as, indeed, it often is. This means that children learning the
language cannot easily distinguish between reflexes of ME /uy/ and
ME /oy/, and the two become confused, as we would expect.

However, although the extension of his rule by simplification of
the structural analysis describes and explains the centralization of

the first element of με ū, it does not explain the development of ME ī.
Chomsky and Halle (1968) incorporate this into the same unrounding
rule by altering the Diphthong Laxing Rule to include switching backness, so that /ey/ → /oy/, and the first element is then unrounded.
But the introduction and subsequent extension of the rules lowering
and unrounding /u/ to /ə/ do not explain this, and in fact I know of
no explanation. In a two-dimensional array it seems very symmetrical and therefore somehow logical that /e/ and /o/ should both centralize together. But perhaps this is only a spurious appearance of logic
and the spatial symmetry is irrelevant, since /e/ centralizes only before /y/, and there is still a lax /e/, whereas ME o lowers to /ɔ/, and
all instances of /o/ present at the time the unrounding rule operates
centralize, whether or not before a glide. Further, when, instead of
looking at the spatial arrangement, one considers the rules as formulated, there is no reason why unrounding and slight fronting of
/o/ should entail retraction of /e/. However, since the two phenomena
do occur together, one would like to link them together more closely
and naturally than the present formulation does.

The Vowel Shift in Old Prussian (cf. Chapter V) also seems to illustrate rule simplification. The earliest monument is the Elbing vocabulary, which is usually dated as being fourteenth century, at the
latest 1400. In this document original i, u, are sometimes represented
as e, o, respectively; however, original ī, ū, are not affected. That
is, there is an optional rule of the form:

$$[+\text{high}] \quad \rightarrow \quad [-\text{high}] \quad \begin{bmatrix} \rule{1cm}{0.4pt} \\ -\text{low} \end{bmatrix} \Big/ \begin{bmatrix} +\text{cons} \\ -\text{voc} \end{bmatrix}$$

In the versions of the catechism, the environment has simplified so
that this rule will apply both to orginal i, u, and to the diphthongs
/iy/, /uw/, from original ī, ū. Since original ē, ō, simultaneously raise
to /ī/, /ū/, I suggested earlier that the Chomsky-Halle Vowel Shift
rules could be used. However, if the change originated with the high
lax vowels and still includes them (as seems to be the case), then the
feature [+tense] must be removed from the specification of the environment. The rule will then predict that the high and mid lax vowels will switch as well as the tense vowels. Since Old Prussian has
no original e, o, this will not produce incorrect outputs. The final Vowel Shift rule for Old Prussian will then be:

$$[\alpha\text{high}] \quad \rightarrow \quad [-\alpha\text{high}] \quad / \begin{bmatrix} \text{\textemdash} \\ -\text{low} \end{bmatrix}$$

Further, the extension to cover the original long vowels should probably be considered a simplification also, if "variables like alpha are higher valued (count less) in the simplicity metric than a specified plus or minus" (King (1969*b*, p. 11)). The rule has then been simplified in two ways. Note that there would then apparently be no reason for ordering Diphthong Laxing to follow Vowel Shift.

I noted earlier (Chapter II) that if we use Bach's neighborhood convention Hoenigswald's example of the gradual disappearance of Greek digamma can be considered a case of progressive generalization of the rule by simplification of the environment. We have another example of this in one of the changes documented by the orthoepists. Quite generally /a/ → /ɔ/ before /w/, regardess of whether the /w/ was part of an original ME diphthong or arose through the rule inserting a back-glide in certain environments. Later we see signs of the gradual rounding of /a/ to /ɔ/ following /w/—gradual, that is, not in the sense that the vowel was first a little bit rounded and then became more so, but in that the rule applied to more and more items. We have, then, the introduction of the rule:

$$a \quad \rightarrow \quad ɔ \: / \: w\text{\textemdash}$$

This can be combined with the earlier rule to give:

$$a \quad \rightarrow \quad ɔ \: / \: w$$

or, more specifically:

$$\begin{bmatrix} +\text{back} \\ +\text{low} \end{bmatrix} \quad \rightarrow \quad [+\text{round}] \quad / \begin{bmatrix} +\text{back} \\ -\text{voc} \\ -\text{cons} \end{bmatrix}$$

This presupposes that ME *a* is still /a/ in the underlying form, and that the restructuring postulated by Chomsky and Halle for Cooper's dialect had not taken place. Further, this would single out the rounding of /a/ to /ɔ/ as a special case, whereas in the Chomsky-Halle formulation it is deeply integrated into the set of rules, since Chomsky and Halle concern themselves only with the major processes in the Vowel Shift. But since the gradual spread of this particular rule is documented by so many orthoepists and becomes so general in the language, and, further, since it seems it can to some extent be explained, I feel it should be taken into account.

SUMMARY OF CONCLUSIONS

It seems then that the orthoepistical, rhyme, and shorthand evidence indicates that ME $\bar{\imath}$, $\bar{u}$, lowered to /ey/, /ow/, before centralizing to /əy/, /əw/, and occasional spellings offer no evidence contrary to this. The only undocumented stage is the diphthongization of the original long tense vowels to /iy/, /uw/. Any other interpretation must be based on theoretical grounds strong enough to outweigh the data, and since the /ī/∼/ey/ and /ū/∼/ow/ alternations are attested in current English and German dialects and also in Czech, it seems unlikely that such a formulation of the change could be proved invalid on theoretical grounds.

There is, however (as noted by Chomsky and Halle), no evidence as to whether the dialect attested by Hart and the other early orthoepists came about by the addition of an exchange rule, except the difficulty of expressing the optionality of such a rule, as in Czech, which is against the addition of such an exchange rule to the grammar; nor, if the exchange rule is the result of restructuring, is there any evidence as to whether the mid vowels raised first, or the high vowels diphthongized and lowered.

The orthoepistical and shorthand evidence all attests that ME $\bar{e}$ remained distinct from ME $\bar{a}$ in Standard English, but that there was some merger in nonstandard dialects. The rhyme evidence shows that there was a variant pronunciation of ME $\bar{e}$ similar to με $\bar{a}$, but it is questionable what status this particular dialect had or how exact the resemblance was. Occasional spellings yield no clear evidence about the exact quality of the sounds. Thus, though there is evidence on both sides, the clearest evidence indicates that ME $\bar{e}$ retained its distinct identity until merging with με $\bar{e}$.

The orthoepistical and shorthand evidence further confirms the traditional analysis of the ME long/short distinction in vowels, and also that the ME diphthongs *ai*, *au*, and *ou* monophthongized. Again there is nothing in the rhyme or orthographical evidence to contradict this point of view, and any contrary theory must be based on purely theoretical grounds, in opposition to the available data.

In general, then, it seems that the facts (as far as they can be ascertained) do correspond more closely to the traditional analysis followed by Chomsky and Halle, and that the rules suggested by them do seem in general to recapture the history of the Vowel Shift at all attested stages—that is, from the time of Hart on—though, as they admit, they have ignored minor changes and also make no claims about the stages preceding Hart. The data examined also provides some support for concepts in the theory of generative phonology in general, in particular exchange rules, the lexical diffusion of a minor rule till it becomes a major rule, and the generalization of a rule by simplification of the structural analysis. There is also some slight evidence in favor of a four- rather than three-vowel-height system.

NOTES

1. The name was apparently coined by Jespersen (1909, p. 231).
2. This terminology and the theory in which it is used will be explained in Chapter II.
3. In fact, the status of such forms is not usually discussed in traditional grammars.
4. This account greatly oversimplifies the process. As Labov's studies show, in New York the trend is **towards** variants which are socially stigmatized; in a recent paper this question is raised and a possible answer suggested (Labov (1970, p. 75)): "Why don't all people speak in the way that they obviously believe they should? ... Careful consideration of this difficult problem has led us to posit the existence of an opposing set of covert norms, which attribute positive values to the vernacular."

CHAPTER I

1. Stockwell's theory is an exception to this.
2. Note that this is **not** what Dobson (1957a, p. 660) calls "the usual theory."
3. This is a very rough approximation to the values implied by Ellis's palaeotype.
4. Kökeritz's discussion of ME $\bar{u}$ is exactly parallel to that of ME $\bar{\imath}$, making the same unexplained reference to modern diphthonging tendencies and postulating totally undocumented stages for which he does not attempt to provide any justification at all (1953, p. 245).
5. Note that (like Chomsky and Halle but unlike Stockwell) in this article Hockett treats centralized vowels as unrounded back vowels.

CHAPTER II

1. The literature on transformational grammar is very extensive. The following account here is necessarily sketchy, and refers to only a handful of the better-known works. However, all of these have full bibliographies. Chomsky (1965, Chap. I) covers most points of interest, though the work in general is concerned primarily with syntactic theory.

2. This is an oversimplification, and more detailed accounts can be found in, e. g., Chomsky (1965, pp. 15-18; 1967a); and Chomsky and Halle (1968, pp. 3-14). One complication discussed in the latter work is that although the output of the syntactic component and the input to the phonological component (p. 9) ". . . do coincide to a very significant degree . . . there are also certain discrepancies. These discrepancies . . . indicate that the grammar must contain certain rules converting the surface structure generated by the syntactic component into a form appropriate for use by the phonological component." These discrepancies entail (amongst other considerations) that a distinction must be made between lexical representation and phonological representation. Chomsky and Halle resolve these discrepancies by invoking the use of "readjustment rules." The status of these is at present somewhat uncertain, but this whole question does not affect in any way the problems with which we are immediately concerned.

3. The necessity (and also the possibility) of ordering the rules in the phonological component of the grammar has been disputed. See Chomsky (1967b) for a discussion and defense of this property of the rules.

4. See Halle (1964) for a brief (though now somewhat outdated) explanation of this.

5. Except, of course, by definition, since it would be possible to define sound change as the addition (extension, etc.) of a classificatory rule using binary features.

6. Wright (§§ 86-87) discusses this phenomenon and gives many examples.

7. See discussion in Bach (1968).

8. The published work does not reflect the chronology of this controversy correctly. These points were first raised by Stockwell in a paper "Realism in Historical Phonology" read before the Winter 1964 meeting of the Linguistic Society of America. Following this paper McCawley wrote to Stockwell supporting some of his arguments, and was quoted in a paper "Problems in the Interpretation of the Great English Vowel Shift" read by Stockwell at a conference at the University of Texas in January 1966. McCawley (1969) incorporates an updated version of McCawley's views, while Stockwell (forthcoming) is a revised paper incorporating the substance of both the 1964 and 1966 (previously unpublished) papers.

CHAPTER III

1. I omit any discussion of the diphthongs consisting of *w*, *y*, plus following vowels, as in, e.g., *ui* (*we*), *iu* (*you*).

2. *de* for *the* occurs three times in these sentences in Danielsson's editions; however, Danielsson does not comment on these examples in his discussion of the phonology (1963, pp. 209-210).

3. *their* is usually transcribed with a long vowel ðēr.

4. Any reference to contemporary French pronunciation is based on Pope.

5. This kind of comparison is quite common in orthoepistical writings, though it is highly improbable that French had a lax [ɪ] sound, or, alternatively, that the /i/ in *until* was tense. However, the pronunciation is still sufficiently similar for them to be equated and contrasted with με ī.

6. It has been suggested to me that the diphthong /ey/ which later became /oy/, as in *moi*, could have passed through an intermediate stage in which it has a centralized first element, and that Bellot was referring to this sound. Against this, however, Pope gives the change of /ey/ > /oy/ as occurring before the middle of the twelfth century, and, further, she does not indicate a stage with a centralized first element (pp. 104-105).

7. Bullokar includes here the half-vowels *l, m, n*; I have completely excluded these from my discussion.

8. Zachrisson (1927, p. 12) adds *ów* here.

9. This may be the same as Cooper's centralizing glide following ME *ā* before *n*, though Mulcaster usually uses *u* to indicate a back-glide.

10. For instance, he lists *yeild, sheild, feild* (p. 153) in his discussion of ME *ai* pronounced *ei*. Mulcaster has simply taken this spelling (in which the vowel symbols are reversed from the order normal today) at its face value.

11. Gil makes frequent references to the speech of the "Mopsae," by which he appears to mean an affected, overfashionable type of pronunciation, of which he is highly critical.

12. *Skolars* seems to be Gil's error for *skolarz*, and is not significant.

13. Other evidence, particularly occasional spellings (cf. Chap. IV), indicates that this variant was not limited to the ultrafashionable, and that it was current much earlier than Gil.

14. In fact, there is evidence for four vowel heights in the descriptions of Cooper and Tiffin (cf. discussion below).

15. *Pre* is presumably a misprint.

16. Here and elsewhere the general text of the quotations from Butler has been converted into normal modern orthography; however, the original spelling is retained for the specific sounds and examples cited, italics being used instead of his modified black letter.

17. Zachrisson (1913, p. 133) believes that Erondelle in *The French Schoole-Maister* (1606) identifies French *e feminine* with the vowel of *come*. However, the quotation is: "What French-men do call *e*, feminine—marke therefor how you sound the second sillable of facere, legere in Latin and pronounce so our *e* feminine at the words end: mark how the common doe sound this English phrase: *Is he come.*" It is then not clear to what Erondelle was referring in the English phrase; he may have meant that unstressed *he* was commonly pronounced with /ə/

(as Zachrisson later suggests himself (1927, p. 56)); an illustration would be the use of *a* for *he* in Mistress Quickly's account of the death of Falstaff (*King Henry V*, Act. II, Sc. III).

18. A possible solution is indicated by a passage in Hunt (1691, p. 10), where we read:

L. 111 what is the difference between *ai*, *ei*, *oi*, with an (*i*) and *ay*, *ey*, *oy*, with a (*y*)? or also between *au*, *eu*, *ou*, with an (*u*) and *aw*, *ew*, *ow*, with (*w*)?

M. This: dipthongs made with (*i* and *u*) are pronounced *short*, those with (*y* and *w*) *long*: . . .

That is, it seems possible that in word-final positions the diphthongs were perceived as longer than the same diphthongs elsewhere. However, later we read (p. 26) that both the so-called "short" diphthongs and also the "long" diphthongs may begin a word, though the "short" diphthongs are more often used in that position (no examples are given). Further (pp. 44-45), both "short" and "long" diphthongs may end words, but usually a "short" diphthong either has an *e* added, e.g. *staie*, *praie*, *boie*, or is turned into a "long" diphthong, e.g. *stay*, *pray*, *boy*. A rule is given here for the spelling (p. 45): ". . . usually the diphthongs with (*i* and *u*) are written in the beginning of words, and those with (*y* and *w*) in the ending of words, especially *if no consonant follow*." The distinction then seems to be purely orthographical. As in Daines, in this discussion *eu*, *ew*, is apparently used for both ME *ēu* and *ēu*, and *ou*, *ow*, for both ME *ou* and *ū*.

19. A facsimile reprint of the first edition of 1653 has now been published by the Scolar Press. I have retained my original references notwithstanding, since presumably the revised edition represents Wallis's final considered opinions, and in some instances has fuller examples; it is quite easy to locate the passages in the earlier edition if necessary. All translations are based on those in Greenwood (1722).

20. With reference to Wallis's powers of phonetic discrimination, note that although he describes voicing quite accurately, he claims that the difference between voiced and voiceless stops and fricatives is caused not by this but by nasalization (Horn Tooke has written *No*! at intervals down the margin of his own copy of the 1765 edition (now in the British Museum) every time this claim is made), and insists on this analysis, instancing [f] and [v], even after other phoneticians had disagreed with him (Wallis (1678, p. 19)). It would not be fair to place too much emphasis on this since all the early phoneticians have similar lapses, but equally we should not consider Wallis gifted above all other early writers on the subject.

21. But, rather surprisingly, in his discussion of diphthongs in *De Loquela* Wallis claims that the diphthong *ei*, *ey*, is pronounced with *e feminine* plus *y* (p. 36), i.e., as /əy/, which does not seem a very likely realization for this.

22. Of this pronunciation, Horn Tooke commented in the margin of his copy, "The Irish pronounce in this manner, but not the Southern English."

23. Horn Tooke objects to *one, none,* as examples of *o rotundum* and says that "The Southern English do not pronounce in this manner." He also claims that the *u pingue* pronunciation of *go* is not used in Southern English.

24. Wilkins uses this symbol here, whereas elsewhere he uses (X).

25. Dobson seems not to have noted this, since he merely mentions as a "surprising feature of Lodwick's system . . . his failure to mention [u] either as the short equivalent of his vowel *oo* . . . or as a separate vowel" and ascribes it partly to the fact that Dutch has only [ū] (1957*a,* p. 278).

26. I am greatly indebted to Jules Levin both for referring me to an account of this (in Alekseev) and for translating the relevant portions. I understand he is working on an analysis of all Kellerman's transcriptions, and, of course, pending such an analysis the inferences suggested here can be regarded only as very tentative.

27. Where only one of Kellerman's versions is given, it is the phonetic transcription, the transliteration being omitted; where both are given, the transliteration comes first.

28. *Orthoepistical* is misquoted as *orthopoetical* in Chomsky and Halle.

29. Chomsky and Halle may perhaps also have been misled by a statement in Cooper on the pronunciation of *I lingual* (p. 6): "The *English* alwayes express this sound when short by *i,* which character also, when taken for the short sound, they never pronounce otherwise, unless before *r,* for the reason aforesaid under *e.*" This refers to the fact that in Cooper's dialect ME lax *i* and *e* had both become /ə/ before *r.*

30. Note how this differentiation of *tear* (*lacrima*) and *tear* (*rend*) agrees with Cooper's.

31. Kökeritz (1953, p. 32 n. 3) claims that Tuite recommends the με *ā* pronunciation; I can find nothing in Tuite to substantiate this claim.

32. It is not clear which words he thought had this *eoo* sound, nor what exactly the sound was, since in his third dissertation he complains at length (pp. 146-179) about the supposed diphthong *iu* in, e.g., *nature, superstition,* and apparently insists that they should have the vowel of *fool.*

CHAPTER IV

1. It seems less likely that Poole would lengthen the first element in ME *ū,* since the general tendency is to lax the first element of diphthongs.

2. Matthews (1943, p. 155) notes that Coles's *Latin Dictionary* (1679) is apparently the first source for ME *ę̄/ę̄* rhymes, e.g. *been/bean, steel/ steal.* Unfortunately, I did not see a copy of Söderholm's study of *The End-Rhymes of Marvell, Cowley, Crashaw, Lovelace and Vaughan* (1970) until this work was in press, so that I was not able to make use of his findings as much as I would have liked. I have, however, incorporated some of his discussion of the development of ME *ę̄* into the notes of

this chapter. Anyone interested in this kind of evidence should certainly consult Söderholm since it seems to me an excellent study, superior to both Gabrielson and Wyld.

3. Söderholm (pp. 77-79) has a useful section on the evidence provided by 17th-century rhymes on the vacillation in pronunciation of ME $\bar{e}$ before r.

4. Söderholm comes to the same conclusion. He says (p. 85):

> . . . it seems perfectly clear that the poets made abundant use of the possibilities offered by the great variety in 17th-c. pronunciation attested also by orthoepists and spellings. The rhymes reflect faithfully most variants on record, often in one and the same poet. . . . Such rhymes simply cannot be based entirely on the poets' own habits of pronunciation, however great the allowance made for variant pronunciations in the speech of one and the same individual.

5. Söderholm concludes that in the 17th century ME $\bar{e}$ was generally still distinct from ME $\bar{e}$, $\bar{a}$, and ai, noting in particular that "Rhymes between $\bar{e}$ and $\bar{a}$, ai [are] clearly avoided" (p. 88), and earlier (p. 24) points out that ". . . it may reasonably be asked why two long e-sounds could not have existed in 17th-c.E ([ɛ:] < ME $\bar{a}$, ai and [e:] < ME $\bar{e}$) as well as in ME ($\bar{e}$ and $\bar{e}$)?"

6. And see n. 22, Chapter III.

7. As discussed earlier in this chapter, Labov has now changed his position on the $\bar{e}/\bar{a}$ merger.

CHAPTER V

1. At this time Orton was a member of the faculty of Armstrong College, Durham University.

2. This is what we would expect, since neutralization of the front/back distinction is usually found in [-high] vowels, so that we would consider vowel systems like (a) natural and (b) less natural:

(a)			(b)		
	i	u		ɨ	
	e	o		e	o
		a		æ	ɔ

This is another argument against position (2) (cf. Chap. VI), since this would require that the [+high] vowels be centralized as the first change. However, it should be noted that Stockwell (who has seen much of the survey material at Leeds University) claims that what is there transcribed [əi] would by an American phonetician be transcribed [ɨi].

3. I have omitted here some variants which seem to me to be obviously reflexes of the mutated plural, e.g. [kai].

4. I am indebted to C. Douglas Johnson for bringing this item to my attention.

5. I have to thank C. Douglas Johnson for the formulation of this rule.

6. In Lass's view, the primary impulse is the raising of the mid vowels; cf. discussion of this in previous section.

CHAPTER VI

1. As suggested in Halle (1962*b*).

2. Labov and Wald have presented evidence to show that in an *r*-less dialect in New York the vowels of word pairs such as *source/sauce* are kept distinct, perhaps on the basis of an underlying *r*, even though the speakers of this dialect claim that the words are homophonous. It seems possible then that ME $\bar{e}$ and ME $\bar{a}$ may have been distinct even in the speech of those who confused their spelling (cf. Chap. IV). Further, ME $\bar{e}$ words could be (and in some dialects regularly were) pronounced as με $\bar{e}$, whereas this was not possible for ME $\bar{a}$ words. Labov has suggested that a sound change which diffuses lexically (as the raising of ME $\bar{e}$ to με $\bar{e}$ seems to have done, *break*, *steak*, and *great* being examples of lexical items which were not affected by the change) "involves the temporary dissolution of word classes." The word class "is defined as the class of lexical items which can vary between X and Y . . ." (Labov (1970, p. 72 & n. 37*a*)), in this case ME $\bar{e}$, which can be realized either as με $\bar{a}$ (or as something very similar to it) or as με $\bar{e}$. Thus even if ME $\bar{e}$ did cease to be a distinct sound and instead merged partially with με $\bar{a}$ (which, in the face of the orthoepistical evidence, seems unlikely), the class of words which originally had this sound could still raise to merge with με $\bar{e}$.

3. I have to thank E. W. Roberts for this example.

4. Chomsky and Halle incorporate this in the Vowel Shift by use of a special condition; whether it is in fact part of the Vowel Shift or a separate process is immaterial here.

BIBLIOGRAPHY

ALEKSEEV, M. P.
  1968. *Slovari inostannyx jazykov v azbukovnike XVIII veka*, Leningrad: izd. Nauka.
ALSTON, R. C.
  1967-68. *English Linguistics 1500-1800* [A series of facsimile reprints of early works on the English language]. Menston, Eng.: The Scolar Press.
BACH, EMMON
  1968. "Two Proposals Concerning the Simplicity Metric in Phonology," *GLOSSA* 2:128-149.
BAILEY, C.-J. N.
  1969. "The English Great Vowel Shift Past and Present," *Working Papers in Linguistics 2*. University of Hawaii, pp. 1-5.
BAUGH, A. C.
  1952. *A History of the English Language*. New York: Appleton-Century-Crofts.
BELLOT, JACQUES
  1580. *The Englische Scholemaster*. No 51 *in* Alston.
BULLOKAR, WILLIAM
  1580. *Book at Large*. London.
BUTLER, CHARLES
  1634. *See* Eichler.
BLISS, A. J.
  1948-49. "Three Middle English Studies," *English and Germanic Studies* II:40-54.
CAMPAGNAC, E. T., ed.
  1925. *Mulcaster's Elementarie*. London: Oxford University Press.
CARTER, RICHARD
  1967. "Some Theoretical Implications of the Great Vowel Shift." Unpublished paper read to the New York Linguistic Circle, March 1967.

CHOMSKY, NOAM
1964. "Current Issues in Linguistic Theory," *in* Fodor and Katz, 50-118.
1965. *Aspects of the Theory of Syntax.* Cambridge, Mass.: MIT Press.
1967*a*. "The Formal Nature of Language," *in* Eric H. Lenneberg, ed., *Biological Foundations of Language.* New York : John Wiley & Sons. Pp. 397-442.
1967*b*. "Some General Properties of Phonological Rules," *Language* 43:102-128.
CHOMSKY, NOAM, and M. HALLE
1965. "Some Controversial Questions in Phonological Theory," *Journal of Linguistics* 1:97-138.
1968. *The Sound Pattern of English.* New York: Harper and Row.
COLES, ELISHA
1674. *The Compleat English Schoolmaster.* No. 26 *in* Alston.
COOPER, CHRISTOPHER
1687. *See* Sundby.
DAINES, SIMON
1640. *Orthoepia Anglicana.* No. 31 *in* Alston.
DANIELSSON, BROR, ed.
1955, 1963. *John Hart's Works on English Orthography and Pronunciation* [Stockholm Studies in English]. Stockholm: Almqvist and Wiksell [1955, Part I; 1963, Part II].
DIXON, DOROTHY
1951. *Alexander Gil's Logonomia Anglica* [Edition of 1621, translated with an Introduction and Critical and Explanatory Notes]. Unpublished Ph. D. dissertation, University of Southern California.
DOBSON, E. J.
1947. "Robert Robinson and His Phonetic Transcripts of Early Seventeenth Century English Pronunciation," *Transactions of the Philological Society* 25-63.
1955. "Early Modern Standard English," *Transactions of the Philological Society* 25-54.
1957*a*. *English Pronunciation 1500-1700.* London: Oxford University Press.
1957*b*. *The Phonetic Writings of Robert Robinson.* Early English Text Society No. 238. London: Oxford University Press.
1962. "Middle English Lengthening in Open Syllables," *Transactions of the Philological Society* 124-148.
DOUGLAS, JAMES
ca. 1740. *See* Holmberg.
EICHLER, A., ed.
1910. *Charles Butler's English Grammar* (*1634*). [Neudrucke frühenglischer Grammatiken, Bd. 4, 1]: Halle.
EKWALL, E., ed.
1911. *The Writing Scholar's Companion* (*1695*). [Neudrucke frühenglischer Grammatiken, Bd. 6]: Halle.

EKWALL, E.
1914. *Historische neuenglische Laut- und Formenlehre.* Berlin: G. J. Göschen.
1958. Review of: E. J. Dobson (1957a), *Review of English Studies,* n.s. 9:303-312.
ELLIS, A. J.
1867-1889. *On Early English Pronunciation.* Early English Text Society Series Nos. 2, 7, 14, 23, 25. London: Trübner.
FODOR, JERRY A., and JERROLD J. KATZ, eds.
1964. *The Structure of Language: Readings in the Philosophy of Language.* Englewood Cliffs, N.J.: Prentice-Hall.
GABRIELSON, A.
1909. *Rime as a Criterion of the Pronunciation of Spenser, Pope, Byron, and Swinburne.* Uppsala: Almqvist and Wiksell.
GIL, ALEXANDER
1621. *See* Dixon; Jiriczek.
GREENWOOD, JAMES
1722. *An Essay towards a Practical English Grammar.* London.
HALLE, M.
1962a. "A Descriptive Convention for Treating Assimilation and Dissimilation," *Quarterly Progress Report* No. 66, Research Laboratory of Electronics, MIT, 295-296.
1962b. "Phonology in Generative Grammar," *in* Fodor and Katz, 334-352.
1964. "On the Bases of Phonology," *in* Fodor and Katz, 324-333.
HALLE, M., and SAMUEL J. KEYSER
1967. Review of: Danielsson (1963), *Language* 43:773-787.
HART, JOHN
1555. *See* Danielsson.
1569. *See* Danielsson.
1570. *See* Danielsson.
HERZOG, GEORGE
1964. "Drum Signaling in a West African Tribe," *in* Dell Hymes, ed., *Language in Culture and Society.* New York: Harper and Row. Pp. 312-329.
HOCKETT, C. F.
1958. *A Course in Modern Linguistics.* New York: The MacMillan Co.
1959. "The Stressed Syllabics of Old English," *Language* 35:575-597.
1965. "Sound Change," *Language* 41:185-205.
HODGES, RICHARD
1644. *See* Kauter.
1653. *Most Plain Direction for True-Writing* [A version of *A Special Help to Orthographie* (1643)]. No. 118 *in* Alston.
HOENIGSWALD, H. M.
1960. *Language Change and Linguistic Reconstruction.* Chicago: The University of Chicago Press.
1964. "Graduality, Sporadicity, and the Minor Sound Change Processes," *Phonetica* 11:202-215.

HOIJER, HARRY
    1949. *An Analytic Dictionary of the Tonkawa Language.* Berkeley
        and Los Angeles: University of California Press.
HOLDER, W.
    1669. *The Elements of Speech.* London.
HOLMBERG, B.
    1956. *James Douglas on English Pronunciation c1740* [Lund Studies
        in English XXVI]. Copenhagen: Munksgaard.
HORN, W.
    1908. *Historische neuenglische Grammatik.* Strassburg: K. J. Trübner.
    1912. "Probleme der neuenglische Lautgeschichte," *Anglia* 35:357-392.
HUNT, THOMAS
    1661. *Libellus Orthographicus.* No. 94 *in* Alston.
HYMAN, LARRY M.
    1970. "How Concrete Is Phonology?" *Language* 46:58-76.
JESPERSEN, OTTO
    1907. *John Hart's Pronunciation of English (1569 and 1570), An-*
        glistische Forschungen 22. Heidelberg.
    1909. *A Modern English Grammar on Historical Principles, Part 1:*
        Sounds and Spellings. Heidelberg: Carl Winter.
JIRICZEK, OTTO L.
    1903. *Alexander Gill's Logonomia Anglica* [Quellen und Forschungen
        zur Sprach- und Culturgeschichte der Germanischen Völker,
        XC]. Strassburg.
KAUTER, H., ed.
    1930. *The English Primrose,* by Richard Hodges (1644) [Germanische
        Bibliothek, Abt. 2, Bd. 82]. Heidelberg.
KIM, CHIN-WU
    1968. "The Vowel System of Korean," *Language* 44:516-527.
KING, ROBERT D.
    1967. "Functional Load and Sound Change," *Language* 43:831-852.
    1969a. *Historical Linguistics and Generative Grammar.* Englewood
        Cliffs, N.J.: Prentice-Hall.
    1969b. "Push Chains and Drag Chains," *GLOSSA* 3:3-21.
KIPARSKY, R. K. P.
    1965. *Phonological Change.* Unpublished Ph.D. dissertation, MIT.
    1968a. "How Abstract Is Phonology?" Unpublished paper, MIT.
    1968b. "Linguistic Universals and Linguistic Change," *in* E. Bach and
        R. Harms, eds., *Universals in Linguistic Theory.* New York:
        Holt, Rinehart and Winston. Pp. 170-202.
KÖKERITZ, HELGE
    1932. *The Phonology of the Suffolk Dialect.* Uppsala: A-b. Lunde-
        quistska bokhandeln.
    1935. "English Pronunciation as Described in Shorthand Systems of
        the 17th and 18th Centuries," *Studia Neophilologica* 7:73-146.
    1953. *Shakespeare's Pronunciation.* New Haven: Yale University
        Press.
    1965. "Dialectal Traits in Sir Thomas Wyatt's Poetry," *in* Jess B.
        Bessinger and Robert P. Creed, eds., *Franciplegius: Medieval*

and *Linguistic Studies in Honor of Francis Peabody Magoun*.
New York: New York University Press. Pp. 294-303.

KUČERA, H.

1958. "Inquiry into Coexistent Phonemic Systems in Slavic Languages," in *American Contributions to the Fourth International Congress of Slavicists*. The Hague: Mouton. Pp. 169-189.

1961. *The Phonology of Czech*. The Hague: Mouton.

LABOV, W.

1963. "The Social Motivation of a Sound Change," *Word* 19:273-310.

1965. "On the Mechanism of Linguistic Change," in *Report of the Sixteenth Annual Round Table Meeting on Linguistics and Language Studies*. Washington: Georgetown University Press. Pp. 91-114.

1966. *The Social Stratification of English in New York City*. Washington: The Center for Applied Linguistics.

1970. "The Study of Language in its Social Context," *Studium Generale* 23:30-87.

Forthcoming. "The Internal Evolution of Linguistic Rules," *in* R. P. Stockwell and R. S. K. Macaulay, eds., *Linguistic Change and Transformational Theory*. Bloomington, Indiana: Indiana University Press.

n.d. "A Quantitative Study of Sound Changes in Progress." A Proposal for Research Project submitted to the National Science Foundation. Department of Linguistics, University of Pennsylvania.

LABOV, W., and BENJI WALD

1969. "Some General Principles of Vowel Shifting." Unpublished paper presented at the Annual Meeting of the Linguistic Society of America, San Francisco, 1969.

LADEFOGED, PETER

1967. *Linguistic Phonetics. Working Papers in Phonetics 6*. University of California, Los Angeles.

LANGACKER, RONALD W.

1969a. "i/e in Proto Uto-Aztecan," *Linguistic Notes from La Jolla* 1:1-15.

1969b. "Mirror Image Rules I: Syntax," *Language* 45:575-598.

LASS, ROGER

1969. "On the Derivative Status of Phonological Rules: The Function of Metarules in Sound Change." Unpublished paper, Indiana University.

LEHNERT, M.

1936. *Die Grammatik des englischen Sprachmeisters John Wallis (1616-1703)* [Sprache und Kultur der germanischen und romanischen Völker, A: Anglistische Reihe, 21]. Breslau.

LODWICK, FRANCIS

1686. "Essay towards an Universal Alphabet," *Philosophical Transactions of the Royal Society* 16:126-137.

n.d. Manuscript notebook, Sloane MS 897.

LOTSPEICH, C. M.
  1921. "The Cause of Long Vowel Changes in English," *The Journal of English and Germanic Philology* 20:208-212.
  1927. "A Single Principle for English and Primitive Germanic Sound-Changes," *The Journal of English and Germanic Philology* 26: 467-470.
LUICK, KARL
  1896. *Untersuchungen zur englischen Lautgeschichte.* Strassburg: K. J. Trübner.
  1900. "Der Ursprung der neuenglischen ai- und au-Diphthonge," *Englische Studien* 27:89-100.
  1901. "Der Ursprung der neuenglischen ai- und au-Diphthonge," *Englische Studien* 29:405-410.
  1914-1940. *Historische Grammatik der englischen Sprache.* [Reprinted 1964.] Oxford: Basil Blackwell.
McCAWLEY, JAMES D.
  1969. "Notes on the Underlying Vowel System of English." Unpublished paper, University of Chicago.
MAŘIK, JOSEPH
  1913. "Ueber die neuenglische Vokalverschiebung," *Englische Studien* 46:188-196.
MARTINET, ANDRÉ
  1955. *Économie des changements phonétiques.* Berne: A. Francke.
MATTHEWS, W.
  1936. "William Tiffin, an Eighteenth Century Phonetician," *English Studies* 13:97-114.
  1943. *English Pronunciation and Shorthand in the Early Modern Period.* Berkeley and Los Angeles: University of California Press.
MULCASTER, RICHARD.
  1582. *See* Campagnac.
NIST, JOHN
  1966. *A Structural History of English.* New York: St. Martin's Press.
ORTON, HAROLD
  1933. *The Phonology of a South Durham Dialect.* London: Kegan Paul, Trench, Trubner.
ORTON, HAROLD, and WILFRID J. HALLIDAY
  1962-63. *Survey of English Dialects: (B): The Basic Material.* [Vol. 1, Parts I, II (1962), and III (1963): The Six Northern Counties and the Isle of Man.] Leeds: E. J. Arnold, for the University of Leeds.
POPE, M. K.
  1934. *From Latin to Modern French.* Manchester: Manchester University Press.
POSTAL, PAUL M.
  1968. *Aspects of Phonological Theory.* New York: Harper and Row.
SANDS, DONALD B., ed.
  1966. *Middle English Verse Romances.* New York: Holt, Rinehart and Winston.

SARRAZIN, G.
1899. "Der Ursprung der neuenglischen ai- und au-Diphthonge," *Englische Studien* 26:229-238.
1901. "Der Ursprung der neuenglischen ai- und au-Diphthonge," *Englische Studien* 29:193-208.
SCHMALSTIEG, WILLIAM R.
1964. "The Phonemes of the Old Prussian Enchiridion," *Word* 20:211-221.
SCHUCHARDT, HUGO
1885. *On Phonetic Laws: Against the Neogrammarians.* Trans. by Burckhard Mohr, *Project on Linguistic Analysis,* Second Series No. 12, February 1971. Department of Linguistics, University of California, Berkeley.
SMITH, N. V.
1970. "The Acquisition of Phonology." Unpublished monograph, School of Oriental and African Studies, University of London.
SÖDERHOLM, TORBJÖRN
1970. *The End-Rhymes of Marvell, Cowley, Crashaw, Lovelace and Vaughan.* [Acta Academiae Aboensis, Ser. A: Humaniora: Vol. 39 nr 2.] Abo.
SOMMERFELT, ALF
1923. "Note sur les Changements Phonétiques," *Bulletin de la Société de Linguistique de Paris* 24:138-141.
STOCKWELL, ROBERT P.
n.d. "English Historical Phonology: Vowel Systems." Unpublished mimeographed handout, University of California, Los Angeles.
1952. *Chaucerian Graphemics and Phonemics: A Study in Historical Methodology.* Unpublished Ph. D. dissertation, University of Virginia.
1959. "Notes towards a Summary of the History of English Sound Change." Unpublished mimeographed handout, University of California, Los Angeles.
1961. "The Middle English 'Long Close' and 'Long Open' Mid Vowels," *Studies in Literature and Language* 2. Austin, Texas: The University of Texas. Pp. 529-538.
1964. "On the Utility of an Overall Pattern in Historical English Phonology," *in* H. Lunt, ed., *Proceedings of the Ninth International Congress of Linguists.* The Hague: Mouton. Pp. 663-671.
1969. "Mirrors in the History of English Pronunciation," *in* B. E. Atwood and A. A. Hill, eds., *Studies in Language, Literature, and Culture of the Middle Ages and Later.* Austin, Texas: The University of Texas Press. Pp. 20-37.
Forthcoming. "Problems in the Interpretation of the Great English Vowel Shift," to appear in the George L. Trager Festschrift, Florida State University.
STOCKWELL, ROBERT P., and C. WESTBROOK BARRITT
1951. *Some Old English Graphemic-Phonemic Correspondences—ae, ea, and a.* [Studies in Linguistics: Occasional Papers 4.] Norman, Oklahoma: Battenburg Press.

SUNDBY, B., ed.
1953. *Christopher Cooper's English Teacher* (*1687*). [Lund Studies in English XXII.] Lund: C. W. K. Gleerup.

SWEET, H.
1888. *A History of English Sounds*. London: Oxford University Press.

TRAGER, GEORGE L., and HENRY LEE SMITH
1951. *An Outline of English Structure*. [Studies in Linguistics, Occasional Papers 3.] Norman, Oklahoma: Battenburg Press.

TUITE, THOMAS
1726. *The Oxford Spelling-Book*. No. 41 *in* Alston.

WALLIS, JOHN
1678. *A Defence of the Royal Society*. London.
1765. *Grammatica Linguae Anglicanae*. London. [A reprint of the revised fifth edition of 1699.]

WANG, WILLIAM S-Y.
1967. "Phonological Features of Tone," *International Journal of American Linguistics* 33:93-105.
1968. "Vowel Features, Paired Variables, and the English Vowel Shift," *Language* 44:695-708.
1969. "Competing Changes as a Cause of Residue," *Language* 45:9-25.

WEBSTER, NOAH
1789. *Dissertations on the English Language*. No 54 *in* Alston.

WEINREICH, U., W. LABOV, and M. I. HERZOG
1968. "Empirical Foundations for a Theory of Language Change," *in* W. Lehmann and Y. Malkiel, eds., *Directions for Historical Linguistics*. Austin, Texas: The University of Texas Press. Pp. 95-188.

WESTERN, A.
1912. "Ueber die neuenglische Vokalverschiebung," *Englische Studien* 45:1-8.

WEYMOUTH, R. F.
1874. *On Early English Pronunciation*. London: Asher.

WILKINS, BP. JOHN
1668. *An Essay towards a Universal Character and a Philosophical Language*. London.

WILSON, R. M.
1963. "The Orthography and Provenance of Henry Machyn," *in* Arthur Brown and Peter Foote, eds., *Early English and Norse Studies*. London: Methuen. Pp. 202-216.

WOLFE, PATRICIA M.
1968. "Exchange Rules and the Impairment of Intelligibility." Unpublished paper presented at the Annual Meeting of the Linguistic Society of America, New York, 1968.

WRENN, C. L.
1943. "The Value of Spelling as Evidence," *Transactions of the Philological Society* 14-39.

WRIGHT, JOSEPH, and E. M. WRIGHT
1928. *An Elementary Middle English Grammar* [Second edition]. London: Oxford University Press.

The Writing Scholar's Companion (*1695*)
1695. *See* Ekwall (1911).

WYLD, H. C.
1923. *Studies in English Rhyme from Surrey to Pope.* London: John Murray.
1927. *A Short History of English* [Third edition]. London: John Murray.
1936. *A History of Modern Colloquial English* [Third edition]. Oxford: Basil Blackwell.

ZACHRISSON, R. E.
1913. *Pronunciation of English Vowels 1400-1700.* [Göteborgs kung. vetenskaps- och vitterhets-samhälles hanlingar, 4. fölkden, XIV: 2.] Göteberg.
1927. *The English Pronunciation at Shakespeare's Time as Taught by William Bullokar.* Uppsala: Almqvist and Wiskell.

ZWICKY, ARNOLD M.
1970. "Greek-letter Variables and the Sanskrit *ruki* Class," *Linguistic Inquiry* 1:549-555.

INDEX